The Southern Mind Under Union Rule

New Perspectives on the History of the South

UNIVERSITY PRESS OF FLORIDA

Florida A&M University, Tallahassee
Florida Atlantic University, Boca Raton
Florida Gulf Coast University, Ft. Myers
Florida International University, Miami
Florida State University, Tallahassee
New College of Florida, Sarasota
University of Central Florida, Orlando
University of Florida, Gainesville
University of North Florida, Jacksonville
University of South Florida, Tampa
University of West Florida, Pensacola

THE SOUTHERN MIND
UNDER UNION RULE

The Diary of James Rumley,
Beaufort, North Carolina, 1862–1865

Edited by Judkin Browning

New Perspectives on the History of the South

University Press of Florida
Gainesville/Tallahassee/Tampa/Boca Raton
Pensacola/Orlando/Miami/Jacksonville/Ft. Myers/Sarasota

Copyright 2009 by Judkin Browning
The Diary of James Rumley is published courtesy of the North Carolina Office
of Archives and History, Raleigh, N.C.
Printed in the United States of America. This book is printed on Glatfelter
Natures Book, a paper certified under the standards of the Forestry Stewardship
Council (FSC). It is a recycled stock that contains 30 percent post-consumer waste
and is acid-free.

14 13 12 11 10 09   6 5 4 3 2 1

Library of Congress Cataloging-in-Publication Data
Rumley, James, 1812–1881.
The southern mind under union rule : the diary of James Rumley, Beaufort, North
Carolina, 1862-1865 / edited by Judkin Browning.
p. cm.—(New perspectives on the history of the South)
Includes bibliographical references and index.
ISBN 978-0-8130-3407-2 (alk. paper)
1. Rumley, James, 1812–1881—Diaries. 2. Clerks of court—North Carolina—Beau-
fort—Diaries. 3. Beaufort (N.C.)—History—19th century—Sources. 4. Beaufort
(N.C.)—Social conditions—19th century. 5. North Carolina—History—Civil
War, 1861–1865—Personal narratives. 6. United States—History—Civil War,
1861–1865—Personal narratives. 7. Beaufort (N.C.)—Biography. I. Browning,
Judkin. II. Title.
F264.B37R86 2009
973.7'31092—dc22   [B]   2009017136

The University Press of Florida is the scholarly publishing agency for the State
University System of Florida, comprising Florida A&M University, Florida At-
lantic University, Florida Gulf Coast University, Florida International University,
Florida State University, New College of Florida, University of Central Florida,
University of Florida, University of North Florida, University of South Florida,
and University of West Florida.

University Press of Florida
15 Northwest 15th Street
Gainesville, FL 32611-2079
http://www.upf.com

CONTENTS

ILLUSTRATIONS

Acknowledgments

No project could be completed without the dozens of individuals who offer assistance and encouragement on both the personal and professional levels. I must necessarily thank many of these people twice but they deserve far more thanks than even these meager acknowledgments can provide. I owe a debt to a great many people.

First, for this project, I would like to thank John David Smith, the editor of the series, for his positive support. He advised me at North Carolina State University and has continued to be a positive presence in my academic career in the ten years since I graduated. I would also like to thank Eli Bortz, who was the original acquisitions editor of the University Press of Florida and encouraged me to submit the manuscript. Meredith Morris-Babb, who replaced Eli, was equally supportive of this work and shepherded it through every stage of the production process. The entire staff at the University Press of Florida has been nothing but very professional, prompt, courteous, and helpful throughout the process. Peter Carmichael and Richard M. Reid both offered helpful suggestions on how to improve the manuscript and were very supportive of publishing the diary.

I would like to thank the staffs of the various repositories that I visited in the course of my research; each provided timely and knowledgeable assistance. These include the Southern Historical Collection and the North Carolina Collection at the University of North Carolina at Chapel Hill; the State Archives and the State Library at the Division of Archives and History in Raleigh, North Carolina; the Rare Book, Manuscript, and Special Collections Library at Duke University; the Massachusetts Historical Society in Boston; the American Antiquarian Society in Worcester, Massachusetts; the Baker Library at the Harvard Business

School in Cambridge, Massachusetts; the Library of Congress; the National Archives, both in D.C. and in College Park, Maryland; the Brown Library in Washington, North Carolina; and the United States Army Military History Institute in Carlisle, Pennsylvania. The interlibrary loan department at my home institution of Appalachian State University has also proved very skilled in acquiring many obscure books in an efficient and professional manner.

Some individuals at these repositories deserve special recognition for going above and beyond the call of duty. At the State Archives, A. Christopher Meekins was very helpful in tracking down records and informing me about collections of the archives. Chris proved an invaluable aide in finding obscure sources that helped illuminate Rumley's personal history and generously sent me copies to save me another trip to Raleigh as a deadline approached. George Stevenson, recently retired from the State Archives, was an instrumental player in this story, helping me to confirm that the true diarist was James Rumley and not Levi W. Pigott. Kim Cumber was very helpful in tracking down a photograph of the elusive James Rumley, something I had been unable to do for several years.

Jason Tomberlin of the North Carolina Collection provided assistance and lunch companionship on my visits to the Chapel Hill area while working on this project. The North Carolina Collection's Newspaper Clippings File was also a treasure trove for locating old newspapers that had crucial information about certain people and events mentioned by James Rumley. Keith Longiotti guided me through the collection's photographs and provided timely reproductions of the images for this volume. At the Carteret County Historical Society in Morehead City, David Montgomery offered much appreciated assistance and promptly provided a reproduction of the photograph of Emeline Pigott.

Any research venture requires the assistance of friends and colleagues who offer places to stay or support for the endeavor along the way. I am indebted to Mike and Corliss Bradley for showing my wife and me such hospitality during our stay in Beaufort, North Carolina; to Mrs. Beverly Kelchner for her hospitality during my stay in Carlisle, Pennsylvania; to my good friend Chris Hoch for opening his doors to me in the D.C. area; to Mike and Rachel Noto for always welcoming me to Raleigh; and to Lindy Aldrich for opening up her home in Medford to me for two weeks of research in Boston, Massachusetts. In addition, I'd like to thank Ed

Pond of Davis Shore, North Carolina, for his encouragement of me in this project. Ronald E. Butchart provided key information about some of the northern missionaries mentioned in this diary. Michael Thomas Smith deserves special mention. Not only did he identify several of these individuals when we co-edited *Letters from a North Carolina Unionist* but he has also been a true friend and colleague in all things academic and otherwise. Finally, I'd like to thank my beautiful wife, Greta, for her continuing support of all my scholarly and nonscholarly endeavors.

EDITORIAL METHOD

Between approximately March 14, 1862, and August 1865, James Rumley wrote 174 dated entries into his diary. Each one of these entries, as far as is known, is included in this volume. The entries have been taken from the two extant issues of *The Look Out*, a Beaufort newspaper in 1910, the surviving issues of the *Beaufort News* from 1937 (which was simply a reprint of the 1910 version of the diary) and from handwritten and typescript copies of the diary, which are available in the Levi Woodbury Pigott Collection at the North Carolina State Archives in Raleigh, North Carolina. The microfilm copies of the newspapers are also at the State Archives. The location of Rumley's original diary is unknown.

Unfortunately, because this volume is derived largely from a copy of a copy of Rumley's diary, made at least 29 years after he died, we do not know the original nuances of Rumley's language—his misspellings and etymological eccentricities. There are three copies available of the diary. The first copyist was the newspaper editor of Beaufort's *The Look Out*, who prepared the diary for publication in serial form beginning on January 7, 1910. Only two issues (January 7 and January 14, 1910) of that paper exist. This serial form of the diary was then reprinted in the weekly *Beaufort News*, which published the diary in fourteen surviving issues from January 14 to April 15, 1937. The editor of the *Beaufort News*, however, did not have an uninterrupted run of *The Look Out* from which to work. As a result, the *Beaufort News* version has gaps in the coverage of the diary.

The second copyist, whose handwritten version is housed in the North Carolina State Archives, made a copy of the newspaper serial form of the diary from *The Look Out*. Regrettably this copyist made numerous mistakes—misspelling words in a variety of ways, copying parts of the same passage, only to cross them out later, and underlining words without any apparent coherent purpose. This second copyist was also extraordinarily fond of commas, and would not hesitate to use 6 or 7 in a sentence often with no clear reason. A comparison with the extant newspaper serial shows that the second copyist misspelled words and added punctuation that was not in the newspaper version, and also deleted sections that were in the newspaper version, reflecting perhaps haste or lack of concentration. A third copyist transcribed the handwritten copy and corrected some (but not all) of the spelling mistakes, made some new spelling mistakes of his or her own, and kept some of the original underlining and punctuation while adding some new ones. Overall, the transcriber made a cleaner copy of the diary, but it was still just that, a copy—or in this case, a copy of a copy of a copy.

Since I could not go to the original source in order to exactly capture Rumley's syntax and style, I have decided to make the diary as readable as possible, while preserving the original intent of the diarist to the greatest extent possible. To this effect, I have removed no words from the body of the diary, in order not to impinge upon Rumley's original. I have silently corrected punctuation mistakes when they disrupt the flow of the sentences. Superscript characters have been converted to a standard font followed by a period. I have also corrected the spellings of common words that the copyist misspelled, on the assumption that Rumley was such a well-educated man he likely would not have misspelled such common words. I have corrected the spelling of some surnames in the text in which it was necessary to identify the individual, while keeping the slight misspelling of others. The newspaper serials and the transcriber spelled the county seat of neighboring Craven County as New Bern, while the second copyist spelled it as Newbern. Since both spellings were common at the time of the Civil War, I have elected to use New Bern, which is the current accepted spelling. The copyist capitalized words like government, county, and country about half the time, with no apparent logic. In order to preserve uniformity, I have transcribed these in the lower case. I have spelled out all ampersands. I have italicized all names of ships and newspapers, to limit confusion to the reader. Occasionally an obvious word is missing from a sentence, and since I cannot know if Rumley left the word out or the copyist did, I have inserted all such words in *italics* inside square brackets [ ].

The copy of the diary is not consistent in how it dates entries. Some entries include the day of the week; others list only the month and not the date. Occasionally there are two entries listed under the same month and year. Also there are two occasions when there are two possible dates listed for an entry. The copyist gave one date as the heading, and at the end of the entry wrote another date. There is no clear indication which of these dates is appropriate. In such instances I use the first listed date, but also acknowledge that the copy has a second date listed. For ease of understanding, I have standardized all dates to include month, date, and year, as well as the day of the week whenever noted in the diary, and have placed these in italics at the beginning of each entry.

INTRODUCTION

James Rumley, an ardent southern sympathizer who lived in Beaufort, North Carolina, at the southern tip of North Carolina's Outer Banks, kept a diary of his experience under Union military occupation during the Civil War. Rumley's diary is an extraordinary journal. It is one of the only published diaries of a secessionist living under Union occupation in the South. Rumley's hometown of Beaufort was occupied by the Union army on March 26, 1862, and remained under continuous Union occupation until the end of the war. As a result, Rumley's diary is an exceptional window into the nature of Union occupation; it records his reactions to the social, cultural, political, military, and economic upheavals that occupation brought to the community. The diary also records the point of view of a decidedly pro-Confederate resident of that occupation, revealing the issues that greatly disturbed the local white population during the occupation, especially the attempt to politically restore the region to the Union, the empowerment of their former slaves, and the imposition of martial law.

The diary that is presented in this volume has an enigmatic history. Though the diary is possibly a redaction of a longer journal, evidence indicates that Rumley recorded only this 41-month chronicle. Two versions of the diary—a handwritten work and a typescript transcription—are available at the North Carolina State Archives, yet neither is original to Rumley nor was their authorship originally attributed to Rumley. The handwritten version is a copy of a serial version published in Beaufort's weekly newspaper *The Look Out* that began on January 7, 1910. Unfortunately, only two (microfilmed) issues of this serialization have survived, for January 7 and January 14. These contain the first two installments of the diary. The typescript version is a transcription of the handwritten copy in which many spelling and grammar errors have been corrected. The editor of *The Look Out* was granted access to Rumley's original diary and arranged the diary for the 1910 publication.[1] It is possible that the editor who published the diary took certain editorial liberties with it (such as inserting James Rumley's name in place of the personal pronoun in the entries for March 17 and March 25, 1862). This would explain the seeming incongruity of Rumley referring to himself in the third person, though that may well have been Rumley's authorial style as a diarist.

It is possible that the editor published the diary in 1910 as part of the spirit of national reconciliation that was sweeping the nation at the turn of the century. However, the content of the diary would not further that aim. Reconciliation demanded that northern and southern antagonists bury the disagreements of the past and emphasized the nobility of the fight on both sides in order to foster a harmonious reunification. Rumley's diary instead characterized a northern occupation as harsh, oppressive, and full of abuses of local whites. It is more likely that the editor wished to publish a local Civil War–themed artifact as the fiftieth anniversary of that conflict approached, and a diary that revealed Yankee misrule during the war would emphasize how much southern whites had persevered during those dark days. The whites in Beaufort had reestablished political domination over blacks, and the diary would show the next generation how much their ancestors had had to endure before they could set things right.[2]

The diary made another appearance in a Beaufort newspaper in 1937, revealing an even more mysterious history. Under a headline titled "Civil War Days in Beaufort," the *Beaufort News* reprinted the diary's serial installments from the 1910 edition of *The Look Out*. The reprinted serial ran weekly from January 14 to at least April 15, 1937. In the initial issue, the editor of the *Beaufort News* claimed that the original diary had been in the possession of a Rumley relative who loaned it to a Beaufort newspaper editor, undoubtedly the editor of *The Look Out*. The editor said that the original diary had never been returned to its owner but that the newspaper clippings from the original serial had been discovered tucked inside another resident's old Bible. He then prepared those clippings for

---

1   *Beaufort News*, January 14, 1937.
2   For more on reconciliation, see Blight, *Race and Reunion*; and Silber, *Romance of Reunion*.

the 1937 serial publication, which matches the 1910 serial in every way.[3] The original diary appears to have disappeared altogether, and only the handwritten, typescript, and brief newspaper serial versions remain.

When the handwritten and typescript copies of the diary were first donated to the state archives in Raleigh in 1995, archivists believed that the diary belonged to Levi Woodbury Pigott, another Beaufort resident during the war. Hence, the diary was processed and originally listed as being that of Pigott, and it is still located in the Levi Woodbury Pigott Collection in the private collections of the state archives. In August 2000, more information came to light to reveal that the author was not Pigott but was instead James Rumley, clerk of the Carteret County court from 1848 to 1881. The confirming evidence that James Rumley was the diarist came from former secretary of the treasury and chief justice of the Supreme Court Salmon P. Chase, who made a brief visit to Beaufort in May 1865. In Salmon Chase's personal diary for May 4, 1865, he wrote that he was visited on board his ship by former North Carolina senator Michael Arendell and "Mr. Rumley Clerk of County Court."[4] Whitelaw Reid, a northern journalist traveling with Chase, similarly recorded that the clerk of the county court met with Chase and his entourage at the wharf. In his diary entry of the same day, Rumley wrote that he had visited Chief Justice Chase on board his steamer, and the descriptions of the ensuing conversation are congruent in all three men's writings.[5] Both Chase and Rumley also referred to Chase's visit to the Carteret County Court House on May 6, and Chase specifically stated, "Mr. Rumley Cl[er]k showed me old records."[6]

Born on November 12, 1812, James Rumley was appointed clerk of the court of pleas and quarters in 1848 and served continuously as the clerk of either this court or the Carteret County Superior Court until he died at midnight on December 15, 1881. Rumley never married. In his obituary, a Beaufort resident reflected on Rumley's bachelor status, writing, "Deprived of the social relations which gladden and expand the nature of the husband and the father, he opened his heart to the love and affection of

3   *Beaufort News*, January 14, 1937.

4   Niven, *Salmon P. Chase Papers*, 1:538.

5   Salmon P. Chase to President Andrew Johnson, May 4, 1865, in Chase, *Advice after Appomattox*, 17–18; Whitelaw Reid, *After the War*, 23–27; Rumley's entry for May 4, 1865.

6   Niven, *Salmon P. Chase Papers*, 1:40; Rumley's entry for May 6, 1865.

his kindred, and extended his sympathies to the poor, the suffering, and the oppressed." His lamenters suggested that he found personal fulfillment in his life of public service: "He was brother to all mankind, ever watchful for an opportunity to do good. He was father to the fatherless, son and brother to the widow wherever found, and his hand was ever stretched out in deeds of kindness and charity."[7]

Rumley first appears in the historical record in the census of 1840, where he is listed as the head of a household that included a female between the ages of 40 and 50. In the 1850 census, the 37-year-old James is the head of a household that includes 62-year-old Abigail Gibble and his 15-year-old niece, Mary Rumley. His relationship to Gibble is unclear. Mary was still living with him in 1860, 1870, and 1880, while Abigail disappears from the record after 1860.[8]

Unfortunately, other details of Rumley's life are unknown. Although the historical sources do not indicate where Rumley received his education, he was obviously a well-educated man. His diary reveals him to be an erudite and extraordinarily well read individual. Rumley quoted many literary and historical texts, and the fact that he often slightly misquoted these works indicates that he was not referencing books at hand but recalling the quotes from memory. Rumley used his education to carve out a respectable life as a responsible public citizen. At the outbreak of the Civil War in 1861, the county clerk was a moderately wealthy individual; he owned $800 worth of real estate, $4,000 worth of personal property, and two slaves—a 60-year-old female and a 15-year-old male. He lost most of his personal estate during the war (most likely with the emancipation of his slaves); he claimed only $200 worth of personal property in the 1870 census.[9]

During the war, we know that Rumley did not take the oath of allegiance when Union forces occupied Beaufort. A letter from military governor Edward Stanly in January 1863 noted that Rumley and others had not taken the oath of allegiance "for good & sufficient reasons." Stanly

7   *Carteret County Telephone*, December 23, 1881.
8   Carteret County Court Minutes, Court of Pleas and Quarters, 1858–1868, vol. 19, State Archives, Raleigh, North Carolina; Sixth Census, 1840: Carteret County; Seventh Census, 1850: Carteret County; Eighth Census, 1860: Carteret County; Ninth Census, 1870: Carteret County.
9   Eighth Census, 1860: Carteret County; Ninth Census, 1870: Carteret County.

ordered Beaufort's provost marshal to allow them to continue to conduct business despite the fact that they had not taken the oath. This greatly annoyed the provost marshal, who felt that he had plenty of evidence to indicate that "none of them are loyal men."[10] Rumley wrote in his diary entry of June 1863 that he was one of eighteen heads of households that had not yet taken the oath. Presumably Rumley took the oath in late June 1863 to avoid being evicted from Beaufort.[11]

After the war, Rumley reclaimed his job as clerk of the superior court and served as Carteret's representative at the state constitutional conventions in 1865 and 1875.[12] He offered testimony supporting the loyalty of several local residents who applied to the Southern Claims Commission for compensation for property taken by Union forces during the war.[13] He also endorsed letters of recommendation describing the loyalty of individual Beaufort residents who sought government offices after the war.[14] When Rumley died in 1881, he was interred at Beaufort's historic Old Burying Ground, ending a life that had seen much turmoil and change for his beloved town and its citizens.[15]

Beaufort was a remote struggling fishing village for much of Rumley's life. Despite its magnificent harbor, Beaufort was never a major commercial port in the state. It had no navigable rivers that allowed access to the interior, and the bogs, swamps, and pocosins that dominated the low-lying country made overland travel prohibitively difficult. These terrain

---

10   William B. Fowle, Jr., to Colonel Southard Hoffman, January 16, 1863, Box 2, Part I, Letters Received, Department of North Carolina, Records of the U.S. Army Continental Commands, Record Group 393, National Archives and Records Administration, Washington, D.C.

11   Rumley's entry for June 1863.

12   John A. Hedrick to Benjamin S. Hedrick, August 11, 27, 1865, Benjamin Sherwood Hedrick Papers; Composite Photo of 1875 Constitutional Convention, Biographical Directory of the General Assembly Photo Collection.

13   Testimony of James Rumley, Claim 15562 (Benjamin Roberson), Carteret County, North Carolina, Records of the Committees Relating to Claims, 1794–1946, Southern Claims Commission, 1871–1880, Disallowed Claims, Record Group 233.8, National Archives and Records Administration, Washington, D.C.

14   John A. Hedrick to Benjamin S. Hedrick, March 10, 1866, Benjamin Sherwood Hedrick Papers.

15   *Cemetery Records of Carteret County*, 162.

features also limited opportunities for large-scale agriculture, prompting local residents from its earliest settlement to seek their livelihoods from the sea. Thousands of acres of estuaries created one of the most productive fishing regions on the Atlantic coast. The 1860 census reveals that 637 of the 1,029 white working men in the county (62 percent) earned their living on the waters.[16]

As a result of its remoteness from the interior of the state, Beaufort had been a commercially unsuccessful town for most of its existence. In 1840, Beaufort had streets and sidewalks that were "continuous banks or drifts of sand," and it had only "a few stores . . . no market house, a courthouse, and but one church." Rev. John Edwards, who preached in Beaufort in 1839, remarked, "Beaufort in those days, was as nearly out of the world as a town could well be."[17] Many Carteret officials and merchants tried to bring a railroad and other technological improvements to Beaufort to take advantage of its harbor and improve their commercial prospects. Rumley led this effort, promising prospective investors that Beaufort citizens would donate $100,000 to help bring the railroad all the way to their town. Despite their best efforts, Beaufort leaders had been successful in getting the railroad only as far as Morehead City by 1860.[18]

The most profitable development for Beaufort residents occurred in the 1850s, when local entrepreneurs began promoting the town as a site for personal recreation. Wealthy socialites from all over North Carolina

---

16   Paul, "Factors in the Economy of Colonial Beaufort," 111–134; Sharpe, "Completely Coastal Carteret," 5, 33; Cecelski, *The Waterman's Song*, 53; Eighth Census, 1860: Carteret County.

17   Rev. John Edwards is quoted in "Beaufort Long Ago Was Quiet and Good," *Beaufort News*, November 29, 1923.

18   Morehead City is only four miles west of Beaufort, but it is across the wide Newport River. For Rumley's promise, see James Manney to Thomas J. Lemay, February 27, 1850, Manney Letter Book. See also "A Bill to Incorporate the Beaufort and North Carolina Railroad," Session 1850–1851, Senate Document No. 74, "A Bill to Incorporate the Atlantic and North Carolina Railroad," Session 1852–1853, House Document No. 30, in *Proceedings of the Annual Meeting of the Stockholders of the Atlantic and North Carolina Railroad*; Brown, *A State Movement in Railroad Development*, 121–122.

chose Beaufort as a vacation destination; they came to enjoy the scenery, the pleasant walks along Front Street, and the cool ocean breezes, which, according to one citizen, "sets in about ten o'clock in the morning & blows with refreshing coolness throughout the day" during the summer months.[19] Soon Beaufort was sporting three luxurious hotels, and many residents were making a living renting out rooms to boarders. Some local businessmen, especially hotel owners, expected to derive handsome fortunes from the growing tourist industry. By 1861, Beaufort was a fairly prosperous port and home to several moderately wealthy merchants as well as many fishermen, small merchants, shopkeepers, and yeoman farmers. Practically no planters lived in this coastal community, and slaves constituted less than 25 percent of the county's population.[20]

Despite the proportion of slaves to the population, Carteret residents recognized that racial slavery was of fundamental importance to their commerce and communal identities. Slavery buttressed a multitude of agricultural, nautical, and forest industries, and racial slavery served as the foundation of white supremacy in the county. In his diary, Rumley declared that the slaves had been satisfied with their lives and had no inclination to change their status until poisoned by Yankees who "[invaded] the sacred precincts of every family, [and robbed] them of their servants, who would be faithful and contented if let alone."[21] Rumley conveniently ignored reality, however. As he and other slave owners knew well, coastal North Carolina slaves had been trying to ameliorate their hardships and establish some sort of control over their own lives for decades before the Union soldiers arrived by surreptitiously seeking education, establishing

---

19 William Geffrey to David S. Reid, August 30, 1858, Reid Papers; William Woods Holden to Miss L. H. Holden, August 6, 1858, in Raper and Mitchell, *Papers of William Woods Holden*, 1:95; "A City by the Sea," by G. F. Stanton, Beaufort Reminiscence, [ca. 1901], Box 2, Alida F. Fales Papers; J. Henry to Thomas Henderson, December 16, 1810, in "One Hundred Years Ago Beaufort Had Big Shipbuilding Industry," *Beaufort News*, February 14, 1929 (quotation).

20 North Carolina, 5:173, 176A, 176E, R. G. Dun & Co. Collection; Eighth Census, 1860: Carteret County.

21 Rumley's entry for January 1, 1863.

as formal a family life as possible, engaging in an illicit "internal economy" with poor whites, running away, or even fomenting revolt.[22]

Whites in Carteret County were constantly on the alert for any improper ideas their slaves might harbor. Several incidents of slave escapes, rumors of potential slave insurrections in the region, and the Nat Turner revolt in southern Virginia in 1831 all exacerbated local residents' anxieties during the antebellum era.[23] Racial slavery intricately intertwined the experiences of elites, yeomen, and even poor whites and created a society that exalted white superiority. While simultaneously granting slaves certain latitudes, whites in the coastal region used slave patrols, militias, intimidation, and the court system to maintain racial boundaries and proper slave behavior. As Rumley's diary reveals, whites in Carteret County were so dedicated to maintaining the racial caste system that any attempts by the Federal government to disrupt the social status quo led to resentment, hostility, and even violence.

In the hotly contested political struggles of the antebellum period, Carteret County residents stood steadfastly by the Whig Party and harbored strong Unionist feelings during the crises of the 1850s.[24] In the election of 1860, Carteret residents supported the Constitutional Union Party ticket of John Bell and Edward Everett.[25] Even after Republican Abraham Lincoln's election, several prominent Beaufort residents opposed immediate secession and held a pro-Union meeting on December 15, 1860. Like conditional Unionists throughout the state and the South, the attendees at the Beaufort meeting did not deny the right of secession but viewed it as the absolute "final remedy—after all other remedies . . . have been tried and failed."[26] Though the county's residents voted in favor of a secession convention in February 1861, they elected a Unionist delegate to represent them, indicating that they did not favor secession as

---

22   Browning, "Visions of Freedom and Civilization Opening before Them," 69–100.

23   For documentation of slaves' escapes, see Parker, *Stealing a Little Freedom*; Schweninger and Franklin, *Runaway Slaves*, 154; and Watson, *A History of New Bern and Craven County*, 157, 207–208.

24   Browning, "Removing the Mask of Nationality," 593–594.

25   Cheney, *North Carolina Government*, 1328–1331, 1400.

26   *Union Banner* (Beaufort, N.C.), December 15, 1860, quoted in *New Bern Daily Progress*, December 20, 1860. For more on Upper South conditional Unionists, see Crofts, *Reluctant Confederates*, esp. 144–152 and 330–341.

a result of Lincoln's election.[27] In October 1860, Governor John W. Ellis wrote, "Some favor Submission, some resistance and others still would *await the course of events that might follow.*"[28] Most Carteret residents favored the last option.

This all changed on April 15, 1861. When President Lincoln called for 75,000 troops one day after Fort Sumter's surrender, Carteret residents reacted angrily, issuing a proclamation that declared, "The honor and best interests of North Carolina demand that her connection with the present Union be dissolved."[29] Some had already acted. Immediately after learning that shots had been fired at Fort Sumter, Josiah Solomon Pender, the 42-year-old owner of Beaufort's Atlantic Hotel, led a small group of friends to capture Fort Macon.[30] Unlike Pender, however, most Carteret men abandoned the Union only after Lincoln's call for troops.

Local young men joined Carteret County companies with the understanding that these companies would remain in their home county, guarding the coastline and manning Fort Macon. Josiah Pender recognized this spirit and organized a company to serve as garrison troops for the fort. His company officially mustered into service as the aptly named Beaufort Harbor Guards on June 1, 1861, enlisting nearly 100 men. Stephen D. Pool, a schoolteacher and former newspaper editor, formed another company in the spring of 1861.[31] When Benjamin Leecraft, a prominent local merchant, attempted to raise yet another company of Carteret men that summer, however, he discovered that local Confederates would serve only under certain conditions. Leecraft lamented that he "could not succeed in raising a company to go any where on Southern Soil to repel the invader" and explained to Governor Ellis that "a large number would enlist for the

---

27   "Voting for Convention," Letter Book, 392–393, Governor's Papers—John W. Ellis. The final vote for Carteret was 415 yeas and 394 nays. Carteret County sent Charles R. Thomas, chairman of the Union meeting in Beaufort on December 15, 1860, as its delegate to the convention. See Cheney, *North Carolina Government*, 386–387, 399–401; *New Bern Daily Progress*, February 28, 1861.

28   John Ellis to William H. Gist, October 19, 1860, in Tolbert, *Papers of John W. Ellis*, 2:469–470.

29   *New Bern Daily Progress*, April 16, 1861.

30   Barrett, *The Civil War in North Carolina*, 10–11; *New Bern Daily Progress*, April 19, 1861.

31   Manarin and Jordan, *North Carolina Troops*, 1:113–137; *New Bern Daily Progress*, August 19, 1860 (Pool as editor); Eighth Census, 1860: Carteret County.

War provided they could have the assurance that they would be retained in the County." Ellis consented to this stipulation, and by October 1861 Leecraft had enlisted sixty-nine men.[32]

Leecraft's difficulty in raising a company reveals that Lincoln's call for troops had not driven everyone unequivocally to the Confederate side. Few other local men joined Confederate companies. While other counties in the state were sending more than 50 percent of their eligible male population into the army—including neighboring Craven County, which sent approximately 73 percent—only 31 percent of Carteret's eligible men enlisted.[33] Many still remained committed to Unionist principles in the face of a secessionist martial furor. In the early days of the war, local Confederate enthusiasts tried to intimidate those who publicly maintained their fidelity to the old Union, using traditional southern methods for community discipline and social control such as social ostracism, humiliation, and violence. Several citizens who vocally opposed the secessionists faced persecution and threats of violence. Therefore, most Unionists kept their sentiments as quiet as possible throughout the first year of the war until the arrival of Union troops in the spring of 1862 allowed them to become more outspoken again.[34]

James Rumley's diary begins around March 14, 1862, when Union troops under the command of General Ambrose Burnside attacked Confederate forces south of New Bern and drove the defenders away from the city. Burnside sent forces toward Beaufort to secure the coast and Fort Macon, which guarded Beaufort's harbor. In the early morning of March 26, two companies of Federal troops marched into Beaufort, beginning an occupation that would last the rest of the war. Almost one month later, Union forces compelled the small garrison of Fort Macon to surrender.

---

32 Manarin and Jordan, *North Carolina Troops*, 1:269–272; Benjamin Leecraft to John W. Ellis, June 25, 1861, in Tolbert, *Papers of John W. Ellis*, 2:875–876 (quotation). This volume cites Leecraft's name incorrectly as "Seecraft."

33 I tabulated the numbers by counting the number of enlisted men from each county, using Manarin and Jordan, *North Carolina Troops*, and then divided that number into the number of men of military age in each county. In Carteret County, there were 1,123 white men and in Craven County 1,522 white men between the ages of sixteen and thirty-nine in the 1860 census.

34 Browning, "Removing the Mask of Nationality," 599–600.

No Confederate military presence remained in the Beaufort area after April 26, 1862, and, to Rumley's dismay, none would ever return.[35]

President Abraham Lincoln and many Federal authorities anticipated that the majority of local white citizens would be loyal and expected to utilize this sentiment to foster a harmonious restoration. Lincoln believed that a show of force and benevolence by the Union army would bring thousands back to the Union fold. Lincoln even appointed a native son, former Craven County representative Edward Stanly, as military governor of the state in May 1862 to help reconstitute self-government and reassure local residents of the Union's benevolent aims. Early results seemed positive, but the nature and depth of white loyalties in Beaufort during the war prove hard to define.[36]

James Rumley argued that the majority of whites in Beaufort felt aggrieved by the Union occupation and were steadfast in their devotion to Confederate North Carolina. In August 1862, Rumley wrote that the white citizens of Beaufort "are not unmindful of the allegiance we owe to our state. Principle grows stronger within us from day to day. The cords that bind us to her, like the child to the parent, are tightening instead of relaxing."[37] Yet when northerners first arrived in Beaufort, they were convinced that loyal inhabitants had been forced by a vocal minority to acquiesce to secession. Daniel Read Larned, General Burnside's personal secretary, found the Beaufort populace to be "loyal to a great extent."[38] U.S. Treasury agent John A. Hedrick arrived in Beaufort on June 12, 1862, and after a week of interacting with the local residents observed, "Some are Secessionists but the greater number are Union men now and I think

35 John G. Parke to Ambrose Burnside, March 26, 1862, Parke to Lewis Richmond, May 9, 1862, Ambrose Burnside to Edwin Stanton, April 29, 1862, all in Scott, et al., eds., *The War of the Rebellion: A Compilation of the Official Records of the Union and Confederate Armies*, ser. 1, 9:279–280, 284, 274 (respectively) (hereafter cited as *Official Records, Army*); Allen, *Forty-Six Months with the Fourth R.I. Volunteers*, 101; Rumley's entry for April 25, 1862.

36 Edwin M. Stanton to Ambrose Burnside, May 20, 1862 and Stanton to Edward Stanly, May 19, 1862, both in *Official Records, Army* ser. 1, 9:391, 396–397.

37 Rumley's entry for August 7, 1862.

38 Daniel Read Larned to Henry Howe, March 26, 1862, Box 1, Daniel Read Larned Papers.

always have been."[39] Yet the assertions of Rumley, Larned, and Hedrick do not adequately encompass the complicated nature of loyalties in the region.

Once Federal forces drove the Confederate army out of the area, many Carteret residents shifted their allegiances back to the United States, though likely for pragmatic reasons more than for ideological ones. Most residents simply wanted the status quo antebellum, complete with Federal protections for southern slavery. An opportunity to reap economic benefits enticed residents back into the Union fold. Union soldiers noted that local residents began warming to their occupiers when northern merchant vessels laden with goods began arriving at Beaufort docks by June 1862. A Rhode Island soldier in Beaufort watched local businesses reopen "with cheerfulness and profit" and found that "many of the most rabid among them soon dropped their patriotic allusion to the Confederacy, and began to consider themselves as part and parcel of the U.S. government once more."[40]

Many businessmen allied themselves with the Union army to protect their economic interests, especially after witnessing how secessionist property was treated. As Rumley recorded in April 1862, northern troops quickly took possession of Josiah Pender's Atlantic Hotel and converted it into a major hospital for much of the war.[41] On June 7, 1862, Rumley denounced the fact that Union officers had confiscated Benjamin Leecraft's home and raided his possessions, but what he did not mention was that the provost marshal gave a northern merchant "permission to occupy the store formerly occupied by Benjamin Leecraft" because "the owner [had] joined the CSA Army."[42] Union actions regarding Pender's and Leecraft's premises forced other merchants in town to quickly assess their own allegiances. George W. Taylor, proprietor of the Ocean House hotel, recognized the economic benefits he would derive from cooperating with a northern clientele. He immediately agreed to operate his establishment as a boarding house for Union officials. Benjamin A. Ensley, proprietor of the Front Street House, did not immediately take the oath of allegiance

---

39 John A. Hedrick to Benjamin S. Hedrick, June 20, 1862, in Browning and Smith, *Letters from a North Carolina Unionist*, 7.

40 Allen, *Forty-Six Months with the Fourth R.I. Volunteers*, 116–117.

41 Rumley's entry for April 1862.

42 Rumley's entry for June 7, 1862; official document from Headquarters Provost Marshal, Beaufort, North Carolina, July 20, 1862, Alfred H. Martine Papers.

and had his hotel confiscated as a result. Ensley, who had a difficult time earning a livelihood in the occupied region, eventually felt compelled to enter the Union fold after a kitchen fire destroyed his residence in October 1863.[43]

Local soldiers also had complex allegiances. Two companies of Carteret County troops surrendered at Fort Macon and were paroled, or allowed to return to their homes, until they were formally exchanged in August 1862. When the exchange occurred, many Carteret residents decided to remain in Union lines. Of the 177 Carteret men who were captured and paroled at Fort Macon, fifty-six (32 percent) did not return to their units after their exchange, and thirty more (17 percent) who did return soon deserted. Similarly, forty-eight of the sixty-nine soldiers who served in Benjamin Leecraft's company at the battle of New Bern abandoned the company during the hasty retreat from the battlefield south of town. Many eventually found their way to Union lines at Beaufort.[44]

While some Carteret County men demonstrated their loyalty by leaving their units or taking the oath of allegiance and resuming business as usual, others actively aided the Union army as pilots, mechanics, or scouts.[45] Several local residents took an even more overt step in demonstrating their loyalty—they enlisted in the Union army. In June 1862, the Federal government authorized the raising of an infantry regiment of native North Carolinians, the 1st North Carolina Infantry Regiment (Union). In November 1863, the government authorized the creation of a second regiment of native white volunteers. One company of the 1st North Carolina and three of the 2nd North Carolina Infantry Regiment (Union) formed in Beaufort. Nearly 1,500 men joined these two regi-

---

43 John A. Hedrick to Benjamin S. Hedrick, June 20, 1862, October 25, 1863, in Browning and Smith, *Letters from a North Carolina Unionist*, 7–8, 163–164; E. A. Harkness to Southard Hoffman, March 5, 1863, Part I, ser. 3238, Box 2, Records of Named Departments, Department of North Carolina, Record Group 393.4, National Archives and Records Administration, Washington, D.C.; B. A. Ensley to J. Jourdan, January 28, 1864, Part II, Letters Sent, October 1863–March 1864, District and Subdistrict of Beaufort, North Carolina, Entry 940, both in Records of U.S. Army Continental Commands, Record Group 393.

44 Manarin and Jordan, *North Carolina Troops*, 1:113–137, 269–272; Benjamin Leecraft to C. C. Lee, March 14, 1862, in Hewett, Trudeau, and Suderow, *Supplement to the Official Records*, pt. 1, 1:598–599.

45 Browning, "Removing the Mask of Nationality," 603–605.

ments throughout the North Carolina coast, earning the soldiers the derisive but obscure nickname "buffaloes" from unsympathetic residents. Thirty-three Carteret men enlisted and many others were refused due to physical disability or age.[46] In October 1862, Rumley bitterly condemned those who took this step as "traitors, who will . . . have the curse of Cain upon them" and proclaimed that they were "induced, by false representations, to sell themselves to the public enemies of their country."[47] Some of these men did have cause to rue their decisions, especially after Confederate forces captured a company of "buffaloes" in February 1864 and executed twenty-two of them as deserters from the Confederate army. Rumley wrote that the remaining locals who had enlisted in the Union army were "poor wretches . . . whose eyes have been opened" by the disaster.[48]

Despite Rumley's view of their motivations, local poor whites took advantage of the Union army's arrival and invitations to improve their economic and physical situations. Whether or not they were ideologically motivated, most poor men recognized the practical advantages of joining the Union army; they could provide food, clothing, shelter, and protection for their families. As Rumley grudgingly admitted, the recruiting efforts "[have] been materially aided by the establishment of a public subsistence store in Beaufort, where the families of volunteers are gratuitously supplied."[49] The opportunity to earn a steady income for their families and provide an acceptable standard of living undeniably led men into the ranks. Lieutenant Colonel James McChesney, commanding officer of the 1st North Carolina Regiment, argued that "the majority of these men have large families who are entirely dependent on the thirteen dollars per month for the supply of all their wants."[50]

---

46 Browning, "'Little-Souled Mercenaries?'" 337–363; Browning, "Removing the Mask of Nationality," 603–604.

47 Rumley's entry for October 1863.

48 Rumley's entry for March 2, 1864; Browning, "'Little-Souled Mercenaries?'" 349, 361–362. For more on the executions at Kinston and their effects, see Collins, "War Crimes or Justice?" 50–83; and Gordon, "In Time of War," 45–58.

49 Rumley's entry for October 1862.

50 J. M. McChesney to Major R. S. Davis, April 6, 1864, Regimental Letter and Endorsement Book, 1st N.C. Infantry, Records Relating to Volunteer Union Organizations, Record Group 94.2.4, National Archives and Records Administration, Washington, D.C.

As the occupation wore on, however, Union agents who thought they had witnessed strong loyalty in the region began to change their tune. One soldier complained in May 1863, "I don't believe that there is a union man in North Carolina."[51] A Massachusetts soldier wrote in late 1862, "They may talk Unionism and take the oath of allegiance, but I have no faith in them, for I think they value their oath no more than they do a piece of blank paper."[52] Even Treasury Agent John Hedrick's attitude toward Union support became more cynical. He commented in August 1863 that he had given up trying to identify a true Unionist among the locals: "The great loyalty, which is said to exist in some parts of the State, I think, exists in the minds of the news writers rather than in reality. . . . There may be a considerable amount of neutrality and a desire to keep out of the war, but this could hardly be considered loyalty."[53]

In March 1863, Rumley asserted that though "some[,] it is true, have strayed from the fold of Israel . . . by far the greater number are as true and steadfast in heartfelt loyalty to North Carolina, as the needle is to the pole."[54] Certainly Rumley remained devoted to the Confederacy, but only secretly. In public interactions with Union officials, Rumley indicated that he was a Unionist. From June 1862 to March 1866, Hedrick met with Rumley several times to consult with him about enticing Unionists to apply for local government offices and discuss certain individuals in the region. Through all their interactions, Hedrick never indicated that he thought Rumley was anything but a loyal Union man. In August 1865, Hedrick recorded that Rumley "is a good man, but slightly tinctured with states' rights."[55] Though Rumley was staunchly loyal to the South, he could project a neutral façade in public interaction with Union officials.

---

51 Joseph Barlow to Ellen Barlow, May 29, 1863, Papers of Joseph Barlow.

52 Spear, "Army Life in the Twenty-Fourth Regiment," 115.

53 John A. Hedrick to Benjamin S. Hedrick, August 9, 1863, in Browning and Smith, Letters from a North Carolina Unionist, 144.

54 Rumley's entry for March 25, 1862.

55 John A. Hedrick to Benjamin S. Hedrick, August 11, 1865, Benjamin Sherwood Hedrick Papers. Hedrick mentioned interactions with Rumley in several of his letters. See John A. Hedrick to Benjamin S. Hedrick, June 20, 1862, and April 17, 1863, in Browning and Smith, Letters from a North Carolina Unionist, 7, 108 and John A. Hedrick to Benjamin S. Hedrick, August 27, 1865, and March 10, 1866, Benjamin Sherwood Hedrick Papers.

Rumley kept his outrage private, spouting his vituperation silently to his diary.

Many Federal agents soon found that sentiment in the region was beginning to prove to be less loyal than they had expected. There are several reasons for this shift in tone among local whites—including proscriptions against trade, destruction of private property, and curtailment of civil rights—but Rumley reveals the primary reason in his diary. Local whites rebelled against a racial policy that they perceived as far too radical. The occupation fundamentally changed the war for local whites and blacks as thousands of slaves flocked to Beaufort and neighboring New Bern from the nearby coastal regions and the state's hinterland, occupying homes that had been abandoned by Confederates when the war began and greatly upsetting the social status quo. (They also lived in tent cities just outside of town.)[56] Horace James, superintendent of Negro affairs in North Carolina, who conducted a census in January 1864, asserted that 17,419 blacks lived under Union protection in eastern North Carolina. Beaufort, whose total black population before the war was about 600 blacks, became home to nearly 2,500 blacks by January 1864, and over 3,200 by 1865, while New Bern housed over 8,500 freedmen in January 1864 and nearly 11,000 a year later (compared to about 3,000 blacks in 1860). Even as the slaves began arriving, local whites continued to hope that all would return to normal when the war ended, regardless of which side ultimately won. However, political developments during the war shattered white hope in the Union as it was.[57]

When President Lincoln announced the Emancipation Proclamation—which was issued on September 22, 1862, and took effect on January 1, 1863—local whites realized that what had been a limited war to restore the Union had become a sweeping, society-changing war.[58] In Beaufort, blacks were granted legal, social, and political rights that had been denied them during slavery. When Rumley repeatedly denounced the Union occupation as a "reign of Niggerism," he was vocalizing the fact that the pillar of white supremacy was being torn down and that white

---

56 For more information, see Browning, "Visions of Freedom and Civilization Opening before Them."

57 Browning, "Visions of Freedom and Civilization Opening before Them," 76–80.

58 Browning, "Removing the Mask of Nationality," 607–612.

former masters were being forced to deal with former slaves as equals. Such actions caused bitterness and increased resistance to occupation in the region.[59]

Though the Emancipation Proclamation granted slaves their freedom de jure, the fact of the matter was that Union soldiers had been granting de facto freedom to slaves from the moment they arrived in the region, despite official pronouncements to the contrary. Rumley noted several incidents of soldiers trying to secrete slaves away and complained that neither Burnside nor Governor Stanly were doing enough to stop this practice. Rumley condemned Burnside as a liar and his February 1862 proclamation (in which the general promised that the Federal government did not intend to interfere with slavery) as "a Yankee trick."[60] Rumley noted on June 7, 1862, that Stanly "deeply lament[ed] the bad effects of the war upon our slave population." But though Stanly had the power to restore fugitive slaves to their loyal owners, Stanly told Rumley that he "deem[ed] it prudent to avoid the exercise of such power to any great extent at present on account of the presence of an abolitionized army."[61] As a result, the local black population began to enjoy numerous freedoms.

With these freedoms came greater legal rights for African Americans. Rumley deplored the fact that blacks could testify or bring charges against white people in military courts. He noted in May 1862 that "in some instances arrests of citizens have been made and property been seized upon negro testimony!" In January 1863, he further bemoaned that the imposition of martial law had replaced all civil courts with military ones. "There," Rumley complained, "a negro, who in our civil courts could not be heard except through his master, can appear as the accuser of any white citizen, and cause the citizen to be arrested."[62]

Rumley and Beaufort residents were appalled when Federal authorities began enlisting African American soldiers into the Union army. Rumley was particularly outraged by the way that Union officials went about enlisting black men. On June 18, 1863, Rumley asserted that "nothing, during

---

59 Rumley's entries for March 25, 1863, August 23, 1863, and March 25, 1864.

60 Rumley's entry for May 1862; Ambrose Burnside, "Proclamation Made to the People of North Carolina," February 16, 1862, *Official Records, Army*, ser. 1, 9:363–364. The Emancipation Proclamation did not take effect until January 1, 1863, eleven months after Burnside's proclamation.

61 Rumley's entry for June 7, 1862.

62 Rumley's entries for May 1862 and January 1, 1863.

our captivity, has shocked the feelings of some of our people more than the act of the military authorities here, converting the court room of our Court House, in Beaufort, into a negro Recruiting office!"[63] Though the clerk of the county court might have more reason to be disturbed by the location of the recruiting office than others, Rumley shared with many whites the fear about what armed black soldiers might do. He envisioned a nightmarish day when "Armies of black negroes may yet be turned upon us, to complete the ruin and desolation that Yankee vandalism has begun." Rumley bewailed, "Visions of armed and infuriated bands of these black traitors, like imps of darkness, rise before us and darken the future."[64] Rumley's fears were undoubtedly compounded in the summer of 1864, when a new Federal law allowed agents to recruit blacks into the army and have that count toward the quota of their home state. The recruiting agents operated primarily out of New Bern and offered a $300 bounty to enlistees, bringing even more black troops into the region.[65]

Rumley and other local whites were equally distressed by the arrival of northern missionaries who sought to elevate the former slaves by providing education for them. Black pupils, hungry for knowledge, were enthusiastic learners, and Union agents began opening schools soon after arriving in the region. Union officers and even some barely literate local blacks had been teaching in schools continuously for over a year before the American Missionary Association opened its first two formal schools in New Bern on July 23, 1863. They extended their efforts far too rapidly for local white tastes. By the end of March 1864, New Bern boasted eleven freedmen schools while Beaufort had three, and nine others existed in the occupied regions of coastal North Carolina; these twenty-three schools enrolled approximately 3,000 black students. Rumley was in earnest when he proclaimed on December 1, 1863: "The solemn tones of the church bells, as they announced, the appointed hours, for the opening of these negro schools, sound in our ears like the death knell of the social and political power of the white race of the south!"[66]

Rumley's diary not only minutely documents the constant racial antagonism in the region, giving voice to white outrage at certain liber-

---

63   Rumley's entry for [June 18, 1863].
64   Rumley's entry for March 25, 1863.
65   Reid, *Freedom for Themselves*, 187–192.
66   Browning, "Bringing Light to Our Land," 5.

ties granted to African Americans, but also reveals the myriad ways that blacks attempted to wield their newfound power over local whites by showing "insolence" to whites, using the army to gain economic and social advantages over whites, and interfering with local white activities. Often the desire of blacks to assert their independence led to confrontations with local whites or Union agents over the nature of what it meant to be free and occupy a place in this new social order. Some Beaufort residents merely voiced their unhappiness with their occupiers. A correspondent for the *New York Herald* wrote of local reactions to Union soldiers teaching blacks how to read in May 1862: "More than one of our old citizens have been heard to declare, that, if it was not for the military, 'the fellow that taught them would have his neck stretched.'"[67] Others took action to intimidate northern teachers and discourage black students from attending schools. In 1864, three white men torched one of the black schoolhouses in Beaufort and threatened the female teacher with violence unless she promised to "never again teach the 'niggers' to read."[68]

Some took out their frustrations on the blacks themselves. Just days after the Emancipation Proclamation took effect on January 1, 1863, an African American woman sought out Joel Henry Davis, perhaps the foremost Unionist in the region and a man she knew well, to insist that her daughter be released from slavery. Beaufort's provost marshal recorded what happened next: "Mr. Davis and Mr. Rieger together tied the woman to a tree her arms over her head and then whipped her severely, the flesh on her arms where the ropes went was badly lacerated and her arms covered with blood when I saw her." Davis, a practical merchant, had taken the oath of allegiance, but he did not welcome some of the government's more radical war aims, embodied in the woman's demand on behalf of her daughter. Davis lashed out at the woman to reinforce the old order of white supremacy and challenge the new sense of freedom that empowered blacks.[69]

In June 1863, after several incidents in which residents were charged with illegally trading with people outside Union lines, the military au-

---

67 *New York Herald*, May 31, 1862, quoted in *The Liberator*, June 27, 1862.

68 James, *Annual Report of the Superintendent*, 20–21.

69 William B. Fowle, Jr., to Major Southard Hoffman, January 14, 1863, Box 2, Part I, Records of Named Departments, Record Group 393.4. Joel Henry Davis and Henry Rieger were prosperous merchants in Beaufort; North Carolina, 5:175, 176L, R. G. Dun & Co. Collection.

thorities issued an ultimatum that all those who had not taken the oath of allegiance be evicted from the town. Rumley would have been one of these evictees. However, the order was later changed to give residents one last chance to take the oath and avoid eviction. Rumley implied in his diary that he would take the oath but would not consider it to be legally or morally binding.[70]

Rumley's diary reveals another form of resistance in which Beaufort residents maintained illicit communications with Confederates outside the Union lines by means of what he termed "the underground rail-ways." He first mentioned the establishment of this line of communication in March 1863, when he wrote that letters and contraband articles had made their way to Confederates outside the lines. He lamented in May 1863 that letters from this pipeline had fallen into Union hands, alerting Union soldiers to the clandestine activity. A year later in June and July 1864, Rumley noted that the underground railway was still going strong, bringing news of Confederate military actions to sympathetic residents in Beaufort.[71]

On February 8, 1865, Rumley documented the arrest of Miss Emeline Pigott, a local woman who had served as a regular conductor of the "underground railway" and was caught carrying contraband goods across Union lines. Living just north of Morehead City, Pigott often illegally carried mail between the lines, writing in her diary on February 7, 1865, "I met Confederate scouts near the Neuse River with a Lady friend—[and delivered] all the news that I knew with letters & papers."[72] On February 8, 1865, she enlisted her brother-in-law to assist her in her latest mission. Underneath her hoop skirt she wore two pairs of Confederate pants and a pair of boots and, remarkably, carried in her voluminous skirt a shirt, a cap, a dozen linen collars and pocket handkerchiefs, 50 skeins of silk, spools of cotton, needles, toothbrushes, combs, knives, razors, gloves, and several letters addressed to Confederates. At about 4:00 p.m. Union soldiers arrested the two and discovered Pigott's hidden contraband. The

---

70   Rumley's entry for June 1863; Mallison, *The Civil War on the Outer Banks*, 119.

71   Rumley's entries for March 25, 1863, May 23, 1863, June 22, 1864, and July 28, 1864.

72   Entry dated February 7, 1865, [Emeline Pigott] Diary, Benjamin Franklin Royal Papers.

soldiers placed her in the Beaufort jail before moving her to New Bern. In protest, some residents caused such a disturbance at a local store that the provost marshal arrested a number of them, closed down the store, and fined each one $10.[73]

In addition to documenting resistance and the local reaction to Union occupation, Rumley also reflected on military matters, including Union expeditions into the countryside and efforts to use Beaufort as a staging area for an assault on Wilmington and Fort Fisher. He also offered a perceptive view of the workings of martial law in the region and the competencies of different commanders in the region. The loyal southerner paid careful attention to Confederate attempts to retake the Beaufort region and the great disturbance this caused among Federal authorities and civilians in Beaufort. Rumley was particularly outraged when anxious Union officers compelled local whites to take arms to repel a suspected Confederate attack in late February 1864. He fumed, "They have summoned every man they could find who is so unfortunate as to be under forty-five years of age, and forced arms into their hands to kill their own brethren and friends with!"[74] Unionist John Hedrick confirmed Rumley's account, writing on March 1, 1864, "All able bodied citizens, present company excepted, were put under arms yesterday evening, for Provost duty." The local citizens were impressed into service for at least the next week. Hedrick wrote on March 7, "All men between the ages of 18 & 45 are enrolled and armed."[75] The commotion soon passed as the Confederate forces abandoned their assault plans for the New Bern–Beaufort area.

Rumley also recorded interactions with nonmilitary enemies; he offered an eyewitness account of the tragic yellow fever epidemic that struck New Bern and Beaufort in the summer of 1864. The fever began in New Bern in September 1864 or perhaps even earlier (John Hedrick referred to a possibility of it in June). Rumley wrote about the dangerous illness

---

73 Calvin Jarrett, "The Spy Was a Lady," *Greensboro Daily News*, September 29, 1963; entries dated February 9, 10, and 17 (quotation February 17), Edmund Janes Cleveland Diary; *Old North State* (Beaufort, N.D.), February 11, 1865; "Sketch of Miss Emeline Pigott," Levi Woodbury Pigott Collection.

74 Rumley's entry for February 29, 1864.

75 John Hedrick to Benjamin S. Hedrick, March 1 and March 7, 1864, in Browning and Smith, *Letters from a North Carolina Unionist*, 188, 189.

for the first time on October 1, 1864.[76] Though the dreaded "black vomit" disease did not claim its first victims in Beaufort until early October 1864, it had been wreaking havoc in New Bern and causing panic among many civilians and military personnel in the region. By October 7, Rumley had realized the seriousness of the situation; he wrote of the grim news from New Bern with dramatic flair: "With steady strides the terrible pestilence walks in darkness, and destroys at noon day, in that scourged and unhappy town."[77] Soon Beaufort was equally unhappy, and over the next six weeks Rumley wrote eight entries dealing with the outbreak in town, identifying many of those who had succumbed to its ill effects. Finally, on November 13, Rumley cautiously noted, "The pestilence has probably taken its final leave of Beaufort." The epidemic had claimed over 1,000 lives in New Bern and Beaufort.[78] The fever caused more casualties in the Beaufort region than any military confrontation in the area during the war.

Rumley closed his diary in August 1865, soon after Union troops had been removed from Beaufort and most of the citizens who had fled in 1862 or had served in the Confederate armies throughout the war had finally returned home. But there was still much uneasiness in the town. Civil law had returned to the county but only under the control of those who could satisfactorily demonstrate their loyalty to the Federal government. As a result, the town had "good and loyal men" serving as mayor, town commissioners, and policemen. True to form, Rumley was able to convince the magistrates of his loyalty and had returned as clerk of the superior court. African Americans, led by the charismatic former slave Abraham Galloway, called for the right to vote. Northern missionaries remained in the region to run several schools established for the freed slave population. Thousands of refugee freedpeople were still living in and around Beaufort. However, the Federal government was rapidly re-

---

76   John A. Hedrick to Benjamin S. Hedrick, June 3 and September 19 and 26, 1864, in Browning and Smith, *Letters from a North Carolina Unionist*, 209, 226, 228; Rumley's entry for October 1, 1864.

77   Rumley's entry for October 7, 1864.

78   Rumley's entry for November 13, 1864; Farnham and King, "'The March of the Destroyer,'" 435–483.

turning all property to former Confederates, which soon escalated tensions in the region.[79]

Beaufort was closing one tumultuous chapter of its existence only to open another, for Reconstruction proved to be a time of much hostility and hard feelings in the region. Yet Rumley—as a white man who felt that the town's residents had endured much abuse at the hands of the "abolitionized army" during the war and who hoped to help lead a return to white man's rule—saw liberation and possible redemption in the end of military occupation. He mused in his diary's final entry: "The dark night which settled upon us in March 1862, is passing away. And though the day upon which we are entering is not clear, and shadows rest upon the horizon, yet we hope, as the day advances, the clouds may roll away, and the skies may grow brighter than the early dawn assures."[80] It is a shame that the diary ends at this point. The Federal government sought to enforce civil rights legislation in regions like coastal North Carolina for the next ten years before eventually abandoning the effort. Rumley's colorful depictions of a tenuous Republican coalition struggling to maintain power among the conservative white Democrats would have been as enlightening as his Civil War journal.

*   *   *

What motivated Rumley to write his diary, especially since he did not begin it until the moment Union troops arrived? In one respect, the diary served a cathartic purpose for Rumley; it provided him an opportunity to privately shout all the outrage that he could not voice publicly. He would not risk openly opposing the Unionists and being evicted. It afforded him an opportunity to manage his feelings and emotions regarding the occupation while giving him a venue to delineate his personal ideologies and political beliefs. It also gave him a sense of purpose. The diary allowed Rumley to convince himself that he was living up to a code of southern honor that he would not risk manifesting publicly. Quite likely, Rumley

---

79 Rumley's entries for July 4, 1865, July 6, 1865, and August 1865. For more on the escalating tensions over land ownership, see Browning, "Visions of Freedom and Civilization Opening before Them," 69–100.

80 Rumley's entries for June 7, 1862 and August 1865.

believed he was serving the cause of the Confederacy by recording the evils of northern misrule as a testament to southern fortitude for future generations. He could wield his pen to assert his and his loyal neighbors' political commitment to the Confederacy even during a time of trial.

Rumley wrote his diary with one eye toward future generations. It appears that he was aware that his diary would likely be read by a future audience, presumably one that would be very sympathetic to the southern attempt at independence. As a result, he crafted some eloquent passages that would be wasted if no one were to benefit from them. What he excluded from the diary is also notable. The diary lacks any personal references to himself or his family. Rumley never once mentioned those who were living in his own household, nor did he reveal any intimate details about himself, preferring to maintain a strictly journalistic approach. He carefully reported each of the abuses heaped on southerners by the Yankee oppressors but glossed over the failures of the Confederacy. He did not denounce the Confederate government for its lack of adequate protection for the coast, its inability to retake the region from the Yankees, or any of its failed policies.

He also carefully refrained from naming many Unionists from Beaufort. The only ones he listed were outsiders who had no strong attachment to the region. He admitted that some lacked faith and joined the Union side, but he repeatedly suggested that the majority of the local residents remained steadfast in their loyalty to the Confederacy. As late as February 1865, after repeated military disasters, Rumley kept his faith in the genius of General Robert E. Lee, writing, "We will not despair while such a man lives in hope."[81] Even when he discussed those who deserted the southern armies, as he did in late November 1863, he absolved the turncoats by saying that they were not fully aware of the danger of the steps they were taking: "They are incapable of appreciating the momentous character of the struggle in which the south is now engaged, and the awful doom that awaits her if she succumbs to Federal power; or they would not desert her standard."[82]

Rumley spent much of his diary criticizing Union military policy from a high Victorian cultural perspective. Rumley saw Yankee misrule

---

81   Rumley's entry for February 28, 1865.
82   Rumley's entry for November 21, 1863.

as largely resulting from the inferiority of the character of northerners. Rumley consciously used negative language to explain northern behavior and Union policy. He considered Union policy to be deliberately antagonistic and used words such as "lying," "tricks," and "fanaticism" (in a very pejorative sense) to depict the character of northerners. In May 1862, angry that General Burnside was not doing more to protect the property of slave owners, he declared that Burnside's "lying proclamation was a Yankee trick."[83] He considered Captain William Fowle, the provost marshal from Massachusetts, to be "a fanatic . . . of the John Brown school."[84] The enlistment of black soldiers was "a diabolical scheme . . . first suggested by northern fanatics."[85] He complained that the slaves, who he insisted had been peaceful and content, had been "filled with venomous hate by the poisonous breath of fanaticism."[86] In fact, Rumley negatively referred to northern fanatics or fanaticism twenty-two times in the diary. In Rumley's construct, those who wished to bring social change to the southern order were not honest men with a high moral purpose but misguided evil men who wished to bring harm and destruction to the South. Hence, Rumley viewed any northern attempts to challenge the status quo antebellum as dishonorable and malevolent. Rumley's diary reveals how a zealous Confederate reconfigured the war through his own cultural and political assumptions.

James Rumley is buried at the southwestern boundary of the tranquil Old Burying Ground at the western corner of the Ann Street Methodist Church, his grave shaded by mature live oaks. His gravestone inscription reads simply "Faithful in all his trusts." Rumley saw himself as such a faithful man—faithful in his court duties as executor of many wills, faithful as financial officer of the county, and, during the war, certainly true to the cause of southern independence. Long after Rumley was laid to rest, members of the United Daughters of the Confederacy placed an iron plaque in front of Rumley's grave. The cross-shaped plaque reads "1861–1865" and has the phrase *Deo Vindice* ("God will defend us") embossed upon it, which was the motto listed on the Great Seal of the Con-

---

83   Rumley's entry for May 1862.
84   Rumley's entry for March 4, 1863.
85   Rumley's entry for May 30, 1863.
86   Rumley's entry for August 4, 1863.

federacy. Rumley is an intriguing recipient of this memorial. All the other graves in the cemetery that bear such a plaque belong to former Confederate soldiers. Rumley would certainly feel the honor was deserved, however. Though he never enlisted, Rumley served the Confederacy in his own way. In his diary, he kept the faith that the South would be victorious, and he consciously constructed the story of the occupation as one of unmitigated Yankee villainy and persevering southern nobility, providing a heroic record that he must have hoped future residents of Beaufort and the South would read and celebrate.

THE DIARY OF JAMES RUMLEY

1862

[Diary Opens, no date]
First page. 1st. And here we begin

On the morning of Thursday the 13th. of March 1862, the inhabitants of Beaufort were aroused by the sound of heavy cannonading in the direction of New Bern, which continued, with slight intermissions, for several hours. This, together with the non-arrival of the cars due from that place the previous night induced the belief that the Federal fleet, known to be in the waters of North Carolina, had ascended the Neuse River and attacked the defensive work below New Bern.[1]

On the morning of Friday the 14th. intelligence reached us that on the previous day the Federal fleet, after thoroughly bomb-shelling the woods, landed a considerable force on the South shore of the Neuse, below the river batteries, and on Friday attacked the works in the rear of the batteries. After a sharp conflict the Confederates retreated. The batteries being evacuated, the fleet then proceeded up the river and captured New Bern.

---

1   General Ambrose Burnside landed a Union expeditionary force south of New Bern on the Neuse River on March 13, 1862. The battle of New Bern occurred the next day, in which Confederates were driven from the city. See Barrett, *The Civil War in North Carolina*, 17–29; Daniel Read Larned to Mrs. Ambrose E. Burnside, March 15, 1862, Daniel Read Larned Papers.

Saturday, March 15, 1862.

The capture of New Bern by the Federal forces under General Burnside[2] cuts off Beaufort and Fort Macon from all communication by mail with the interior, and probably seals their destiny for the present war. This shuts the back door of retreat upon Beaufort and Fort Macon, which being blockaded and closely watched by sea and sound, may be considered captured.

The clouds that have long been darkening the horizon are gathering over us. The night, whose shades long darkening the Southern skies, foretold its coming, is closing upon us. When will the morning come?

Monday, March 17, 1862.

The Confederate steamer *Nashville* left this port at 8 o'clock P. M. After passing the bar in safety she was fired upon by the blockading vessels outside, but probably escaped. She had lately arrived at this port from England, via Bermuda, running the blockade. After the fall of New Bern she had no alternative but to risk the guns of the blockading vessels again, or submit to capture. It was quite dark when she moved from her moorings.

On Friday and Saturday, the 21st. and 22nd. of March, 1862, General John G. Parke,[3] U.S. Army, with about 1,500 troops from New Bern, occupied Carolina City, in Carteret County. On Sunday, the 23rd., he sent a flag of truce to Fort Macon[4] with a proposition to the Commandant[5] to surrender the fort. On Monday, 24th., several Federal officers, under a flag of truce from General Parke, came to Beaufort to invite some of the citizens to a conference with Genl. Parke at Carolina City. On the same

---

2   Ambrose Everett Burnside (1824–1881) commanded the successful Federal expedition to North Carolina that seized much of the state's coast between February and April 1862. Warner, *Generals in Blue*, 57–58.

3   John G. Parke (1827–1900) served as a brigadier general in Burnside's North Carolina expedition. Warner, *Generals in Blue*, 359–360.

4   Fort Macon was a masonry fort constructed between 1826 and 1834 that was located on Bogue Banks and protected Beaufort harbor. Heidler and Heidler, *Encyclopedia of the American Civil War*, 2:739.

5   Lieutenant Colonel Moses J. White was commandant of Fort Macon in the spring of 1862. Branch, *The Siege of Fort Macon*, 9.

day Col. J.H. Taylor,[6] Benjamin L. Perry[7] and James Rumley,[8] proceeded to Morehead City, where they received from Genl. Parke a message to the citizens of Beaufort, requiring an answer.

Tuesday, March 25, 1862.

James Rumley and Robert W. Chadwick,[9] by request of the committee of safety, proceeded to the headquarters of Genl. Parke at Carolina City, to bear an answer to his message of the day previous; and had an interview with him touching the situation of Beaufort during the contemplated investment of the fort.

During the night of the 25th. of March, two companies of U.S. troops, under command of Major John A. Allen[10] of the 4th. Regiment Rhode Island Volunteers, occupied the town, and the next day established a Military Government over the town and vicinity. A few days after this, another company was added to the garrison.

All persons leaving town are now required to have written passes. To obtain these, an oath of allegiance has to be taken by each applicant. Very

---

6   James H. Taylor (b. ca. 1802) attended the University of North Carolina from 1827 to 1828 but did not graduate. In 1860, he was a farmer who owned twenty-three slaves. Eighth Census, 1860: Carteret County; Grant, *Alumni History of the University of North Carolina*, 611.

7   Benjamin L. Perry (1811–1869) was a merchant, insurance agent, and former county clerk. *Cemetery Records of Carteret County*, 160; Eighth Census, 1860: Carteret County; *Halcyon and Beaufort Intelligencer*, October 10, 1854; North Carolina, 5:163, 170, R. G. Dun & Co. Collection.

8   James Rumley (1812–1881), the author of this diary, served successively as clerk of the superior court and the court of pleas and quarters during the period 1848 to 1881. This third-person reference is either his own style or a later editor's insertion. *Cemetery Records of Carteret County*, 162; Eighth Census, 1860: Carteret County.

9   Robert W. Chadwick (1826–1884) was a graduate of Emory and Henry College in Emory, Virginia, and director of the Beaufort Male Academy. He served as clerk of the county court from 1856 to 1860. Muse, *Grandpa Was a Whaler*, 34; *Cemetery Records of Carteret County*, 150; Eighth Census, 1860: Carteret County; *Halcyon and Beaufort Intelligencer*, November 7, 1854.

10 Major John A. Allen was a commander of the 4th Rhode Island Volunteers. He took a leave of absence soon after Union forces captured Fort Macon and eventually resigned from the service on August 11, 1862. Branch, *The Siege of Fort Macon*, 96.

few citizens do this willingly. Some are compelled by their situation to do it. Persons from the country who come to town, not knowing what regulations exist here, are not allowed to return to their homes without a pass; and they are thus forced to take the oath. Most of them regard the oath under such circumstances as compulsory and not binding on the conscience. In some instances passes are obtained without any oath, and in others, by the oath of neutrality. But most of the citizens, feeling an utter abhorrence of either oath, keep within the limits of the town, rather than procure passes on the conditions required.

All communication between Beaufort and Fort Macon is cut off.

April [n.d.], 1862.

That deception which is known to belong to the Yankee character, has been severely practiced upon the people of Carteret county, by the Federal army. When this army came here, they offered assurances of ample protection to persons and property, and avowed their determination to have nothing to do with the slaves, and to do nothing which would encourage insubordination among them, or in any way disturb the relations existing between them and their owners. Such assurances of a conservative and conciliatory policy, following upon the heels of an awful and imposing proclamation of their commanding General Burnside, allayed, somewhat, the fears of the inhabitants, and inspired the hope that their invaders, while they hated the South, would nevertheless see the manifest policy of respecting the institutions and laws of the State.[11]

Well, what shall the record say, for the few weeks these professed Union savers have had the control of this town? Their first act, upon their entrance into the town, was the seizure of a vacant private dwelling house belonging to a widow residing in the town, for a barrack for their soldiers. Without ascertaining from the owner whether they could get the keys or not, they broke open the doors, took possession of the premises, and hoisted the United States flag over the roof of the house. At any other point on the harbor, within range of the guns of Fort Macon, this act would have provoked a fire from the fort.

---

11   General Burnside issued a proclamation on February 16, 1862, stating that he wished to protect native interests and property and did not seek to confiscate anything, including slaves. *Official Records, Army*, ser. 1, 9, pt. 1:363–364.

Their next act, worthy of notice, was to press into their service, chiefly as boatmen, fifteen or twenty slaves, without consulting their owners, who were then residing in the town. These slaves aver that the Federal officers promised to pay them and not their owners, for their services. We judge this is true, and that other secret influences are aiding to corrupt the slaves, from the fearful signs we see of a growing excitement among them. They evidently think a jubilee is coming.

The next act of outrage upon private rights, was the seizure of the Atlantic Hotel in Beaufort, the property of Capt. Pender.[12] In this building was a great deal of valuable furniture. Capt. Pender was absent on private business. Mrs. Pender[13] had lately died. The building was occupied by a lady who remained there in charge of three of Mrs. Pender's children, infants of tender years.[14] The building was entered by officers, soldiers and negroes and robbed of its most valuable furniture, which was carried off. As there was no act of the Federal Congress authorizing a seizure of property in this way, it will of course not be accounted for to the government, and will, no doubt, be appropriated to the private use of officers, soldiers and negroes.

The premises of Dr. King[15] have been entered and searched under an order from the Military Commandant[16] of the town. The ostensible

---

12 Josiah Solomon Pender (1819–1864) was a merchant who organized the first company of Confederate troops from Beaufort and led the capture of Fort Macon on April 14, 1861. He was dismissed from the Confederate military in December 1861 for being absent without leave due to his wife's fatal illness. Pender then served as a blockade-runner until his death from yellow fever on October 25, 1864. *New Bern Daily Progress*, April 16 and 19, 1861; *Cemetery Records of Carteret County*, 160; North Carolina, 5:176A, R. G. Dun & Co. Collection; Powell, *Dictionary of North Carolina Biography*, 5:62–63.

13 Marie Louise Pender (1826–1861) died of an undisclosed illness on December 18, 1861. Unprocessed papers, Box 3, F. C. Salisbury Collection.

14 Betsy Harper was the housekeeper of Pender's Atlantic Hotel and had charge of Pender's children while he was away. The three children are likely Mariah Pender (b. ca. 1859), America Pender (b. ca. 1854), and Paul Pender (b. ca. 1851). Unprocessed papers, Box 3, F. C. Salisbury Collection; Eighth Census, 1860: Carteret County.

15 Dr. Francis Lathrop King (1805–1874) was a physician who lived in Beaufort with his wife and two teenage daughters. Eighth Census, 1860: Carteret County; *Cemetery Records of Carteret County*, 157.

16 Major John A. Allen, 4th Rhode Island Volunteers. Branch, *The Siege of Fort Macon*, 42; *Official Records, Army*, ser. 1, vol. 9, 291.

object was to look for powder, supposed to be in the Doctor's possession, but the real object doubtless was to annoy the family for their well known hatred of the Yankees. Not satisfied with a fruitless search for powder and the plunder of 15 barrels of corn from the private stores of the family, this Military commandant, or Military Governor as he is styled, has posted two armed sentinels in this gentleman's private yard, to interdict communication between his family and the citizens of the place.

Wednesday, April 23, 1862.

Attention was directed today to a Federal steamer which appeared in the eastern channel of the harbor, and sent a flag of truce in the direction of Fort Macon, bearing to the Commandant of the post, it is supposed, notification of an intended attack and a proposition for a surrender of the fort. The flag of truce was met by a boat from the fort. After having apparently, a short parley, the latter returned to the fort. Late in the evening they met again.

Thursday, April 24, 1862.

The flags of truce were out again this morning, attracting all eyes on the harbor. Gen. Burnside, the Federal Commander, and Col. White,[17] the Commandant of the fort had an interview in person, on Shackleford's Banks. Col. White declined to surrender the fort.

Order has been given to the Federal batteries on Bogue Banks to commence firing on the fort.

Friday, April 25, 1862.

At an early hour this morning the Federal batteries on Bogue Banks, comprising one battery of four 8-inch siege mortars, one of five 10-inch siege mortars, and one of three rifled siege guns, opened fire on the fort;

---

17   Moses J. White (1835–1865) finished second in his class at West Point (1858). After resigning from the U.S. army, he took command at Fort Macon on October 5, 1861. Suffering from epilepsy, White died in Natchez, Mississippi, on January 29, 1865. Heitman, *Historical Register*, 1:1028; Manarin and Jordan, *North Carolina Troops*, 1:40; Branch, *The Siege of Fort Macon*, 9.

the farthest battery being about 1300 yards distant. The garrison at the fort vigorously returned the fire. About 10 o'clock A.M. three Federal steamers at sea drew up within good range of the fort and opened a heavy fire of bombshells. One of them soon received a shot from the fort, which went through her; and they all backed out of the fight. This naval exploit hurt nobody. But the shots from the batteries; made the dust rise in clouds from the embankments and walls of the fort; while now and then the smoke of bursting bombshells within the fort, could be seen rising above the walls. The bombs were thrown with little precision from batteries or ships, and sometimes burst high in the air, and scattered their fragments over land and sea. Their explosions were like peals of thunder; discharges from the heavy cannon and mortars jarred the earth beneath us, and shook every tenement around. The day seemed suited for holier work. The sun was shining brightly, and the wind was blowing softly from the sea, while the fight was going on. But the scene was one of painful interest to the inhabitants of Beaufort, many of whom had husbands, brothers or sons in the doomed fortification.

About 5 o'clock P.M. the firing ceased at the fort. Soon after, the batteries ceased to fire. A parley ensued.

Saturday, April 26, 1862.

This morning, the garrison surrendered and were released on parole,[18] and Fort Macon is now occupied by a Federal garrison. The loss in the garrison was eight killed and fourteen wounded. The Federal loss was one killed and a few wounded. So say the Federal officers.

The long expected contest for the possession of Beaufort Harbor is over. The flag of the United States now waves over its shores and its waters. But that flag, once the cherished symbol of our national glory, excites no enthusiasm in us now. Borne and polluted by the hands of fanatics and tyrants it has become the most loathed and hated ensign that ever waved over any people.

General Burnside visited Beaufort today. Some of the citizens presented him with a petition, setting forth the spirit of insubordination daily manifesting itself, and the desertions occurring among the slaves;

---

18   *Official Records, Army*, ser. 1, 9, pt. 1:276; Browning, "Removing the Mask of Nationality," 600.

arising from an undue excitement produced among them by the presence of his army, which is threatening our country with ruin. The petition reminded him of his offers of protection, in his proclamation to the people of this state, and requested him to make an order prohibiting slaves hereafter from entering the lines of his army at their several stations on this harbor, and thus avoid the difficulty created by a late act of the Federal Congress prohibiting the surrender of fugitive slaves after they have entered the lines of the army.[19] He received the petition very courteously, and promised to grant the request.

May [n.d.], 1862.

Within a few days after the fall of Fort Macon, the town of Beaufort was occupied by six companies of the 4th. Regiment of Rhode Island Volunteers. A military governor, Col. Rodman,[20] and a Provost Marshal, Major Allen, have been appointed for the town.

Civil liberty has now fled. The presence of armed sentinels within and without the town, indicate the reign of military despotism. The darkness of night, starless and rayless, enshrouds us. Between us and our Southern friends the curtain is drawn, through which no ray of light nor even of sympathy can reach us. Our minds are groping in a wilderness of gloomy thought. The past, bright with the memories of a once glorious country, rises before us, at times in mournful contrast with our present state of political darkness and ruin; which, o'er the dark abyss of the future hope scarcely throws a beam of light.

Slaves are now deserting in scores from all parts of the county, and our

---

19   The First Confiscation Act (August 6, 1861) granted the president power to seize any property used to aid the rebellion. It also ended masters' claims over their slaves if they had used those slaves to assist the Confederate military. The act did not define the status of released slaves, however. Lincoln did not vigorously prosecute the law. Heidler and Heidler, *Encyclopedia of the American Civil War*, 1:477.

20   Isaac Peace Rodman was colonel of the 4th Rhode Island Regiment from October 30, 1861, until April 28, 1862. On the latter date he was promoted to brigadier general. He became a division commander in the IX Corps before the Battle of Antietam. Rodman died on September 30, 1862, of wounds received at the Battle of Antietam on September 17, 1862. Heitman, *Historical Register*, 1:841; Warner, *Generals in Blue*, 409–410.

worst fears on this subject are likely to be realized. The order which General Burnside promised to make, to prevent them from entering his lines, has not been made. His lying proclamation was a Yankee trick. These runaway Negroes are allowed to pass the sentinels at any time, even in the night. Often white citizens are required to retire to their homes. They are welcomed at the different quarters by officers and soldiers, while the lying scoundrels who receive them declare they do not encourage them to come among them and do not want such nuisances. An infamous law of the Federal Congress, prohibiting the surrender of fugitive slaves, enables these fanatics to make their quarters perfect harbors of runaway negroes.[21] Officers employ them in various capacities and pay them for their services, ignoring the rights of the owners and violating the law of the state.[22] They get information from them as to the political opinions and conduct of the owners, and in some instances arrests of citizens have been made and property been seized upon negro testimony.

The soldiers go, without hesitation, into the kitchens among the negroes and encourage them to leave their owners. Some of them have been seen promenading the streets with negro wenches.

The inhabitants are filled with loathing and disgust by the presence of this pestilent army. The disastrous effects of their conduct towards the slave population have been represented to Gen. Parke, who has taken up his quarters here for the present. He has promised to correct this evil; but does not do it.

June 7, 1862.

The Hon. Edward Stanly,[23] Military Governor of North Carolina, arrived here today. He deeply laments the bad effects of the war upon our slave population. He is clothed with power to restore fugitive slaves to

---

21 Rumley is referring to the First Confiscation Act.

22 The Revised Slave Code of 1855, Chapter 107, Section 31, forbade slaves from, among other things, trafficking in goods with others without their master's permission. Johnson, *Ante-Bellum North Carolina*, 498–499.

23 Edward Stanly (1810–1872) was born in New Bern and represented North Carolina in Congress before moving to California in the early 1850s. Lincoln appointed Stanly military governor of North Carolina in April 1862. Stanly arrived in New Bern on May 26 to take office. Powell, *Dictionary of North Carolina Biography*, 5:423.

their owners, but deems it prudent to avoid the exercise of such power to any great extent at present on account of the presence of an abolition- ized army; and will direct his efforts mainly to the establishment of such regulations at the different posts, as will prevent the escape of slaves from the state, until peace is restored, when he thinks they will be returned to their owners. He will establish a Custom House and post office.

Most of the vacant dwelling houses in town have been taken by the Federal officers for barracks for their soldiers or quarters for themselves. Among others, the house of Mr. E.H. Norcom,[24] who is absent with his family, has been occupied by 10 or 12 officers, the Provost Marshal among them, who has his office there. Nearly all the house furniture of the fam- ily has been left there, even Mrs. Norcom's[25] wardrobe. The kitchen and backyard have become a perfect den of thieving runaway negroes. These have had free access to every part of the dwelling. They have appropriated to themselves such articles as they wanted, especially bed furniture and table furniture; they have taken the whole of the lady's wardrobe; and even her bridal dress has been worn by negroes. A big buck negro was lately seen seated in the parlor, thrumming on Mrs. Norcom's piano.

At the house owned by Mr. Benjamin Leecraft,[26] which is also occu- pied by officers, negroes have been allowed to take furniture and even the dresses of Mr. Leecraft's deceased wife[27] and child,[28] which had been left there by him. These have been worn by negroes.

The mask, which concealed at first the hideous features of fanaticism,

---

24   Edmund Halsey Norcom (1824–1867) was an 1847 University of North Caro- lina graduate, former state legislator, and merchant. *Cemetery Records of Carteret County*, 160; Battle, *History of the University of North Carolina*, 1:801.

25   Laura Dusenberry Norcom (b. ca. 1827), who hailed from Lexington, North Carolina, married Edmund Halsey Norcom in 1847. They had six children together. Browning and Smith, *Letters from a North Carolina Unionist*, 71; Eighth Census, 1860: Carteret County; Ninth Census, 1870: Carteret County.

26   Benjamin Leecraft, Jr. (b. ca. 1823), was a dry goods merchant in 1860. He or- ganized a company of Confederate troops from Beaufort in October 1861. He resigned his commission as captain on April 16, 1862, and never returned to Beaufort. Manarin and Jordan, *North Carolina Troops*, 1:269; Eighth Census, 1860: Carteret County; North Carolina, 5:163, R. G. Dun & Co. Collection.

27   Mary E. Arendell Leecraft (1826–1858), was the daughter of Bridges and Sarah Arendell. *Cemetery Records of Carteret County*, 158.

28   Wilbur Leecraft (1846–1858). *Cemetery Records of Carteret County*, 158.

is now thrown off, and the conduct of the troops in reference to the slaves, has become alarming to the inhabitants. Those fanatics feel a bitter hatred towards slaveholders, and the lying stories the slaves have told them of the cruelty of their owners has made their hatred stronger. If any citizen were to chastise a disobedient slave, he would run the hazard of being mobbed by ruffianly soldiers. If an owner attempts to recover a runaway slave, he runs the same risk. Owners have permission to take their slaves wherever they find them, if they can do so without using forcible means. If the slave is willing to go the owner can take him along with him. If not the soldiers will interfere and protect the slave. The consequence is very few runaways are recovered. Citizens in search of their slaves have been threatened with violence and compelled to desist.

A few days ago, while some of the troops were embarking on board a steamer at King's wharf (supposing they were taking their final leave of Beaufort), they attempted to take off with them a number of slaves belonging to citizens of this county. Some of the owners, who were present, discovered their slaves and seized them. The ruffians who were engaged in this attempt to kidnap them immediately attempted to rescue them, and would have done so but for the timely efforts of an officer, Capt. King[29] (the only one out of a number present), who manfully exercised his authority, and prevented the outrage. Then troops, for some unknown cause, were ordered back to town. When they returned two of them went forcibly into a private dwelling in town where one of the negroes referred to was tied, seized the negro, a boy, and carried him off to their quarters. The other negroes, who had been wrested from the soldiers succeeded in getting back to them.

These thieving soldiers on attempting a second time to embark, contrived a new mode of kidnapping. They boxed up the negroes and carted them to the wharf, with their baggage, unobserved. In this way four negroes were conveyed on board the Steamer *Empire City* lying in the harbor. They were discovered, however, by the master of the vessel and were sent back to Beaufort.

29 Captain John N. King was brigade quartermaster and commissary for Brigadier General John G. Parke's 3rd Volunteer Brigade, which helped besiege and capture Fort Macon. General Parke praised King for his efforts in the Battle of New Bern on March 14, 1862, and his assistance in the investment of Fort Macon. *Official Records, Army,* ser. 1, 9:235, 286; Heitman, *Historical Register,* 1:599.

On Sunday, the 6th. of July, the whole Regiment of Federal troops stationed in Beaufort embarked on board the Steamer *Empire City*, for parts unknown—probably Virginia.[30]

On this occasion the wretches threw off all restraint, and while they were assembling on board the steamer *Union*, at the county wharf, publicly invited the negroes, who had crowded the wharf, to go with them. In some instances, they seized negroes and dragged them on board, in presence of their owners and the officers of the Regiment. Some negroes went voluntarily and boldly on board, before the eyes of their owners. Some were conveyed on board concealed in boxes and casks. Altogether, about fifteen were taken were taken off. The owners dared not interfere. The soldiers insulted and defied them, and even threatened them with bayonets; the officers present showed no disposition to check these outrages. The United States flag was flying on the boat where this disgraceful scene occurred.

Three of the Negro women taken off on Sunday, were sent back to Beaufort before the *Empire City* left the fort. The males were retained.

We learn that a Connecticut Regiment which embarked from Morehead City on the fifth of this month forcibly carried off about thirty slaves.

[*July [n.d.], 1862*]

On the third of July, advices reached here by a special train from New Bern, that Richmond had fallen. So reliable was the intelligence considered, the Commandant at Fort Macon fired a national salute. Soldiers in town manifested their joy by wild huzzas. More recent and reliable advices inform us that the Federal troops, instead of taking Richmond,

---

30 Burnside received formal orders on July 5 to depart North Carolina "with as large a force as possible" and join Union general George B. McClellan's Army of the Potomac outside Richmond, Virginia. Burnside left with 8,000 men the next day. *Official Records, Army*, ser. 1, 14:300, 305.

were repulsed with great slaughter.[31] "Better not to hollow till you get out of the woods."[32]

Beaufort is now occupied by five companies, composing the 5th. Battalion of Rhode Island Volunteers, under command of Maj. Wright.[33]

August [n.d.], 1862.

About the first of this month the 5th. Battalion of Rhode Island Volunteers, left this place for New Bern, and two companies of troops from the 9th. New Jersey Regiment, under command of Capt. Curlis,[34] occupied the town.

August [n.d.], 1862.

Among the military orders emanating from the Federal authorities in this state is one called "General Order No. 28" issued by the command of Major General Burnside, restricting the freedom of speech. The following is a copy of part of the order:

---

31 From June 25 to July 1, 1862, in a campaign dubbed the Seven Days' Battles, General Robert E. Lee's Confederate army drove General George B. McClellan's Army of the Potomac away from Richmond. Confederates suffered approximately 20,000 casualties, compared to the Union army's 16,000. McPherson, *Battle Cry of Freedom*, 464–471.

32 Rumley is misquoting a line from Thomas B. Thorpe's *The Hive of "The Beehunter."* The actual line reads: "Never holler till you get out of the woods." Thorpe, *The Hive of "The Beehunter,"* 51.

33 Major John Wright was the commander of the 1st Battalion of the 5th Rhode Island Infantry Regiment in Brigadier General John G. Parke's 3rd Volunteer Brigade. He resigned from the service on August 25, 1862. *Official Records, Army*, ser. 1, 9:232, 239–240; Branch, *The Siege of Fort Macon*, 97.

34 William B. Curlis was elected captain of Company F, 9th New Jersey Infantry Regiment on November 9, 1861. He was promoted to major on January 8, 1863, and to lieutenant colonel on May 24, 1864. He was discharged for a disability on February 11, 1865. Curlis was appointed provost marshal of Beaufort on August 4, 1862, a post he held until December 4, 1862. Drake, *The History of the Ninth New Jersey Veteran Vols.*, 83, 97, 422.

"Whoever, after this issue of this order shall, within the limits to which the Union arms may extend in this Department, utter one word against the Government of these United States, will be at once arrested and closely confined."[35]

Among the unpleasant scenes we are compelled to witness here, it is [not] uncommon to see a gang of black negroes, dressed in naval uniform, walking our streets, they are sent ashore by the Federal war steamers lying in this port, who have stolen them from the coast, or harbored them as runaways. Some of the rascals are armed. Among them are sometimes seen fugitives from this place, whose masters reside here. The scoundrels who send them ashore deserve to be shot for thus insulting a southern community whom for the present they have in their power.

The military force now stationed in Beaufort comprises five companies of the 9th. New Jersey Regiment.

Thursday, August 7, 1862.

This is the day designated by the laws of North Carolina on which to hold an election for Governor, Members of the General Assembly and Sheriff.

Being under martial law, we hold no election. As to a Governor, one will be elected without our aid. But this is the first year that Carteret County has ever failed to have a representative in the popular branch of the Legislature of the state. Jones County, not being entirely overrun with Federal troops, may elect a senator for the district of Carteret and Jones. As to a sheriff of this county, the law fortunately provides that the present incumbent shall continue in office until a successor shall be appointed. Our old friend Dill,[36] therefore, should his life be spared, will continue to have a legal existence as sheriff, though with suspended powers, having but little trouble, and as little pay, until the day shall come when he can exercise his civil functions.

But how melancholy is the reflection that while we are geographically

---

35   General Ambrose Burnside issued General Orders No. 28, which declared the region to be under martial law, on April 28, 1862. Rumley quotes the order correctly. *Official Records, Army,* ser. 1, 9:380.

36   George W. Dill (b. ca. 1795). Eighth Census, 1860: Carteret County.

within the limits of our own beloved state, we are virtually lopped off members of her political body, subjugated and held by a foreign power, which takes special pleasure in treating her laws with contempt. Not even in the old Revolution, nor the war of 1812, was civil government so completely annihilated anywhere in the state, as it is here now. Under all this, we are not unmindful of the allegiance we owe to our state. Principle grows stronger within us from day to day. The cords that bind us to her, like the child to the parent, are tightening instead of relaxing. The sword of the invader cannot cut them asunder.

October [n.d.], 1862.

"Watchman: Tell us of the night.
　What the signs of promise are!"[37]
　Tell us when the dark political night that is upon us shall pass away. It drags its slow length along, heavy, cheerless, wearisome, as the long night of the arctic regions. Its shadows have long hung around the spirit like a pall of death. Occasional gleams of light, it is true, have shut athwart the gloom, from the battle fields of the South. But like flashes of lightning over a stormy sky, they served only to reveal for a moment the terrible face of the war cloud that was over us and then passed away. We still grope through the darkness. Weary of its oppressiveness, we look, but look in vain, over the dark horizon, for some glimpse of the morning light; and often unconsciously cry out,
　"Watchman, tell us of the night;
　What the signs of promise are."
But no watchman answers! For it is the night of Revolution, whose duration no mortal now can measure; and no watchman can tell the hour. No starry lights traverse its dark sky, to tell us when its zenith is passed, and when we may look for the approach of day. It is one of those seasons of darkness that sometimes settles down upon a nation like the night of death; when a withering despotism sways its iron scepter over a scourged and unhappy people, and the Genius of Liberty, clothed in torn and bloody garments, sits weeping over her fall. That this fearful darkness

---

37　"What of the Night?" is an English hymn by John Bowring. Stedman, *A Victorian Anthology, 1837–1895*, 173.

will pass away, and the sunlight of liberty and peace return, we doubt not. But, how many fields may stream with blood; how many moons shall wax and wane; how many seasons, nay, how many years, shall circle round, ere that day shall dawn, God Almighty, and He alone can tell.

"Oft may glowing hope expire;
"Oft may weary love retire;
"Oft may sin and sorrow reign."[38]

Ere that hour shall come.

Arming citizens against the State.

Treason now stalks abroad at noon day. Protected by a thousand Yankee bayonets, it has come forth from its hiding places, and walks with impunity the highways where but a little while ago it dared not rear its head. Our Court House has been polluted by its presence. Union meetings, so called, have been held there, for the avowed purpose of encouraging the enlistment of citizens of the county in the military service of the public enemy. There, a few deluded citizens, and a crowd of Yankee soldiers, have several times assembled, to hear Union speeches from the notorious Charles Henry Foster[39] and one poor fanatic of this place. These speeches have been full of abuse of the "Slave holding aristocracy of the South" and what the speakers are pleased to call the "infernal rebellion." The court room has rung with the shouts and hurrahs for Lincoln and his reprobate crew, and groans of derision for the friends of southern rights.

Now, a recruiting office is opened in a house on Front Street, where traitors are invited to enlist. Over the door hangs a sign with the words "Volunteers Wanted" printed on it. If permitted to make an addition to

---

38   This verse is from an old English Protestant hymn that is sometimes titled "When Shall We All Meet Again?" Nye and Demarest, *Psalms and Hymns and Spiritual Songs*, 181–182.

39   Charles Henry Foster (1830–1882) was born and raised in Maine. He moved south and in 1859 became editor of the *Citizen*, a newspaper in Murfreesboro, North Carolina, in which he expressed pro-southern sentiments. By 1861, however, he had become an active Unionist. He attempted unsuccessfully to win a seat in Congress from Union North Carolina during the war. Foster served as recruiting agent for the 1st North Carolina Regiment (Union) and as lieutenant colonel of the 2nd North Carolina Regiment (Union) until banished from the army in 1864. Powell, *Dictionary of North Carolina Biography*, 2:227.

the sign, I would add the words which David saw over the portals of Hell:

"All hope abandon, ye who enter here."[40]

The place is indeed none other than the house of Satan and the very gate of hell. Some poor deluded wretches enter there, and are induced, by false representations, to sell themselves to the public enemies of their country!

If the Southern Confederacy establishes its independence (of which we cannot entertain a reasonable doubt) the condition of these men, or such of them as may survive the war, will be fearful to contemplate. If by treaty stipulations they are saved from public execution as traitors, they will still have the curse of Cain upon them and like that "fugitive and vagabond in the earth," they may each cry out with fear, "every one that findeth me shall slay me";[41] and if perchance they escape the violence of an incensed populace, the fires of public indignation which will centre upon them, will scorch them, and blast them and their posterity, while their names shall be remembered.

And yet no loyal citizen here will venture to warn these men against the fearful leap in the dark which they are making. No person can do it without subjecting himself to arrest under military law.

The enlistment of men in this county in the service of the public enemy has been materially aided by the establishment of a public subsistence store in Beaufort, where the families of volunteers are gratuitously supplied. Other citizens of the county who cannot otherwise procure subsistence are authorized to get supplies at this store.

November [n.d.], 1862.

If anything has been needed to demonstrate the ample capacity of this harbor for a great maritime commerce, it has been afforded the arrival of two huge Steamers, the *Mississippi* and the *Merrimac*, which now float on the magnificent stream that flows along the west side of the harbor. These noble vessels are each about 2000 tons burthen, and over 280 feet

---

40 This passage is from Canto III of Hell, in Dante's *The Divine Comedy*. Eliot, *The Divine Comedy of Dante Alighieri*, 13.

41 Genesis 4:14. Rumley's quotations from the Bible are all from the King James Version.

in length! They were recently built at Boston to run as merchant vessels between that city and New Orleans, but are now employed by the Federal government to transport troops to North Carolina.

Vessels ranging from 1,000 tons to 1,500 tons burthen have frequently visited this port since its occupation by the Federal Army.

In 1828 the author of the Carlton Essays[42] called attention to the fact, as one of great importance to North Carolina, that vessels of three hundred tons burthen could enter the harbor of Beaufort with their cargo. In 1839 the ship *Napoleon* of 940 tons burthen was laden at this port and sailed for Europe. This was then supposed to be the largest vessel that had ever entered the waters of this state; and no one expected to see vessels over 1000 tons enter the harbor in safety. Since that time, however, vessels of much heavier burthen have entered with their cargoes; and now we witness the safe arrival and departure of splendid steamships of 2,000 tons; as large surely as the wants of the most extended commerce can ever require.

The depth and capacity of this harbor were doubtless underestimated as late as 1828, and it might have been truly stated at that time that vessels of 500 tons, as they were then constructed, could have entered Beaufort Harbor, with their cargoes. The average draft of water of loaded vessels of that burthen was probably at that time eighteen or nineteen feet. But these steamers of 2,000 tons now only draw about this depth of water. This great increase of bulk, with so little increase in draft of water, is the result of a change in the construction of the vessel, by which the length and width are increased in a greater ratio than the depth of the hold, while the bottom is flattened.

December [n.d.], 1862

On Thursday Dec. 4th. 1862, the New Jersey troops who have occupied this town since August last, left here for New Bern. Their thieving propensities were exercised for sometime previous to their departure, in rob-

---

42   Joseph Caldwell (1773–1835), a mathematician, Presbyterian minister, and first president of the University of North Carolina, wrote *Letters of Carlton* in 1828, in which he strongly advocated internal improvements for the state of North Carolina. Powell, *Dictionary of North Carolina Biography*, 1:303–304.

bing hen roosts about town; and their officers, not satisfied with having used the private dwellings of citizens for their quarters without pay plundered them of their most valuable furniture, and carried it off.

A company of Massachusetts troops,[43] together with a company of North Carolina troops, commonly called "Buffaloes,"[44] now occupy the post.

We now have Massachusetts masters to rule over us, for the Commandant of the Post (Fowle)[45] and the Provost Marshal (Sanderson)[46] are both from Massachusetts, a state the most abhorred by us of any in the North. They say they can give no protection to persons who refuse to take the oath of allegiance, and as a general rule will grant no papers except upon that oath. Their way of dispensing justice shows their bias in favor of the negro, if the case which lately came before them, called the hog case affords a fair specimen. Mrs. D., who lives a short distance from town, owned a hog. A slave negro in town stole the hog, or by some unfair means got possession of it, penned it and claimed it as his own, two months more, unknown to the owner. It was finally discovered and identified as the property of Mrs. D. by credible witnesses, who appeared with evidence before the Provost Marshal, and requested the restoration of the property. The negro's plea was that the hog was given to him by a soldier, that he had fed it two months, and fattened it, and therefore he claimed it as his own property. His own declaration was admitted by the Provost, in proof of his plea; and the Provost decided that, as the negro had fed the hog two months, he was entitled to it.

---

43 Company C, 43rd Massachusetts Militia Volunteers. Massachusetts Adjutant General's Office, *Massachusetts Soldiers, Sailors, and Marines*, 4:240.

44 "Buffaloes" was a derisive term used to refer to native North Carolinians who joined the Union army. Its etymological origins are unknown. Browning, "'Little-Souled Mercenaries?'" 337–340.

45 William B. Fowle, Jr., was the 36-year-old captain of Company C, 43rd Massachusetts Militia Volunteers. His unit mustered in on September 22, 1862, and mustered out on July 30, 1863. Hewett, Trudeau, and Suderow, *Supplement to the Official Records*, Part II, 29:378–380; Massachusetts Adjutant General's Office, *Massachusetts Soldiers, Sailors, and Marines*, 4:240.

46 Augustine Sanderson was the 27-year-old first lieutenant of Company C, 43rd Massachusetts Militia Volunteers. He was commissioned on September 22, 1862, and mustered out on July 30, 1863. Massachusetts Adjutant General's Office, *Massachusetts Soldiers, Sailors, and Marines*, 4:240.

December [n.d.], 1862.

Our town is crowded with runaway negroes. Not only the able bodied, but the lame, the halt, the blind and crazy, have poured in upon us, until every available habitation has been filled with them. Even the Methodist Parsonage, and the Odd Fellows Lodge, have been desecrated in this way, and are now filled with gangs of these black traitors.

1863

January 1, 1863.

This will be long remembered as the day on which Lincoln's Emancipation Proclamation[1] goes into operation, and an election is held, by order of the Military Governor of the state, to elect a Representative from the 2nd. Congressional District, under the districting of 1851 to the 37th. Congress of the United States![2]

Many reflecting minds have for several months past looked forward to this day with deep concern, on account of the slave population in our

---

1 Lincoln issued the preliminary Emancipation Proclamation on September 22, 1862, and declared that it would take effect on January 1, 1863. It proclaimed the slaves in eight seceded states to be forever free. It also authorized enlisting African American soldiers in the Union armies. The proclamation did not apply to the border states, to Tennessee, or to parts of Louisiana or Virginia then under Union control. Heidler and Heidler, *Encyclopedia of the American Civil War*, 2:650–652.

2 Voting occurred only in Carteret, Craven, and Hyde counties. The election pitted Charles Henry Foster against Jennings Pigott (1811–1882), a Carteret County native and former Whig member of the North Carolina legislature. Of the 864 votes cast, Pigott received 595. Foster challenged Pigott's election on the grounds that Pigott had not lived in the county for many years and that pro-southern officials had permitted Confederate sympathizers to vote while prohibiting some Unionists from casting ballots. The committee and subsequently the House voted against seating Pigott. No representative from the region sat in the U.S. House of Representatives during the war. Harris, *With Charity for All*, 70; Norman D. Brown, "A Union Election in Civil War North Carolina," 388, 394–400; Browning and Smith, *Letters from a North Carolina Unionist*, 66–82; *Cemetery Records of Carteret County*, 160.

midst. They could hardly believe that so remarkable an epoch could arrive without producing some commotion among the negroes, some tumult, some shock to society. That the shackles should suddenly fall from the hands of thousands of slaves, as silently as snowflakes fall upon the earth, and the slaves move on in their new atmosphere of freedom, with no signs of uproar, no fandangoes, no shouts, no jubilant songs to express their joy or insult their former owners, and with no more stir among them than might be produced on any New Year's Day, by a transfer from one set of masters to another, was not to be believed by any who knew what sudden emancipation once caused among this race in the Island of St. Domingo.[3] Yet this is precisely the state of things we behold around us this day. The Emancipation Proclamation has taken effect today and has sundered, so far as military law can do it, the bonds that united the slave to the master, without producing a ripple on the face of the waters. This peaceful and quiet transition from slavery to freedom must find its explanation, to a great extent, in the fact that the Federal Army in this section of the state had long since, by their conduct towards the slaves, anticipated the Proclamation and virtually set them free. Besides this, the slaves may not be entirely certain that their freedom is permanent, and may have some secret dread of the approach of Confederate power.

But the Election. Oh! the farce, the burlesque upon the right of suffrage—the miserable mocking of a once precious civil right. Here we are voting at the ballot box, under the dark shadow of military despotism, and under the martial law of a power with whom the state of North Carolina is at war; and voting for a Representative to that very power! The act is treason against our own state. And yet we are compelled by the circumstances that surround us to commit the act. We did not want the election. We refused to petition for it when solicited to do so. But the Military Governor has ordered it. Under the auspices of Charles Henry Foster, and under the baleful influence of this Revolution, a po-

---

3   The Santo Domingo revolt was a successful slave revolt that erupted in 1791 in the modern-day nation of Haiti, which was a French colony at the time. About 25,000 whites were killed in the revolt before it finally concluded with Haitian independence in 1801. Elkins and McKittrick, *The Age of Federalism*, 649–662.

litical party[4] has been organized in our midst, the most dangerous that ever reared its head in a southern state. It is abolition to the backbone, egregious, destructive. Its members, looking upon slave holders as a class hostile to their interests, and, upon slavery as the cause of our present evils, have declared an eternal war upon both. Some of them outstrip Greely,[5] and Giddings[6] and Garrison,[7] in their fanaticism. They scout the idea of a Southern Confederacy, and doff its power.[8]

Foster is the candidate of the party, in this election. If he should be elected, who [is] so blind as not to see, that this party will be strengthened and encouraged by the event, and our condition be made worse than it is. If the party can be checked in this first grasp at political power, it may be checked forever. The arm of the Confederate government cannot reach us to crush this poisonous serpent in our midst. We must fight it, ourselves, at the ballot box. All persons who are qualified according to the constitution and laws of North Carolina are allowed to vote without an oath of allegiance.

The duty of all friends of Southern rights and of law and order is plain in this case; although it may appear disloyal to the State of North

---

4   Charles Henry Foster organized local free labor associations in occupied eastern North Carolina. These organizations, which were loosely construed as a party, advocated compliance with President Lincoln's Emancipation Proclamation. Delaney, "Charles Henry Foster and the Unionists of Eastern North Carolina," 348–366.

5   Horace Greeley (1811–1872) was editor of the *New York Tribune,* a Republican newspaper. Greeley was a radical abolitionist who used his newspaper to urge the Lincoln administration to authorize Union officers to liberate slaves wherever possible. Heidler and Heidler, *Encyclopedia of the American Civil War,* 2:876–877.

6   Joshua Reed Giddings (1795–1864), an Ohio congressman, was one of the founding members of the Republican Party. A former antislavery Whig, Giddings was instrumental in helping Lincoln win the presidential nomination at the 1860 Republican National Convention. Heidler and Heidler, *Encyclopedia of the American Civil War,* 2:839.

7   William Lloyd Garrison (1805–1879) was the staunch abolitionist editor of the *Liberator* of Boston, Massachusetts. Garrison proclaimed John Brown to be a martyr after his failed slave raid in 1859 and called for emancipation to be a Union war aim from the outset of the war. Heidler and Heidler, *Encyclopedia of the American Civil War,* 2:815–817.

8   Rumley is using the word "scout" in its older meaning of "mock" or "deride" or "reject scornfully."

Carolina, they will be justified by the law of self-preservation, in voting for a candidate who will do the county no harm, if he can do it no good, and by this means checking this dangerous and odious party in it first step to power, and placing themselves in a condition to avoid proscription hereafter, which may fall with a heavy hand upon those who refuse, at the ballot box today, this miserable mock manifestation of loyalty to the powers that be.

We must plead hereafter, in justification of the act, that necessity which, Blackstone[9] says, so "constrains a man's will" as to "oblige him to do an action which without such obligation would be criminal. That is when a man has his choice of two evils set before him, and being under a necessity of choosing one, he chooses the least pernicious of the two."[10]

One of the sad results of the military occupation of this county is the suspension of our civil courts. No judge of the Superior Court has ventured to come within the Federal lines in this Judicial circuit, since the Yankee army made its appearance here, and the justices of the county, who might hold the County Courts by permission of the Military Governor are not inclined to do so. All disputes, therefore, arising between citizens, and all cases of violations of the civil or military law, have to be heard, if heard at all, before the Provost Marshal or Commandant of the Post. There, a negro, who in our civil courts could not be heard except through his master, can appear as the accuser of any white citizen and cause the citizen to be arrested. Arrests of this character were made before the negroes were declared free.

A short time since a very respectable white boy of tender years, threw some missiles at a negro on the street, to resent the negro's insolence to

---

9   Sir William Blackstone (1723–1780) was a famed English jurist who produced the definitive treatise on English common law, *Commentaries on the Laws of England*, from 1765 to 1769. Matthew and Harrison, *Oxford Dictionary of National Biography*, 6:10–16.

10 Rumley is slightly misquoting William Blackstone's dictum on the legal rights of a man who has to choose between two evils. The passage reads: "There is a third species of necessity, which may be distinguished from the actual compulsion of external force or fear; being the result of reason and reflection which act upon and constrain a man's will, and oblige him to do an action which, without such obligation, would be criminal. And that is, when a man has a choice of two evils set before him, and being under necessity of choosing one, he chooses the least pernicious of the two." Blackstone, *Abridgement of Blackstone's Commentaries*, 415.

the boy's mother. The negro reported him to the Provost Marshal and caused him to be arrested and confined in the Guard House. Any justice of the peace within the Federal lines with six months' experience in trying warrants could dispense justice to a southern community better than these ignorant usurpers.

Some years ago, G. executed to P. a deed of sale for [*copy missing*] court as this. The commandant orders that L. be ousted from the land and G. put in possession.

But, bad as the present military rule really is, and revolting to those who have heretofore lived in the sunshine of civil liberty and law, it is nevertheless not entirely unmixed with good. Justice is sometimes measured out. Its demands are often unsatisfied by the long delays of the civil law. But here, once decreed, the execution is swift and sure. No processes of judges or justices of the peace can arrest it. Bayonets if necessary enforce every decree. The man who is seen drunk in the streets or is caught selling liquor without license is not allowed to wait six or twelve months for indictment and trial, but is taken immediately to the Guard House. So with others who disturb the peace of the community. Sudden and radical changes in the social system of a people are well known to be impolitic and dangerous. None but crazy enthusiasts, or mad fanatics, ever dream that such changes can advance the general interests of society.

The sudden enfranchisement of an entire servile race, millions in number, living in the midst of the superior race, where the relation has subsisted for ages, and forming a part of the household of thousands of families, would be regarded, we would suppose, by the true friends of humanity everywhere as a most hazardous experiment, and a project which none but a fool or a madman would seriously meditate. It has been universally admitted that in the southern states, where African slavery exists, gradual emancipation is the only practical mode of removing the evil—if evil it be. Our ablest men have agreed, that sudden emancipation would ruin both races. And all, with one voice, have declared that the question, whether emancipation in any form be practicable or desirable, is one which the states wherein slavery exists, and they alone, have the right to decide. No sane man, acquainted with the history of its formation, ever supposed that the Federal government had any right to interfere with the institutions of slavery in the several states; and never, before the present war, did it enter into the conceptions of men that a President of the United States, under any circumstances, unless he had actually run mad, would ever conceive himself to be clothed with such a power as that of emancipation in the states, or attempt to exercise it; for in no constitutional monarchy in Europe, we believe, would the sovereign, in peace or war be allowed this high prorogation. Yet history must record the past, that this more than kingly right, this most unconstitutional and despotic power, has been assumed by the present Executive of the United States; and in a Proclamation dated the 1st. day of January 1863, he de- clares all persons heretofore held as slaves in ten southern states (except a few districts) to be forever free! That this astounding stretch of power which this functionary calls a necessary war measure, is prompted by the vindictiveness which repeatedly baffled attempts to conquer us have inspired, and is designed to light the fires of insurrection, and produce an upheaval of society in the south, there is little doubt. We are happy to believe, however, that before this diabolical purpose can be accom- plished, a wall of southern bayonets must be broken down. Within that wall this infamous Proclamation, which cannot be read to a slave there but under the penalty of death, will fall as harmless as an edict of the Emperor of China or the Pope of Rome. But not so within the territory occupied by the armies of the United States. Here this paper has, for the present, all the force of a constitutional legislative act. And here appears the total want of justice and impartiality on the part of its author in the enforcement of this measure. Here, where the armies of this despot have subjugated the people and induced thousands, by offers of protection, to remain with their slaves at home; here, where the people have submit- ted quietly to his government, and trusted in its protection, this usurper, not satisfied with the evils which an army of abolitionists and highway robbers have already inflicted on them, now, like a lawless robber and incendiary, invades the sacred precincts of every family, robs them of their servants, who would be faithful and contented if let alone, and then offers the servant arms to butcher the white man of the South! A miscreant

"Oh, for some secret curse, some hidden thunders,
Red with uncommon wrath, to blast the wretch!"[11]

---

11   This is a slightly incorrect quote of the opening scene of Joseph Addison's *Cato: A Tragedy*. The actual verse reads, "Oh Portius, is there not some chosen curse, / Some hidden thunder in the stores of heav'n, / Red with uncommon wrath, to blast the man." Addison, *Cato: A Tragedy*, 14.

who thus tramples constitution and sacred personal rights in the dust.

The consequences of this disruption of the bonds of servitude, though not as bad as were anticipated, are serious to many families. Drudgeries, to which they have never been accustomed, have now to be performed by delicate women and aged men, while the negroes look on with indifference. Some of the latter work for a support. Others are idle and do not seem to know what use to make of their newborn liberty. Some of them are fed by the Yankees. Many of them exult, and also there are white devils among us who exult in this cruel outrage upon slave holders.

The bitter cup drank in apparently quiet submission. And looking merely at the surface of society, we see no signs of serious jostle or disturbance. But oh! The deep fires of indignation that burn below, and the wrath that is treasured up against the day of wrath! Who can measure them?

January 25, 1863.

During the last four weeks a Federal fleet, chiefly of transports with a few armed vessels, has been gathering in this harbor as a place of rendezvous, preparatory to an attack on some point south of this.

The number of vessels has been gradually increasing until they amount to about one hundred. The harbor is beautifully studded with steamers, barges and schooners lying at anchor, stretching along a line three miles in length, somewhat of a crescent form, from a point east of Fort Macon to a point half a mile north of Morehead City. Many of them are laden with troops, others with munitions of war. Looking on them from this place, without knowing the hostile character of their mission, one might suppose them to be the richly freighted argosies of commerce, and himself to be standing near some great emporium of trade. And we are not sure that this long array of stately vessels may not prefigure, more truly than the uninspired pencil of the artist can do it, the aspect this harbor may wear in years to come, when war shall have ceased its havoc, and a peaceful commerce, sped on by wind and steam, shall enliven our southern waters.

But it saddens the spirit to look upon their long black hulks, as they cloud the horizon, and think of their mission of death. Their decks are covered with an armed foe, and their holds filled with the engines of destruction. They are about to sail.[12] While we write their fires are smoking, and their sails are spreading to bear them away.

O, for Prospero's magic power,[13] to pursue them with spirits from the vastly deep, "to call forth the mutinous winds, And ' twixt the green sea and the azure vault, set roaring war."[14]

March 4, 1863.

The company of Massachusetts troops, who have occupied this town since the 4th. of December last, left here today for New Bern.[15] In exchange for them, two companies of another Regiment (51st.) of Massachusetts Troops have been sent here. These, with a company of North Carolina troops heretofore mentioned, commonly called "Buffaloes," now constitute the military force stationed here. Major Harkness[16] is Provost Marshal.

The whole community were rejoiced to see the abolition pests who lately had control here, take their final leave. The non-commissioned officers and privates of the company behaved better than any Yankee troops

---

12   Major General John Foster sailed from Beaufort with approximately 10,000 troops and 600 artillery, arriving at Port Royal, South Carolina, on February 1, 1863. The troops were sent from North Carolina to South Carolina to assist in the attack on Charleston. *Official Records, Army*, ser. 1, 14:394.

13   Prospero was the protagonist of William Shakespeare's play *The Tempest*. He was the Duke of Milan and a powerful magician who used his powers to stir up the sea to punish his enemies. "*The Tempest*: Synopsis," in Wright, *The Complete Works of William Shakespeare*, 1297–1298.

14   *The Tempest*, act 5, sc. 1, in Wright, *Complete Works of William Shakespeare*, 1321.

15   Company C, 43rd Massachusetts Volunteer Militia. Massachusetts Adjutant General's Office, *Massachusetts Soldiers, Sailors, and Marines*, 4:229.

16   Major Elijah A. Harkness had served as first lieutenant and adjutant for the 25th Massachusetts Infantry Regiment. He was mustered into service on October 27, 1861. He was promoted to major of the 51st Massachusetts Militia Regiment on November 11, 1862. In this capacity, he served as provost marshal of Beaufort in the spring of 1863. *Official Records, Army*, ser. 1, 9:96, 219, 346, 18:129; E. A Harkness to Southard Hoffman, March 5 and April 1, 1863, Box 2, Part I, Department of North Carolina, Letters Received, ser. 3238, Records of Named Departments, Department of North Carolina, Record Group 393.4; Massachusetts Adjutant General's Office, *Massachusetts Soldiers, Sailors, and Marines*, 3:3, 4:548.

who have been stationed here. But their captain, Fowle, is a fanatic, it is believed of the John Brown[17] school, and deeply prejudiced against slaveholders and everything Southern. Sanderson, the Provost Marshal, was formerly, it is said, a butcher, and lately a Detective officer of the Boston police. Both were as unmannerly as boors and so destitute of gallantry that they required even ladies to go in person to their quarters to get permits to leave the town for a few hours and treated them there with no politeness whatever. They were both guilty of the low act of eavesdropping under the window of a young man's office in town, after night, and generally were guilty of a good many mean things, but nothing meaner, perhaps, than the imprisonment of three boys of tender years, who, being tired of Yankee rule and imagining they could do good service to the Southern Confederacy, struck out for "Dixie," but hungry stomachs and two nights of exposure to winds and pelting rains, having tried their patriotism too severely, they voluntarily returned where these two worthy representatives of niggerdom, instead of complimenting the bold and enterprising spirit of the boys and ordering them to their homes, put them in a dungeon in the county jail!

On the 14th. of this month, precisely twelve months from the capture of New Bern, a heavy cannonading was heard in the direction of that place, from early morn till late in the day. Some thought the Yankees were celebrating the anniversary of that fatal day, on which New Bern fell. But the very irregular firing which we could distinctly hear did not indicate that sort of celebration. Some thought that General Hill[18] might have concluded to celebrate the day by saluting the Yankees with bombshells. Rumors soon reached us that the Confederates had attacked the town. Fear, which could not be concealed, seized upon the military authorities here. The guards were strengthened, and all communication between the people of the town and those of the country around interdicted. There was a flutter among the Yankee traders residing here, and many of them

---

17 This is a reference to John Brown, who led an attempted slave insurrection in Harpers Ferry, Virginia, in October 1859. The raid failed, and Brown was executed in November 1859. McPherson, *Battle Cry of Freedom*, 201–213.

18 Daniel Harvey Hill (1821–1889) was a major general in independent command of the Confederate forces in North Carolina in the spring and summer of 1863. He was appointed a corps commander in the Army of Tennessee after the fall of Vicksburg in July 1863. Heidler and Heidler, *Encyclopedia of the American Civil War*, 2:975–976.

set to work "packing up," ready for flight whenever a Confederate face should make its appearance anywhere near the harbor.

The negroes began to wonder at the mighty power of the "rebels," with fearful misgiving, that the great Yankee "nigger" government, after all its displays of ships and big guns and mighty "armies with banners," might not be able to shield them from the wrath of an outraged people. But the threatened storm did not come. The Confederates made a demonstration on the north side of the Neuse River, opposite New Bern, and caused a terrible fright among the vile brood of soldiers, and Yankee traders and negroes in the town.[19] But what further they did we cannot [say].

March 24, 1863.

We are saddened to day by the appearance in the harbor of the large steamer *Nicholas*,[20] laden, it is said, with arms and munitions of war; captured by some of the Yankee fleet while trying to run the blockade at Wilmington, and brought hear as a prize. She is English.

March 25, 1863.

Precisely one year has been added to the records of time since this town was first cursed with the presence of an abolition army. It has been the most remarkable year in the annals of the place; a year of gloom and sadness, the darkest, we hope, that will ever blur its history. During that gloomy period, we have seen the civil law, the only sure guardian of our

---

19   On March 13, 1863, Confederate troops under D. H. Hill launched an unsuccessful attack against New Bern. This included a March 14 assault on Union-held Fort Anderson, located across the Neuse River from New Bern. The attack on the fort was repulsed with the aid of Union gunboats. Barrett, *The Civil War in North Carolina*, 151–156.

20   The *Nicholas III* was a sidewheel steamboat that the Confederates purchased from Great Britain and fitted out in Dublin, Ireland. The *Nicholas III* loaded with supplies in Liverpool, England, in November 1862 in order to run the blockade into a Confederate port. The boat was laden with 170 cases of rifles, 1,400 bags of salt, 30 cases of wire, 1,320 quarter-barrels of gunpowder, earthenware, and clothing. United States Naval War Records Office, *Official Records of the Union and Confederate Navies in the War of the Rebellion*, series 1, 7:433; 8:267–268 (hereafter *Official Records, Navy*).

rights, trampled in the dust, and martial law, which is no law at all, but the will of one man in authority, substituted in its place. We have seen the flag of the Confederacy struck down by a victorious foe, and the flag of the most detestable government on earth hoisted in its place. We have seen legions of the armed hirelings of that government landed upon our shores, to carry on this damnable war against us; while their piratical fleets have darkened our waters.

We have seen our entire slave population turned loose in our midst, and efforts made to introduce an era of "niggerism," as revolting to the soul of every Southerner, as that of St. Domingo; and this by the very scoundrels who had solemnly assured us they did not intend to interfere with the rights of slave holders. We have seen almost the whole of this population in the country, under the baleful teachings of abolitionism, turned into traitors and spies against their legitimate masters.

We have seen white citizens of the county, forgetting their allegiance to their own state, arming and joining the invader against her, showing as little respect for her laws as they would for those of the Hindus; acting as spies and informers, and with the aid of their black allies and the countenance and cooperation of their abolition masters endeavoring to inaugurate over the loyal citizens of the county a reign of terror.

We have seen citizens arrested and imprisoned, and private property seized, often upon the information of negroes—contrary to all the instincts of justice and humanity when military necessity did not require it, and only to gratify an abolition vindictiveness of the basest character, and a spirit of private plunder worthy of a band of highway robbers.

These are some of the memories of the past year; which the retrospect, today, calls to mind; and which will render the year memorable, among the inhabitants of the town, for ages to come.

History may not record them, but tradition will transmit them to generations yet unborn.

This is the reign of "niggerism." The scoundrels in authority here know very well that the African race is the only one whose loyalty they can trust, as their negro-stealing government has forfeited all claim to the loyalty of any decent white man. The negroes they can trust. They tell them they have come here to fight for them and, like Moses, to deliver them from their Egyptian bondage. The deluded wretches, lured by the sweet sound of liberty, hail these desecrators of our soil as their deliverers. Nothing can shake their faith in the Yankee. On the other hand, nothing can shake the Yankee's faith in the negro. They seem to have strong affinities for each other and are very natural allies. All the Yankee lacks to make him a negro is a black skin with a woolly head. With these marks of African upon him, his identity with the sooty race would be quite sufficient to consign him to a southern cotton field, where, if he had his deserts, he would certainly be. His intellect is less stolid than the negro's, but is generally exercised in contrivances for cheating, and in meddling with other people's business, while in vandalism and thieving propensities he certainly excels the negro. He excels also in hatred of the slave owner. The negro would have but little of this feeling if let alone, but is easily tutored in it when the Yankee plies his art to corrupt him, which he has not failed to do.

Worthy allies, these, in the unholy crusade against southern society which northern "Niggerism" is now carrying on. But what bitter thoughts, what scorn and indignation stir the [*illegible*] of white men and women against the miserable "Niggerism" to which the fortunes of war have for season subjected them.

While the white man, as a general thing, is eyed with suspicion, and deprived of privileges which his own slaves were never refused, and is probably a subject of negro espionage; runaway negroes are the special objects of protection and favor with the nigger government here. Any mark of African blood is a passport to favor with that government. *Mr.* George Ramsey, *Mr.* Perry Pigott, *Mr.* Brister Davis,[21] are greater men in the eyes of these disciples of John Brown, than the greatest Southern man, saint or sinner, that now lives.

Their negro mania renders them incapable of dispensing justice between the negro and the white man. A respectable white citizen once went to the office of the Provost Marshal and complained that a negro boy had behaved with great insolence toward him, and had threatened him with personal violence while on board the white man's own boat. The Provost was reminded of the law of the state in the case. But he gave

---

21   Rumley is referring to former slaves of local citizens. George Ramsey was likely the former slave of Isaac Ramsey, a Beaufort merchant who owned eighteen slaves in 1860. While there was only one Ramsey who owned slaves in Carteret County, numerous Davises and Pigotts owned slaves. Eighth Census, 1860: Carteret County.

the citizen no satisfaction, while another Federal officer present openly advised the negro, when a white man molested him, to use the weapons God had given him. This was before the negroes were declared free. Another citizen, G. was summoned before the late Commandant, Fowle, upon a charge made by a negro, that he, G., had passed him a counterfeit dollar bill. G. appeared before the officer, where he was met by the negro with the bill of money. The negro produced no witness to prove his charge. G. declared he had never seen the negro or the bill of money before in his life. But the negro's word could not be questioned, and the officer decided that G. should take the bill from the negro and give him a good dollar!

Like the fanatic Hunter[22] in South Carolina, the negro loving scoundrels take great pains to provide homes for the crowds of runaways who assemble here, and have seriously annoyed white citizens by crowding these nuisances near them, while they manifest no concern about the comfort of poor white families. They have established schools for the gratuitous education of negro children, in violation of the laws of the state, but care nothing about the education of poor white children.[23]

They often refuse permits to white citizens to carry to their families, in the country, articles of necessity, from real or pretended fear that portions of it might find its way to the "rebels," but they refuse no such favors to negroes. Their guards often search the persons of white citizens passing to and from the town, to see if they have letters or anything "contraband" secreted upon them, but they perpetrate no such indignity upon the per-

---

22 General David Hunter (1802–1886) issued an emancipation edict on May 7, 1862, declaring all slaves in his Department of the South (South Carolina, Georgia, and Florida) to be free. On May 19, 1862, President Lincoln repealed Hunter's edict, saying that he had overstepped his authority. Hunter was soon reassigned to command in Washington, D.C. Heidler and Heidler, *Encyclopedia of the American Civil War*, 2:1019–1020.

23 Northern agents established two evening schools for freedmen in New Bern in April 1862 under the direction of Superintendent of the Poor Vincent Colyer. Military Governor Edward Stanly closed the schools in May 1862, but they were reopened in July. Schools were opened in Beaufort as well, and several Union officers served as teachers. The American Missionary Association formally set up its first two schools in New Bern in July 1863 and opened several in Beaufort and Morehead City later in the summer of 1863. Jones, "'A Glorious Work,'" 45–51. See also Browning, "'Visions of Freedom and Civilization Opening before Them,'" 69–100.

son of a negro, unless it be one who is known to be faithful to his master. Amid the general faithlessness and treason of the race, there are a few who remain faithful to their owners.

Verily, this is the reign of "Niggerism." But bad as it is, it may become worse. On the horizon of the future rises a portentous cloud blacker far than any that has yet darkened the vision and charged with an element of war more horrible than any that has yet been let loose upon us. Armies of black negroes may yet be turned upon us, to complete the ruin and desolation that Yankee vandalism has begun. Visions of armed and infuriated bands of these black traitors, like imps of darkness, rise before us and darken the future. We are passing through the shadow of a dark eclipse—a frightful political and civil obscuration.

When we emerge from its overshadowing darkness and hail the long obscured light again, we shall doubtless look upon this gloomy period as the mariner who has gained the sunny shore looks back upon a long night of storms and darkness on the Arctic sea, and shall characterize it while memory lives as the dark reign of "Niggerism."

Two abolitionists from the north said to be brothers, of the name of "Means,"[24] lately came to North Carolina to teach the negroes; in violation of the laws of the state. One of them died about a fortnight ago at New Bern, and was boxed up and sent back to "niggerdom." Last night (April 23rd.) the other died at Taylor's Hotel,[25] in Beaufort; and will be likewise boxed up and sent in the same direction. We doubt whether any

---

24 Rev. James Means (1813–1863), a Congregationalist minister and former teacher from New Hampshire, was appointed superintendent of contrabands in New Bern in the spring of 1863. He died of typhoid fever on April 6, 1863, in New Bern. I have not been able to identify his brother. James Means to Southard Hoffman, March 3, 1863, and National Freedman's Relief Association to J. G. Foster, May 1, 1863, both in Box 2, Letters Received, Part I, Records of Named Departments, Department of North Carolina, Record Group 393.4; Horace James to the O. S. Sabbath School, May 25, 1863, Horace James Correspondence; Carter, *The Native Ministry of New Hampshire*, 23.

25 George W. Taylor (b. ca. 1814) was a farmer and the proprietor of the Ocean House Hotel in Beaufort. He had moved to Beaufort from New Bern in 1854. Eighth Census, 1860: Carteret County; North Carolina, 5:173, R. G. Dun & Co. Collection.

more of that family will be sent to meddle with other people's business, during the war.

The "Oath of Allegiance."

A most disgusting subject to the loyal citizens of this county, is the "Oath of Allegiance" required by the Federal authorities to place the citizens *rectus in curia*[26] with them. Every intelligent citizen knows that his allegiance is due to his own state, and he cannot conscientiously abjure it. The law of the state forbids [*it*]. Public opinion generally forbids it. But the Yankees, who care nothing about our state laws, and scout the idea of state allegiance when opposed to their nigger government, cling to the oath as a political touchstone to test the loyalty of every man to the government, and will grant very few privileges without it. What, then, are people to do, who without taking the oath cannot go a mile from their homes to attend to business, though starvation may stare them in the face! Many have already suffered inconveniences, privations and losses, rather than take the detestable oath. But many have felt compelled to submit to the formality of the oath, believing it did not bind them morally, and would not, in the slightest degree, impair their loyalty to the South. Such persons are just as loyal to the south now as they ever were, and continue to render aid to the Confederates whenever they find an opportunity to do so.

The Yankees are badly deceived if they suppose they have secured the loyalty of a single man by forcing this despotic oath upon him against his will, for, says Dante,

"The will that wills not still survives unquenched,
And doth as nature doth in fire;
Though violence doth wrest it a thousand times,"[27]
and it cannot be bound by a compulsory oath of allegiance. They forget

---

26 *Rectus in curia* is Latin for "right in court." According to John Bouvier's *Law Dictionary*, "When a person outlawed has reversed his outlawry, so that he can have the benefit of the law, he is said to be *rectus in curia*." Bouvier, *A Law Dictionary*, 2:428.

27 The verse is from Canto IV of Paradise, in Dante's *The Divine Comedy*. Eliot, *The Divine Comedy of Dante Alighieri*, 299.

that while oaths generally, being very solemn appeals to the Almighty, have been recognized in all ages as very necessary to bind the consciences of men, if an oath to become a traitor to his own state be taken by a man against his will and the dictates of his conscience, and under circumstances amounting to compulsion, he cannot, by the universal consent of mankind, be morally bound to perform it.

So thought the Saxon king, Harold, eight hundred years ago, when reproached by the Duke of Normandy for violating an oath taken, under great solemnities, to support the pretensions of the Duke to the crown of England. Harold informed the Duke that the oath which he had taken was extorted by the well grounded fear of violence, and could never be regarded as obligatory.[28]

Enlightened men of the present day regard a compulsory oath, affecting a man's allegiance, as this king of England did eight centuries ago, and as Robert Bruce regarded his oath of allegiance to England when Scotland required him to arm against Edward.[29] Hard, indeed, have the abolition scoundrels who rule here tried to make the citizens "loyal" to their nigger government; to make them turn their backs upon their struggling brothers and sons in the Confederacy; hold no communication with them, and send them nothing to "aid and comfort" them in their day of trial. To this end, they had forced oaths of neutrality and oaths of allegiance upon them; threatened them; sent spies and detectives out to watch them; searched their houses, and sometimes incarcerated them. But all in vain. Nature revolts at the thought of such loyalty, and the unconquerable will spurns the idea of submission. Letters will come and go,

---

28   In 1065, Harold, the son of King Edward the Confessor of England, was compelled by William, duke of Normandy, to take an oath supporting William's claim to the English throne when King Edward died. Harold, threatened by force, took the oath but reneged when Edward died. William invaded England and defeated Harold's army at the battle of Hastings in 1066. Thierry, *History of the Conquest of England by the Normans*, 1:148–156.

29   In the revolt against the English occupation of Scotland in 1297, Robert Bruce, the future king of Scotland, renounced the oath of fealty he had pledged to England's King Edward I in August 1296 as being made under duress and therefore not binding. Bruce was a participant in the revolt that eventually led to Scottish independence from England in 1316. Matthew and Harrison, *Oxford Dictionary of National Biography*, 47:98–107.

and many little contraband articles to "aid and comfort" the Confederates find their way across the Federal lines by what is secretly known as the underground rail-ways.

Never were the people of this county more attached at heart to the laws and institutions of their own state than they are now. We mean the majority. Some, it is true, have strayed from the fold of Israel. But by far the greater number are as true and steadfast in heartfelt loyalty to North Carolina as the needle is to the pole. They acknowledge no government, on this soil, which she does not acknowledge. In the darkest hours of this dark despotism that is over us, their hearts turns instinctively to her. "When we forget thee, Oh Jerusalem, let our right hand forget her cunning."[30]

April [n.d.], 1863.

The Hon. Edward Stanly, late Military Governor of part of North Carolina, has resigned his office, and left the state.[31] He accepted this appointment, and came to this state, with very mistaken views of the temper of the people and the condition of things generally in the state, and especially within the Federal lines. He thought there was a deep seated Union sentiment among the inhabitants within and without the lines; and he expected to find at New Bern most of his old friends and townsmen ready to cooperate with him in measures to develop the Union sentiment, and gradually restore the former relations between the state and the Federal government. But alas, for the fallacy of human hopes. When he arrived at New Bern, he found nearly all his old friends had fled before the storm that had swept over the place, and their homes desecrated by Yankee soldiers and runaway negroes; and he soon learned that the Union sentiment, wherever he went, was too dead to be galvanized into even a

---

30 Psalms 137:5. Rumley is slightly misquoting the actual verse, which reads: "If I forget thee, O Jerusalem, let my right hand forget her cunning."

31 Edward Stanly submitted his resignation in early February. He was informed on March 4, 1863, that President Lincoln had accepted it, effective March 1. Stanly left New Bern in March. He traveled to Washington, D.C., where he met with Lincoln in April before going to California. Brown, *Edward Stanly*, 250, 252–253; Browning and Smith, *Letters from a North Carolina Unionist*, 88, 94–95.

transient life. But worse than all, he soon perceived that the army which surrounded him, instead of being a band of patriots, as he had supposed they were, were a vile horde of abolitionists and highway robbers, hostile to him, and in some instances refusing obedience to his orders. The late measures of the Federal government were entirely against his views.[32] Under the circumstances he felt constrained to leave his post. His mission had failed. And perhaps he saw that the fabric of Federal power was falling and it was better to fly, than to perish in its fall.

May 4, 1863.

Thursday, the 30th. of April 1863, was Lincoln's appointed day of fasting and prayer[33] for the success of his abolition, nigger-worshipping and thieving army. Of course none but the Yankees and a few of their friends observed the day. But the night was signalized by an attempt of Capt. Warren, an officer of Lincoln's navy, to commit the atrocious crime of violating the person of a white girl under twelve years of age, the daughter of Capt. Carr, his brother officer in the Navy.[34] The circumstances are too shocking and revolting for detail here. Warren is over fifty years of age. He had been a frequent visitor and guest, at the house of his friend Carr, who resides in this place. He commanded the Steamer "*Daylight*," and had been in the blockading service at Cape Fear. The old brute steamed out of the harbor and went off early on the morning of the 1st. of May. He will probably be arrested and brought to trial for his infamous crime.

    Change, change, change, marks the track of time. The two companies

---

32   Edward Stanly opposed the Emancipation Proclamation and resigned in protest over it. Stanly, *Military Governor among Abolitionists*, 46–47; Harris, *With Charity for All*, 70.

33   On March 28, 1863, President Lincoln issued a proclamation designating Thursday, April 30, 1863, as a day of fasting and prayer to appeal for God's divine favor in the war and "to confess our national sins, and to pray for forgiveness and clemency." *Official Records, Army*, ser. 3, 3:106–107.

34   Rumley is referring to Acting Master Joshua P. Warren and Acting Master Henry P. Carr. No record of this case has been discovered. Carr disappears from the *Official Records* after February 1863; Warren was still on duty as late as February 1864 although he was no longer in the North Atlantic Squadron. *Official Records, Navy*, ser. 1, 8:138, 216, 255, 358, 468, 487; 9:609, 703; 15:260.

of Massachusetts troops[35] who have occupied the town since the 4th. of March last, left here today (the 4th. of May 1863) and two companies of the 81st. regiment of New York troops take their places, with Major Curlis of the 9th. New Jersey Regiment, as Provost Marshal.[36]

May 13, 1863.

A flag of truce left here this morning for Swansboro, in charge of a Federal officer. Several ladies and 4 children from this place, with Capt. Slaight[37] from Morehead City, went along with it on their way to Dixie. The officers who superintended the matter were not at all disposed to annoy the party by searching their baggage closely, and no small quantity of merchandise to aid and comfort the Confederates was carried along in trunks and boxes. One good lady carried, concealed on her person a pound of calomel![38]

The steam mill in Beaufort, belonging to Mess. Perry and Co., was almost entirely destroyed by fire on the night of the 2nd. inst.[39] It was doubtless the work of an incendiary. The Yankee army had been in the habit of taking whatever they wanted from the mill, in the shape of lumber, tools, &c. But not satisfied with this, after the mill was burnt, the

---

35   Two companies (one of which was Company C) of the 51st Massachusetts Militia Regiment.

36   Companies E, I, and K of the 81st New York Regiment served as the provost guard in Beaufort in May 1863. De Forest, *Random Sketches and Wandering Thoughts*, 235–236.

37   Rumley is likely referring to Samuel C. Slate (b. ca. 1802), a merchant who lived in Morehead City. Eighth Census, 1860: Carteret County.

38   Calomel, or mercurous chloride, was one of the most widely prescribed drugs during the Civil War despite its extremely dangerous side effects, which included mercury poisoning. Physicians believed it was effective as a disinfectant and laxative (among many other things) despite its potentially fatal effects. Morris, *The Better Angel*, 93–94.

39   The Steam Mill Company was a large profitable sawmill owned jointly by local merchants Benjamin L. Perry, John P. C. Davis, Thomas Duncan, and Isaac Ramsey. North Carolina, 5:176B, R. G. Dun & Co. Collection. A letter by a Union soldier corroborates Rumley's suggestion that the mill was a victim of arson, claiming, "We had quite a fire here last, a Steam Saw Mill was burnt down, probably was set on fire by someone." George Frederick Jourdan to wife, May 3, 1863, Box 1, Folder 9, Civil War Collection.

asst. Quarter Master seized all the machinery, bricks, timber &c, that survived the fire, worth about $1500, for, (as he says) government use, and on the ground that one of the owners (whose interest is only one fourth) is in the Confederate lines and supposed to be aiding the "rebels."[40] These harpies seize property without the slightest authority in the confiscation act[41] or any other law of the Federal Congress. They have no court here to make a decree of confiscation. And in the instance referred to, they wantonly disregard the law concerning partnerships, and rob the whole company to punish one partner. They do not allege that there is any military necessity for this act. That is the plea, however, under which they generally plunder.

May 18, 1863.

The northern mail today brings the sorrowful news of the death of General Thos. J. Jackson[42] of the Confederate army. It has fallen heavy upon the hearts of loyal citizens here, and has produced a general feeling of sadness and despondency, notwithstanding the accompanying intelligence of the splendid victory of the Confederates over Hooker,[43] which cost the precious life of Jackson. This hero was one of the brightest lights that shone upon the Confederacy. And to him the eyes of millions had

---

40   Since all four men can be identified as remaining in Beaufort during the occupation at various times, it is not known which of the four Rumley is referring to.

41   The First Confiscation Act (August 6, 1861) and the Second Confiscation Act (July 17, 1862) granted the president power to seize any property used to aid the rebellion. It also ended masters' claims over their slaves if they had used those slaves to assist the Confederate military. Heidler and Heidler, *Encyclopedia of the American Civil War*, 1:477–479.

42   Confederate general Thomas J. "Stonewall" Jackson was mortally wounded by Confederate soldiers at the battle of Chancellorsville, on May 2, 1863. He died eight days later of pneumonia. Furguson, *Chancellorsville*, 201–206, 329.

43   General Joseph J. Hooker led the Union Army of the Potomac against the Confederate Army of Northern Virginia, crossing the Rappahannock River on April 30, 1863. Robert E. Lee's Confederates subsequently defeated the Federals at the battle of Chancellorsville. The Union army had retreated back across the Rappahannock by May 5, 1863. Foote, *The Civil War*, 2:261–316.

turned, as a bright particular star that had risen over a dark horizon to light the way to liberty and independence.

"The paths of glory lead but to the grave."[44]

May 23, 1863.

A number of letters have been distributed among citizens of the town to-day, from the Provost Marshal's office, the contents of which plainly show that they were sent by the "Underground rail way," but which, by some mischance, have fallen into the hands of the military authorities here, and have been examined. The writers of course say many hard words against the Yankees. One of them (a gentleman holding a commission in the Confederate army) discloses some facts which ought not to have been known by the Yankees, and which he, no doubt, supposed would be carefully concealed from them. Another writes to a young lady, threatening direful vengeance upon certain disloyal citizens of the town when the Confederates drive out the Yankees and take charge of Beaufort again.

May 25, 1863.

Some time since the 4th inst., a third company of the 81st. Regiment of New York troops was added to the garrison here. Three companies now occupy the town. Yesterday afternoon these troops, after their dress parade, on Front Street, were addressed by the Chaplain of the Regiment.[45] He urged them not to shrink from the war, but to fight on, and told them that the United States government would never give it up, until the flag of the Union waved triumphantly over every Southern state. He told them the Union armies had triumphed on nearly every battlefield during the war, and that in the late affair on the Rappahannock Hooker lost nothing, except in men, and that the rebel loss was twice as great as

---

44 The verse is from "Elegy (Written in a Country Courtyard)," a poem by Thomas Gray (1716–1771). Stuart, *A Treasury of Poems*, 534.

45 Rev. Isaac G. Duryee was commissioned as chaplain of the 81st New York Regiment on October 17, 1862. He served in this capacity until mustering out with the unit at the end of the war. Duryee died on February 8, 1866, "from disease contracted in the service." De Forest, *Random Sketches and Wandering Thoughts*, 260.

his! He told them that Grant[46] had lately fought the rebels four times in the southwest, and whipped them every time, and that glorious news from that region was expected soon.[47] The reverend liar then prayed and, among other things, asked God to "teach" their "hearts to war" and their "fingers to fight!"[48]

Arming the Blacks! May 30, 1863.

"To this complexion have we come at last."[49] Who would have believed it two years ago? Who, then, could have imagined that the land of Washington in the year 1863, was to be cursed by the tramp of negro armies, set on foot by one who occupied the seat which Washington himself first hallowed by his presence, to butcher white citizens of the country? When the diabolical scheme was first suggested by Northern fanatics, the civilized world appeared to be shocked at the thought of it. Such has long been the feeling of all but fanatics and murderers on the subject. Fifty years ago, when Sir Charles Napier proposed to the British government, then at war with this country, to arm the slaves against us, that government rejected the proposal as barbarous and inhuman.[50] It was left for the United States government to disgrace itself and blacken the history of the age by this infernal measure. This work has been going on for some time past on the coast of South Carolina and at other points in the south.

---

46   Union general Ulysses S. Grant.

47   Duryee's statement that Grant had been successful four times in the West was accurate, but his statement that the Confederates had lost twice as many men as Hooker at Chancellorsville was not correct.

48   Rumley is slightly misquoting from Psalms 144:1, which actually reads: "Blessed be the Lord my strength which teacheth my hands to war, and my fingers to fight."

49   I have been unable to find the originator of this quotation. It was quoted frequently by Rumley's contemporaries in the nineteenth century.

50   Sir Charles James Napier was a general in the British Army who was most widely known for conquering the Sind region of India. In 1812, from Bermuda, Napier proposed a plan to arm an army of southern slaves, with himself as its commanding officer, that would march on Washington, D.C. The British government rejected the plan. Matthew and Harrison, *Oxford Dictionary of National Biography*, 40:156–162.

This day it commences here. The old church, now known as the African Church, built by our forefathers near a half century ago, and consecrated by them to the worship of God, under the white man's government, and standing within the very enclosure where their ashes lie, has this day been desecrated by Yankee recruiting officers, and prostituted to the most unholy and damnable work of raising negro volunteers for the armed service of the Yankee government!

June 1, 1863.

A recruiting office has been opened by the Yankees, today for negro volunteers on Front Street, near the residence of the late Marcus Thomas,[51] where the black traitors are gathering in considerable numbers. Before the door waves the United States Flag, that once "gorgeous ensign of the Republic," so loved and lauded by Mr. Washington, now polluted by fanatics, and hence prostituted to the vilest purpose that ever disgraced a civilized nation. The spectacle is deeply painful to loyal inhabitants of the town. It is especially so to the women. When these think of their husbands and brothers and sons, who may fall at the hands of these black savages, no language can express their horror, or the fiery indignation that burns in their bosoms. They are constrained to be silent where Yankee ears can hear them, but they may well exclaim in secret, like the woe stricken lady in the tragedy of King John,

"O, that my tongue were in the thunder's mouth;
Then with a passion would I shake the world."[52]

That hated oath of allegiance is the constantly recurring question of the hour, with a number of our citizens in this place, and others in the country. The thought of it is revolting, perplexing, harassing; and haunts us like a spectre by day and by night. We have long dreaded it.

---

51 Marcus Cicero Thomas (1801–1853). Seventh Census, 1850: Carteret County; *Cemetery Records of Carteret County*, 164.

52 This is a quote from Shakespeare's *The Life and Death of King John*, act 3, sc. 4, in Wright, *The Complete Works of William Shakespeare*, 429.

A few weeks ago we were notified by Brigadier Gen. Negley[53] who, under Foster,[54] commanded in this county, that all persons suspected of disloyalty shall be required to take the oath, or leave the Federal lines.[55] Now, a humbug of a general, named Spinola,[56] has come here, in Negley's

———

53   Henry Morris Naglee (1815–1886) was commander of the District of Virginia and Norfolk in the summer of 1863. He had a disagreement with the governor of the "Restored Government of Virginia" over confiscation of property of disloyal citizens. The governor, Francis Harrison Pierpont, demanded that all those who refused to take the oath of allegiance to the United States and the restored government forfeit their property to the government. Naglee refused to enforce this order and was subsequently relieved of command on September 23, 1863. Warner, *Generals in Blue*, 340–341.

54   John Gray Foster (1823–1874) was a brigadier general in Burnside's North Carolina expedition. In July 1862, Foster was assigned as commander of the Department of North Carolina. He was assigned to the Department of the Ohio in the fall of 1863. Warner, *Generals in Blue*, 157–158.

55   Rumley is referring to Naglee's issuance of General Order No. 1 on April 27, 1863, in which he stated: "Any person who shall refuse to take the oath of allegiance, or having taken the oath of allegiance, shall utter disloyal sentiments, or who shall hold communication verbally with any persons who may cross our lines, or by letter with any persons residing within the lines of the enemy, shall be forthwith sent from the Department of the 18th Corps or be more severely punished." General Order No. 1, April 27, 1863, District of Beaufort, George H. Johnston Papers. Naglee was following the directive of his commander, General Foster, who on April 17, had issued his own order that stipulated, "All persons guilty of uttering disloyal sentiments, or known to be inimical to the Union cause, will at once be arrested and sent beyond the lines." "Head-quarters, 18th Army Corps, Newbern, N.C. April 17, 1863: Special orders, No. 111," broadside, American Antiquarian Society, Worcester, Massachusetts.

56   Francis Barretto Spinola (1821–1884) of New York commanded a Federal brigade in North Carolina from January to June of 1863. He was later court-martialed and allowed to resign from the army in January 1865. Warner, *Generals in Blue*, 467–468.

place; and as he ran from the Confederates not long since,[57] it is thought he will have to do something here, where his carcass is safe, to show his spunk; and it is whispered about town that he intends to regard Negley's order as a final notice, and to order out of the lines every man who has not taken the oath at the date of his order. Now every decent white man in this community who has not taken this oath would as willingly swear allegiance to the Negro government of Hayti, or the king of Dahomey, as to the vile crew of negro worshipping thieves and murderers, who control the government at Washington. But it is next to impossible for most of them to leave here now. What then, are they to do? If they take the oath they will treat is as a nullig—

"It is great sin to swear unto a sin;
But greater sin to keep a sinful oath."[58]

June 18, 1863.

Nothing during our captivity has shocked the feelings of some of our people more than the act of the military authorities here, converting the court room of our Court House in Beaufort into a negro Recruiting office! On the nights of the 16th. and 17th. inst., the black traitors held meetings there to muster recruits. It is an epoch in our history worthy of record. The orators were negroes imported by the Yankee recruiting officers. What these Samboes had to say, the writer of these lines did not venture to hear. Report says their cry was for blood—the blood of the "rebels." Armed sentinels were posted in the Court yard to preserve order.

---

57 Rumley is referring to General Spinola's poor performance in a skirmish at Blunt's Mills in eastern North Carolina. On March 30, 1863, Confederates under D. H. Hill laid siege to the Union garrison at Washington, N.C. General Spinola was ordered to leave New Bern and march overland to Washington to break the siege. Spinola was turned back by a smaller Confederate force at Blunt's Mill in April 1863 and was heavily criticized for his lackluster efforts. *Official Records, Army*, ser. 1, 18:211–216, 245–246; Browning and Smith, *Letters from a North Carolina Unionist*, 135.

58 *The Second Part of King Henry VI*, act 5, sc. 1, in Wright, *The Complete Works of William Shakespeare*, 71.

All this was done under the authority and in the name of the government of the United States.

> "What a fall is here, my countrymen,
> Since he, miscalled the Morning Star,
> No man, nor fiend hath fallen so far."[59]

It is scarcely possible to realize the state of things to which we have come. We have reached it by such gradual approaches that we have become prepared to behold its frightful realities without that horror and dismay which their sudden appearance would have been calculated to produce. And as scene after scene is unfolded to view, in the terrible drama through which we are passing, though they reveal in darker and darker shades the barbarous character of our foe, we can look upon them without emotions of terror, as only the manifestations of the impotent rage of devils who are hurrying on to their dire doom under the withering curse of the Almighty. That His arm of power is against the wretches who wage this barbarous war against us, many of their own people believe. While none whose hearts are with the South permit themselves to doubt for a moment the success of her cause. Though the tempest rages with fearful violence, and strange and frightful phenomena appear in the sky, yet He, whose spirit rides upon the whirlwind and directs the storm, will doubtless control, in his own wise way, the angry elements, until the fury of the storm shall pass away.

[June n.d., 1863]

The 23rd., 24th. and 25th. of June, were sorrowful days in Beaufort. The devils in authority here, with General Spinola at their head, resolved upon the expulsion beyond the Federal lines of every white male citizen of the town who had not taken the oath of allegiance, with his family! The number of heads of families in town (among whom the writer of these notes

---

59   The first line of poetry Rumley wrote is a slight misquoting from *The Tragedy of Julius Caesar*, act 3, sc. 2: "O, what a fall was there, my countrymen!" Wright, *The Complete Works of William Shakespeare*, 649. The other two lines are slightly misquoted from Lord Byron's poem "Ode to Napoleon Buonaparte" (1814). They are the concluding lines of the first stanza: "Since he, miscall'd the Morning Star, / Nor man nor fiend hath fallen so far." Bryant, *A Library of Poetry and Song*, 712.

was included) who had not taken the detestable oath had been gradually reduced to eighteen. There were also eight or ten young men under the ban of proscription.[60] The announcement of the despotic and inhuman order for their expulsion broke upon the community like thunder. Even defenseless women were not entirely exempt from this proscription. Two highly respectable widows of advanced age, with their families, were ordered to leave with the others at 10 o' clock A.M. of the 27th. inst.[61] Sadly flurried were the proscribed parties, and their numerous friends, by the sudden prospect of exile for a period of time, also uncertain and through which no eye but God's could penetrate.

The general in command was appealed to for a reconsideration of his order. He consented to modify it as to most of the persons it was directed against so far as to permit them to take the oath of allegiance and remain at home, but insisted that some should be expelled.

While the fate of these people hung suspended on the decision of this brute, who was doubtless inclined to ape some of the tricks of the infamous Butler,[62] he was suddenly called away, by the threatening aspect of affairs in Pennsylvania, to different fields of action. The rule adopted then was that those who had been ordered to leave should take the oath

---

60 Rumley appears to be referring to individuals who had been expelled from Beaufort under orders.

61 A specific example of this order, addressed to Rev. John Rumley, reads, "You and your family will be sent beyond the lines at 10 o'clock A.M. on Saturday, June 27, 1863." It is unclear whether John Rumley was actually expelled or whether he took the oath. The original of the letter is in a private collection. Headquarters District of Beaufort to John Rumley, July 23, 1863, Private Collections of Henry Rumley, Esq. of Washington, N.C., quoted in Mallison, *The Civil War on the Outer Banks*, 126. I have not been able to establish any clear relationship between John Rumley and James Rumley.

62 Benjamin Franklin Butler (1818–1893) was appointed military governor of Louisiana in May 1862. His headquarters were in the occupied city of New Orleans. After a controversial term of office—during which Butler, among other things, ordered southern white women who insulted Union officers to be treated as prostitutes—he was recalled from his command in Louisiana in December 1862. He did not receive another command until November 1863, when he became head of the Department of Virginia and North Carolina. Garraty and Carnes, *American National Biography*, 4:90–93; Warner, *Generals in Blue*, 60–61; Rable, "'Missing in Action,'" 134–146.

of allegiance within four days or be sent, with their families, beyond the Federal lines, and personal notices were issued accordingly.

This so-called oath of allegiance is really no oath at all, according to the law of North Carolina, for the "holy gospels" are not kissed or even touched or referred to in the administration of it or by the party taking it; and there are no Quakers or other sects here who are conscientiously opposed to taking a book oath of any other kind. But if all the legal solemnities were observed, the oath could not bind the consciences of the person upon [*whom*] it is forced. He does not mentally or morally assent to it, but repudiates and abhors it. The act which, if voluntary, would be criminal, being forced against the will, is no crime at all. The so-called oath requires the party taking it to renounce all allegiance to the Southern Confederacy. In this he renounces nothing at all. He owes no such allegiance. To the state of North Carolina, and to her alone, he owes allegiance. Every public officer of the state has sworn to "be faithful and bear true allegiance to the state of North Carolina."

This allegiance the oath referred to does not require him to renounce. But he is required to support the constitution and government of the United States, render all aid in his power to put down the "rebellion" &c, which, if he is a friend of the South, he will take good care not to do, and which the Federal officers themselves do not expect him to do. Indeed the Federal army expect nothing of a private citizen under this oath but passing obedience. If he takes office or employment under the government or army, something nearer to a literal compliance with the oath is required. Most of the men who were marked for expulsion will take this so called oath, but regard it as entirely compulsory; they are determined that it shall not, mentally or morally, affect their allegiance and shall make no change in their principles. They are, as they have been for many months, in a situation where they can render no service to the Confederates, and they have resolved to render none to the Yankees.

During sixteen months these men have struggled, beneath the gloomy shadows of Federal despotism, to live "faithful and bear true allegiance" to their own state, unmoved by the frowns, the menaces, or the blandishments of power. And their strongest desire now is that they may pass through the dreadful ordeal with hands unpolluted by any act of disloyalty and with garments unsullied by treason.

June [n.d.], 1863.

The cruel and despotic practice of the Federal Commanders, expelling citizens from their homes and seizing their property because they refuse to take their hated oath of allegiance, recalls to mind the history of the melancholy fate of the French inhabitants of Acadia, or Nova Scotia, in 1735.

By conquest and diplomacy the British government had acquired, as early as the Peace of Utrecht, the sovereignty of that Province.[63] But while these people submitted to British authority, they loved France and would not fight against its standard or renounce its name. Years rolled on, and events transpired which caused fresh suspicions as to their loyalty to Britain. They manifested a willingness to take an oath of fealty to England, but refused to pledge themselves to bear arms against France. They were ordered by a Council at Halifax to take the oath of allegiance in the common form before the council. The deputies who had been sent to the council to negotiate on the subject "entreated leave to return home and consult the body of their people." But the next day "foreseeing the sorrows that menaced them,"[64] they offered to swear allegiance unconditional. They were then told that having once refused they could not [be] permitted to take the oaths. An order of expulsion followed. Seven thousand of these persecuted people were forced, at the point of the bayonet, on board of ships and scattered among the English Colonies from New Hampshire to Georgia, while all their property, except their money and household goods which they carried with them, was confiscated. Their tenements were destroyed, and their beautiful country reduced to a solitude. While only the faithful watch dog was left round the ashes of their

---

63   In 1755 (not 1735, as Rumley states), British authorities forcibly expelled the French Acadians from the British territory of Nova Scotia. New England militia troops had taken Nova Scotia from French authorities in 1710 during Queen Anne's War. The Acadians had lived under British control peaceably since the 1713 Treaty of Utrecht ended Queen Anne's War and permanently made Nova Scotia a British territory. But by 1755, in the wake of continuing conflict with France in North America, the British doubted their neutrality. They deported approximately 11,000 Acadians, dispersing them to the other thirteen colonies. About 2,500 migrated to the Spanish colony of Louisiana. Ciment, *Colonial America*, 1:74–75.

64   Bancroft, *History of the United States*, 4:201.

cottages, "vainly seeking the hands that fed him;"[65] the poor exiles them-selves were pursued by misfortune wherever they fled. "I know not" (says Bancroft) "if the annals of the human race keep the record of sorrows so wantonly inflicted, as fell upon the French inhabitants of Acadia."[66]

July 2, 1863.

A flag of truce left here today for Swansboro, carrying a number of citi-zens of the town who refuse to take the so-called "oath of allegiance," and who were compelled under the late order of expulsion to go beyond the Federal lines. Since writing the above, the whole party have returned. They proceeded as far as Morehead City, when they received orders from General Heckman[67] (now in command) to return to Beaufort. There is evidently a flutter in the Yankee camp, caused by some movements of the Confederates unknown to the citizens here. The whole garrison of the town were suddenly called away last night, and today the place, for the first time since its capture, is clear of Yankee troops, except a few inva-lids at the Hospital and a few officers. An extraordinary order is posted on the street, prohibiting all citizens outside the town from coming in, and forbidding all persons, except commissioned officers, to carry "goods" from the town.

July 3, 1863.

The negro recruiting business, in Beaufort, seems to be dead. The Court House was occupied for the purpose only two nights. The office on Front Street is closed; and the negro sentinels that graced it have disappeared. Not more than sixty volunteers were obtained, and very few of these

---

65   Ibid., 4:206.

66   Rumley is slightly misquoting George Bancroft's *History of the United States.* Bancroft actually wrote, "I know not if the annals of the human race keep the record of sorrows so wantonly inflicted, so bitter and so perennial, as fell upon the French inhabitants of Acadia." Ibid., 4:206.

67   Charles Adam Heckman (1822–1896), who was promoted to brigadier general on November 29, 1862, served in Burnside's North Carolina expedition and held a variety of commands in North Carolina, including commander of the District of Beaufort from May to July of 1863. Warner, *Generals in Blue,* 226–227; Boatner, *The Civil War Dictionary,* 391–392.

were Beaufort negroes. May the place never be cursed by their presence again.

The blindness of fanaticism was never more strikingly displayed, than in this barbarous measure of arming negroes against the south. The mutterings of discontent which are heard from officers and soldiers of the white army of the Federals plainly indicate that this negro which has been introduced among them, stings their pride, quenches their ambition, and is actually disintegrating the already broken fragments of the once massive and powerful army of the Union.

July 8, 1863.

The fourth of July 1863 is upon us. It was ushered in by the dull ringing of bells by a few boys. At noon, the fort and some vessels in the harbor let off a national salute. There are no other demonstrations by army or navy to mark the day, except the display of flags on the vessels in port. No signs of enthusiasm are visible anywhere, except among the negroes. No decent white man or woman of the south has any respect for the day now as a national holiday. The national Union, whose birth the observance of the day was intended to commemorate, is dissolved forever, and the day may as well be stricken from our political calendar.

A disgraceful system of espionage has been kept in operation by the Yankees here for some time past, by means of which the conversations of unsuspecting citizens have been reported to the invisible head of this machinery. Secret detectives and spies have infested the public streets and stores, and eavesdropped under the windows of private families, and have heard, of course, a great many hard things said against the Yankee government and many sympathies expressed for the Southern Confederacy. These have been reported and noted in a book, the existence of which Federal officers have lately acknowledged. Negroes, and worst of all, white citizens of our town and country it is believed, have played a part in this game of secret villainy. The constant dread of these secret foes is painfully embarrassing to men of Southern sympathies. When they meet on the streets to talk over the latest news, they fear to speak in tones above a whisper, until they "look this way and that way,"[68] like Moses before he slew the Egyptian, to see who are near. If they hear good news,

---

68 Exodus 2:12.

they manifest no signs of joy until they get where no soldiers, negroes, or white traitors can see or hear them. On one occasion an express order was issued by the commandant of the post to arrest any citizen who rejoiced over the defeat of the Federal arms. By the order of General Burnside, before referred to, it is treason to utter one word against the government of the United States. Hence the necessity for great caution. This is military despotism. But what a sad condition to be in, when contrasted with the by-gone days of liberty.

July 20, 1863.

The troops who were suddenly called away from this place on the night of the 1st. inst. have returned. Our southern citizens, generally, shun their presence as they would the loathsome lepers. It is difficult for such to learn much as to their late doings. It is quite certain however that they have been on a freebooting expedition, under the direction of General Foster. It is whispered here that the cavalry portion of the force, which went from New Bern, penetrated the interior as far as Warsaw,[69] where they tore up ten miles of the railroad track and stole some money and about 250 negroes.

For several weeks past the condition of Vicksburg[70] has excited the deepest solicitude. Accounts reached through Northern sources, of affairs in the vicinity of the beleaguered city, have caused serious apprehensions as to its fate. On the evening of the 10th. inst, a telegraphic dispatch was received at Morehead City, from Gen. Foster, announcing its fall. The next evening, New York papers were received containing particulars purporting to be the terms of the capitulation of the garrison, the number of officers and men &c. The same papers contain frightful

---

69 Warsaw is a town on the Wilmington and Weldon Railroad in Duplin County. It is about ninety-five miles west of Beaufort and seventy miles southwest of New Bern. Powell, *The North Carolina Gazetteer*, 518.

70 Union general Ulysses S. Grant began a siege of the city of Vicksburg on the Mississippi River in May 1863. On July 4, 1863, after exhausting nearly all of the food supplies and realizing that no rescue attempt would be made, Confederate general John C. Pemberton surrendered the city and its garrison. Heidler and Heidler, *Encyclopedia of the American Civil War*, 4:2021–2027.

accounts of disasters to the Confederate force under General Lee, at the three days' fight near Gettysburg.[71] Never were earthly hopes more suddenly clouded. The deepest despair and mortification settled upon every loyal heart; and every countenance "gave signs of woe that all was lost."[72]

In a day or two, other papers came from the North. They brought no further light from Vicksburg, but put a much better face upon affairs in General Lee's army. It was concentrating at Hagerstown and was far from being the broken and routed army it was supposed to be.

Days rolled on and no official dispatch from the Federal Commander at Vicksburg announced its capture. Nor did the Richmond papers, six or seven days after the reported fall of Vicksburg, contain any intimation of such a disaster. Men doubt its fall, and a flickering hope revived that its brave garrison might hold out until the Confederates could raise the siege.

Recent intelligence confirms the report of its fall. Port Hudson[73] has also yielded to the Federal arms. And darkness has settled down upon the south west.

---

71 General Robert E. Lee began leading the Confederate Army of Northern Virginia in an invasion of the North on June 3, 1863. From July 1 to 3, 1863, Lee's army engaged in battle with Union general George G. Meade's Army of the Potomac near Gettysburg, Pennsylvania. Lee's army was defeated and began retreating from Pennsylvania on July 4. Heidler and Heidler, *Encyclopedia of the American Civil War*, 2:827–838.

72 This quote is from John Milton's *Paradise Lost*, bk. 9, line 784, in Eliot, *The Complete Poems of John Milton*, 280.

73 After Vicksburg surrendered on July 4, 1863, Confederate general Franklin Gardner surrendered the Confederate garrison of Port Hudson, Louisiana (located on the Mississippi River about twenty miles north of Baton Rouge) to a combined Union army and naval force on July 9, 1863. Heidler and Heidler, *Encyclopedia of the American Civil War*, 3:1546–1549.

July 25, 1863.

Col. Emory[74] of the 17th. Massachusetts Regiment, acting Brigadier General, now commands this District, and has established his headquarters at Beaufort.

Among the officials located here, at present, is Mr. David Heaton,[75] Supervising Agent of the Treasury Department of the United States, "to regulate the coasting trade of this Federal District, and take charge of abandoned property, &c." He commenced the performance of his duties in Beaufort by seizing and appropriating to himself the dwelling house of C.R. Thomas, Esq.,[76] who was a member of the late state Convention, and is now within the Confederate line.

The steamer *Catawba* arrived today and landed at Morehead City over a thousand negro troops, destined for New Bern.[77] Persons who

---

74   Colonel Thomas J. C. Amory (1828–1864) of the 17th Massachusetts Infantry was commander of the Sub-District of Beaufort from August 1 to 14, 1863 and from June 27 to October 7, 1864. He died in Beaufort on October 8, 1864, from yellow fever. Boatner, *The Civil War Dictionary*, 12–13; Dyer, *A Compendium of the War of the Rebellion*, 1:393; Browning and Smith, *Letters from a North Carolina Unionist*, 230.

75   David Heaton (1823–1870), a former member of the Ohio and Minnesota state senates, was appointed as a special agent for the treasury department in 1863. During Reconstruction he played an active role in the North Carolina Republican Party, serving as a delegate to the state's 1868 constitutional convention and representing the state in the U.S. Congress. *Who Was Who in America*, 1:244.

76   Charles Randolph Thomas (1827–1891), a Beaufort native, was North Carolina's secretary of state from January to August 1865. He had also been a leading Unionist in the county before secession and was elected to serve as Carteret County's delegate to North Carolina's secession convention in February 1861 (which failed). Powell, *Dictionary of North Carolina Biography*, 6:20; Cheney, *North Carolina Government*, 181, 193, 386–401.

77   The 55th Massachusetts Infantry Regiment, an African American regiment under the command of Colonel Norwood P. Hallowell, arrived in New Bern in July 1863 with 974 officers and men. *Official Records, Army*, ser. 1, 27, pt. 3:819; 28, pt. 2:75.

saw them describe them as a degraded looking set of wretches of various colors from the light mulatto to the sooty black, filthy as hogs in their persons, hideous in their forms and faces, cowardly looking in their general aspect, and with the look of demons in their eyes. They have been raked up from the filthy kennels of Massachusetts and Ohio, and have come here, they say, to hunt down the "rebels."

July 26, 1863.

The U.S. Steamer *"Penobscot,"* arrived in port this morning, having on board James Howard,[78] E. Hurt[,][79] David Sabiston[80] and others, taken as blockade runners, on board the Confederate Steamer *"Merrimac"*[81] outward bound from Wilmington N.C.—The *"Merrimac"* had passed the blockading squadron, and though chased by one of the steamers, was triumphantly plowing her way towards the gulf stream, when she was unexpectedly met by a United States steamer bound towards the Wilmington blockading station, and was captured. She was laden with cotton and naval stores.

---

78 James Howard (b. ca. 1837) was a ship's carpenter from New Bern. Eighth Census, 1860: Craven County.

79 Edward H. Hurtt (1822–September 20, 1864) was listed as a merchant and as a mechanic from New Bern in the 1850 and 1860 censuses, respectively. He died in New Bern, likely from yellow fever. He is buried in Cedar Grove Cemetery in New Bern. Seventh Census, 1850: Craven County; Eighth Census, 1860: Craven County; Stapleford, *Cedar Grove Cemetery*, 35.

80 David Sabiston (b. ca. 1839), a mariner, was the son of Beaufort fisherman John Sabiston. Eighth Census, 1860: Carteret County.

81 The CSS *Merrimac*, an iron paddle-wheel steamer of nearly 635 tons, was captured at 10 a.m. on July 24, 1863, about forty miles east of the Masonboro Inlet near Wilmington, by the U.S. steam sloop *Iroquois*. The *Merrimac* was loaded with 642 bales of cotton, nine barrels of spirits of turpentine, and over seventy-seven kegs of tobacco. *Official Records, Navy*, ser. 1, 9:131–132.

July 30, 1863.

About five hundred negro troops, North Carolina volunteers, arrived at Morehead City from New Bern today and embarked in a steamer for Port Royal.[82] A brother of Henry Ward Beecher[83] accompanied them.

Sunday, August 2, 1863.

A negro preacher, chaplain to the negro regiment[84] lately sent from Massachusetts to this state, preached to the negroes of Beaufort in the African Church today.

Thursday night, August 4, 1863.[85]

A captain of a negro company from New Bern, occupied the Court House for the purpose of enlisting negroes, and although aided by a negro orator brought with him, failed to obtain a single volunteer.

Thursday the 6th. of August is Lincoln's appointed day of thanksgiving,[86] for his late escape from total ruin at the hands of General Lee.

---

82   The 1st North Carolina Colored Volunteers arrived in Beaufort en route to Port Royal, South Carolina, to assist in an offensive against the port city of Charleston, South Carolina. Richard M. Reid, *Freedom for Themselves*, 40–41.

83   The 1st North Carolina Colored Volunteers was commanded by Colonel James. C. Beecher and was part of the African Brigade raised by General Edward A. Wild in the spring of 1863. Beecher (1828–1886) was half-brother to Harriet Beecher Stowe, author of *Uncle Tom's Cabin*, and Henry Ward Beecher (1813–1887), an influential antislavery minister from New England. Richard M. Reid, *Freedom for Themselves*, 25; Finding Aid, Papers of James Chaplin Beecher; Heidler and Heidler, *Encyclopedia of the American Civil War*, 1:202–203.

84   William Jackson (b. ca. 1824), a clergyman from New Bedford, Massachusetts, was commissioned as chaplain of the 55th Massachusetts Infantry Regiment (Colored) on July 10, 1863. He resigned and was discharged from the service on January 14, 1864. Massachusetts Adjutant General's Office, *Massachusetts Soldiers, Sailors, and Marines*, 4:717.

85   August 4, 1863, was a Tuesday.

86   On July 14, 1863, President Lincoln issued a proclamation designating Thursday, August 6, 1863, as a "day of national thanksgiving" in order "to render homage to the Divine Majesty" for the victories at Gettysburg and Vicksburg. *Official Records, Army*, ser. 3, 3:492–493.

The negroes are celebrating the day, in the African Church, with all the enthusiasm which such an occasion is calculated to inspire among the deluded and excited race. With hymns of praise to God are mingled prayers for the success of the "Union Armies," and for the speedy downfall of the "rebellion." These are the foes the south has nursed and reared on her own sunny fields; harmless, were faithful to her when let alone, but easily converted into traitors, and filled with venomous hate by the poisonous breath of fanaticism.

These demonstrations among the negro race suggest sad and solemn thoughts. They point with fearful significance to the true character of this war. That it is a grand crusade against African slavery; every negro in the Federal lines perfectly understands. Abolitionism is the power that now sits enthroned at the north and wages this war. And although its complete ascendency at Washington damaged for a while the armies of the Federal government, yet it is doubtless now the real animus of the war. Fanaticism is now the element that fires the heart, and nerves the arm, of the Federal soldier. His drawn sword and his bayonet are flashing in its lurid light. It is heard in his battle cry of "freedom," and in his songs of hallelujah to the memory of Old John Brown.[87]

August 15, 1863.

About five hundred Federal troops arrived this week in a steamer at Morehead City. They are the first reinforcements furnished by the Northern Conscription.[88] Nearly the whole of them are hired substitutes of persons drafted in Rhode Island. They exhibit a great deal of rowdyism,

---

87 Rumley is referring to a popular northern song from the time known as "John Brown's Body." The song began "John Brown's body lies a-mouldering in the grave" and ended with the line "His soul goes marching on." In November 1861, Julia Ward Howe, a New York reformer and author, crafted new lyrics to the song to create the famed "Battle Hymn of the Republic." Heidler and Heidler, *Encyclopedia of the American Civil War*, 1:191–192; 2:1010–1011.

88 Lincoln signed the Enrollment Act into law on March 3, 1863, which called for the drafting of males between the ages of twenty and forty-five. The act had several exemptions, including allowing drafted men to hire substitutes to serve in their stead. The act was primarily a tool to stimulate voluntary enlistment. The first draft was held in June 1863. Only about 6 percent of all Union soldiers were draftees. Heidler and Heidler, *Encyclopedia of the American Civil War*, 1:487–488.

and were no doubt the genuine *sans cullotte*[89] of the northern cities. But they manifest no hatred toward the south. They drive the negroes from their presence whenever they encounter them, and call the "secesh" their friends. Fifteen or twenty of them deserted immediately after their arrival, and went in the direction of Neuse River. On the arrival of the main body at New Bern, one of them loudly hurrahed for Jefferson Davis!

Major Curlis has been called away, and is succeeded in the office of Provost Marshal of Beaufort by Capt. Bartlett,[90] who belongs to the Massachusetts regiment.

Sunday, August 23, 1863.

About fifteen negroes—men, women and children—arrived here today by sea in a small open boat, from Snead's Ferry in Onslow County. They are fugitives in search of freedom. By the law of "Niggerdom" they are free here.

September [n.d.], 1863.

Our political night grows darker. The light which, a little while ago, was breaking from the Peace party of the North and rising like a bright aurora above the northern horizon, has been suddenly obscured and succeeded by the blackness of midnight; and the voice of peace is heard no more, while far over the water, where millions of the south have long bent their anxious looks and fondly imagined of late the day star of their hopes was rising, clouds and shadows darken the sky; and over head and all around,

---

89   The term sans culotte ("without kneepants") refers to working-class citizens during the French Revolution who could not afford the high fashion of the nobility.

90   George W. Bartlett (b. ca. 1836) was a lawyer from Greenfield, Massachusetts, who enlisted as a first lieutenant and adjutant of the 27th Massachusetts Infantry Regiment on September 25, 1861. He was promoted to captain of Company K on May 2, 1863. He resigned his commission and was discharged from the service on September 12, 1864. Massachusetts Adjutant General's Office, *Massachusetts Soldiers, Sailors, and Marines*, 3:122.

a cloud-like, starless canopy bounds the vision. But it is not night to all, even in a political sense.[91]

There are men who are perfectly satisfied with the present military despotism, while it bears not heavy on their persons or property, and they can gratify their lust of gain. They can say in their hearts, with Pope:

"For forms of Government let fools contest;

That which is best administered is best."[92]

And this is best administered for them.

There are others who loathe the presence of abolition masters, and would hail with joy the restoration of Southern rule, but have gradually become accustomed to military law and the presence of bayonets, and weary of the monotony of their captivity, and sick of hope deferred, have sought the excitement of business, and in the pursuit of money have caused to contemplate the awful night of suffering and sorrow that rests upon their country.

October [n.d.], 1863.

Since the fall of Vicksburg, the friends of Southern Independence have been at the lowest point of depression, and fast settling down in a night of despair. But light breaks from the West, and from the bloody field of Chickamauga[93] comes a voice of encouragement; a voice which cries, in

---

91 Rumley is likely referring to the calls for peace from the Peace Democrats, or Copperheads, who were strongest in the midwestern states of Ohio, Indiana, and Illinois and were led by Ohio politician Clement Vallandigham. They reached a crescendo in the spring of 1863 before many were arrested and Vallandigham was banished from the United States in May of that year. Heidler and Heidler, *Encyclopedia of the American Civil War*, 3:1470–1471.

92 This is a slight misquotation of Alexander Pope's *Essay on Man*, epistle III, verse VI, lines 303–304. The actual verse reads: "For forms of government let fools contest; / Whate'er is best administer'd is best." Pope, *An Essay on Man*, 123–124.

93 Confederate general Braxton Bragg's Army of Tennessee defeated Union major general William Rosecrans's Army of the Cumberland near Chickamauga Creek in northern Georgia on September 19–20, 1863. McPherson, *Battle Cry of Freedom*, 672–676.

tones which we can readily understand, "Resistance till the last armed foe expires."[94]

From Charleston too comes the cry of "resistance unto death"; and all the intelligence we get from the brave defenders of that city indicates that they are animated by a spirit as heroic, and as deadly in its determination, as that of Saragossa.[95] We await the result of the operations now going on against that point, with profound anxiety.

Charles Henry Foster has come again! By a dogged perseverence worthy of a better man and a better cause, he has at last procured a commission. He is now "Captain and Recruiting officer, second Regiment Loyal North Carolinians,"[96] as his printed circular shows. He is trying to raise more Buffalo Troops. On a late raid of the Yankees, which he accompanied, in the direction of Murfreesboro, he found his wife who had formerly repudiated him. He brought her to Beaufort, where, true to Yankee instincts, he took possession of an absent lady's dwelling house and furniture, and has quietly quartered himself and lady there—without pay.

It is painful to see this man and his satellites dogging the poor men of the county, to get them to enlist in a service which their southern instincts incline them to abhor. They tell the benighted creatures the "rebellion" is fast on the wane, and they will have nothing to fear from the south. They appeal to them by their old love for the American flag, and the former glory of the American name; and not forgetting to assure them that God will prosper the cause they address to them the persuasive language of

---

94   Rumley is paraphrasing a verse from the poem "Marco Bozzaris" by British poet Fitz-Greene Halleck. The actual verse reads, "Strike—till the last armed foe expires." Dana, *The Household Book of Poetry*, 392.

95   The city of Saragossa, in northern Spain, suffered through two long sieges by the French army during the Napoleonic Wars. In the first siege of June–August 1808, the Spanish defenders outlasted the French besiegers and forced them to withdraw. The Spanish army was supplemented by thousands of civilians who took up arms to defend their city. The second siege, from December 1808–February 1809, was characterized by brutal fighting in which the French finally captured the city after killing almost all of its defenders. Over 50,000 Spanish died defending the city. Ward, Prothero, and Leathes, *The Cambridge Modern History*, 9:438–448.

96   The 2nd North Carolina Infantry Regiment (Union) began mustering into service in November 1863. In all, five companies were formed before the 2nd North Carolina was consolidated into the 1st North Carolina Regiment on February 27, 1865. Browning, "Little-Souled Mercenaries?" 341–342.

Moses to Hobab, "come thou with us."[97] But they do not come except a few who are lured into the net by the prospect of food and clothing.

Many of those who were caught in it twelve months ago would now give the world to get out of it. They offer no encouragement to others to enter into the same snare, but like the rich man in hell,[98] they would rather, if they could, send messengers to testify unto their brethren lest they also should come to that place of torment.

Change again! Gen Heckman's Brigade has been suddenly called to Virginia. This call takes away the troops from Beaufort. Their place is supplied by a portion of the 158th. Regiment of New York Infantry. No change in the office of Provost Marshal.

October 17, 1863.

This post being the only "Port of Entry" in this Military District, a great deal of merchandise is imported here. Most of it is taken by railroad to New Bern direct from the vessels. The residue (except such as stops at Morehead City) is landed at Beaufort, by Yankee traders who have followed the army here, and by our own merchants. Here many people from Craven and other eastern counties come to procure supplies. The officers and soldiers of the army, and the officers and marines from the United States Naval vessels that visit the harbor, contribute to swell the number of purchases. At the same time, the people of this county find here a ready market for their agricultural products, fish, and every living thing from beneath the water. From these causes a brisk trade has sprung up in Beaufort. Every store or shop in the front part of the town fit to receive merchandise has been occupied by traders.

Turpentine, tar and resin, with the spirits of turpentine, enter largely into this trade. When the Yankees first occupied this county, the owners of piney land, generally, seeing their delicate and critical position, were strongly desirous to avoid the production of these articles for the benefit of their enemies. But some were driven to it by necessity. Others, seeing their lands would be taken and used by the Yankees, negroes and other

---

97　Numbers 10:29.

98　Rumley is referring to Jesus's parable of the rich man and Lazarus. When in Hell, the rich man asked Abraham to send Lazarus to his father's house to warn his brothers of the torments of Hell. Luke 16:22–28.

traitors, concluded to take the business in their own hands, and are now engaged in a traffic, which their sense of duty to the south, and the laws of the Confederate States, forbid. Turpentine has sold in this market as high as $30 per barrel, and the other naval stores proportionally high.

But this whole trade is about to receive a severe check. The United States government now claims the exclusive right to purchase these naval store products; and through their agent, Mr. Heaton, have issued orders prohibiting the sale of such products to any person except a government agent. They have scaled the price down to $12 per barrel for Turpentine, $3.75 per barrel for tar, $1 per barrel for rosin, and per gallon for spirits of turpentine, thus robbing the producer of the difference between these prices and those which private individuals are willing to give. In the meantime, Mr. Heaton is about to impose new restrictions on the trade of the store keepers, limiting the amount of their purchases and sales, and requiring a very stringent oath touching their loyalty to the United States.

At the Custom House, likewise, the restrictions upon the export and import trade are very severe. The Treasury Department at Washington has resorted to every conceivable means short of absolute prohibition of trade, to prevent the passage of merchandise across the Federal lines. But in this they have failed. And until their abolitionized, nigger government can conquer the hearts of these subjugated and indignant inhabitants of this region, who hate that government as they do the Devil, all the oaths and restrictions it can impose—nay, a Chinese wall erected along the lines—cannot bar their intercourse with their friends beyond.

October 30, 1863.

On the morning of the 25th. of October, long before day, our town was visited by an awful fire, unprecedented in its ravage in the history of the place. It broke out in the kitchen of Mr. Ensley,[99] adjoining the prem-

---

99 Benjamin Ensley (1830–1879) was a resident of Craven County who owned and operated Front Street House in Beaufort. By 1870, he had relocated to Hyde County. Eighth Census, 1860: Craven County; Ninth Census, 1870: Hyde County; North Carolina, 5:176E, R. G. Dun & Co. Collection; New Bern *Daily Progress*, September 1, 1860; Lewis, *The Carteret County Cemetery Book*, 1:B8.

ises of Dr. King[100] now occupied by Dr. Martin[101] on Front Street. This was not fifty yards from the Military Guard House, where a sentinel constantly stands and other soldiers are always on duty. Several soldiers were at that time patrolling the town. With all these safe guards, the fire was suffered to progress so far that it baffled all the efforts of citizens, officers and soldiers, who came as soon as they heard the alarm, to extinguish it, until five dwelling houses with outhouses, and a great deal of other property, were consumed. The dwellings and outhouses of Mrs. Jane Ward,[102] Mr. Ensley, Dr. Martin, Mr. Taylor,[103] and Capt. Fulford,[104] and Dr. Martin's Drug store all perished. After Mr. Taylor's hotel took fire, Capt. Fulford's dwelling was blown down, with powder, to stop the fire in that direction. Capt. Bartlett, the Provost Marshal, and the officers, physicians and soldiers of the post, with citizens, after they reached the scene of the fire, made the most vigorous efforts to extinguish it. The dampness of the weather, caused by a previous rainy spell, favored their efforts. They succeeded in saving Mr. R.S. Hall's dwelling house,[105] and stopped the flames at that point, even after the house and kitchen, and a tree in his yard, had taken fire! The dreadful fire cast a lurid, unearthly glare over the face of the harbor, while the dark clouds all round the horizon assumed a hue of frightful blackness, presenting a scene which made a deep impression upon the mind of every beholder.

On the night of the 26th. of October a daring attempt was made, by some devil in human form, to burn the dwelling house of Mr. James

---

100 Francis Lathrop King.

101 Dr. Lafayette Martin (1826–1880), a native of Virginia, operated an apothecary shop in Beaufort. *Cemetery Records of Carteret County*, 159; Ninth Census, 1870: Carteret County; Browning and Smith, *Letters from a North Carolina Unionist*, 164.

102 Jane Bell Ward (b. ca. 1786–1868). *Cemetery Records of Carteret County*, 165; Eighth Census, 1860: Carteret County; Jesse Ward and Jane Bell, Marriage Bond, March 8, 1825, Carteret County.

103 George W. Taylor, owner of Ocean House hotel.

104 William Fulford (b. ca. 1786) had been a lighthouse keeper in 1850. Seventh Census, 1850: Carteret County.

105 R. S. Hall (b. ca. 1797) was a local farmer. Eighth Census, 1860: Carteret County.

Bisk,[106] in Beaufort, where Mr. B. and family and several boarders were sleeping. The wretch entered the house and robbed it of what he could find to suit him, and then took a small trunk of papers, broke it open, and finding no money in it, carried it out, placed it under the weather boarding of the house and kindled a fire in it, which destroyed the papers and would have set the house on fire had not a lady being near, who happened to be up at that moment, discovered the fire and gave the alarm.

Other houses have been entered within the last few nights; and we have alarming evidences that robbers and incendiaries are among us. The Provost Marshal has called out a citizen patrol for night service, for the safety of the town.

There are but few soldiers at this point, and some of them are suspected of being discharged convicts from northern penitentiaries, and ripe for crime.

October 31, 1863.

Our citizens were startled today by the sudden appearance in town of James W. Bryan Esq.,[107] who lately came to New Bern from the Confederate lines under a flag of truce, and was called on business to the Provost Marshal's office in Beaufort. No living man could have been more welcome to us in our dreary captivity. His visit was short—very short, but long enough to remind us forcibly of those better days when he towered among us in the light and liberty of civil law—days that are gone forever by, but now in the retrospect, look bright as Heaven compared with the present starless night.

---

106 James Bask (b. ca. 1800) was a sailmaker in Beaufort. Eighth Census, 1860: Carteret County.

107 James West Bryan (1805–1864) was a state senator from Carteret County in 1835–1836 and a delegate to the 1835 state constitutional convention. He died in New Bern of yellow fever in October 1864. Powell, *Dictionary of North Carolina Biography*, 1:255; Browning and Smith, *Letters from a North Carolina Unionist*, 229.

November 3, 1863.

Another small company of troops belonging to the 158th. New York Infantry was added to the garrison here today. Some of them have a very ruffian like aspect; and if reports as to their character can be trusted, we had as well have among us so many of the Huns and vandals who plundered Italy. They look as though
> "Some rugged rock's hard entrails gave them form,
> And raging seas produced them in a storm."[108]

The citizen patrol is to be discontinued.

November 9, 1863.

Two Confederate steamers, the *Lady Davis* and *Robert E. Lee*,[109] were brought in here as prizes today. They were bound to Wilmington, laden with munitions of war, when captured. Crowds of people were attracted to the wharves to view them as they glided mournfully up the channel.

November 10, 1863.

Another steamer from England bound to Wilmington, is brought into this port today, as a prize to the Yankee blockading vessels. *Ella and Anna*[110] of Charleston.

---

108 Rumley is slightly misquoting a passage from Homer's *Iliad*, Book 16, lines 50–51. The verse actually reads, "Some rugged rock's hard entrails gave thee form, / And raging seas produced thee in a storm." Pope, *The Iliad*, 749.

109 The USS *James Adger* captured the Confederate steamer *Lady Davis* (previously known as the *Cornubia*) on November 8, 1863, near New Inlet, North Carolina. The following day the same Union ship seized the *Robert E. Lee* off Cape Lookout Shoals, North Carolina. *Civil War Naval Chronology*, 3:153, 6:294.

110 The correct name of the captured blockade-runner was the *Ella and Annie*. It was seized by the USS *Niphon* near Masonboro Inlet, North Carolina, on November 9, 1863. *Civil War Naval Chronology*, 3:154; *Official Records, Navy*, ser. 1, 9:291–292.

November 11, 1863.

Another Steamer is brought into port today as a prize. Her name is *El-la*.[111] All these unfortunate vessels were last from Bermuda, and laden chiefly with munitions of war.

The Yankee blockaders have struck a stream of good luck. They are in high glee over the prospect of the prize money they are to get. And they vainly imagine that in taking those blockade runners, they are rapidly "crushing the rebellion." They do not seem to know that a large portion of the people in the Confederacy—perhaps a large majority—are opposed to the whole system of blockade running and would be glad to see it annihilated. The propriety of permitting its further continuance is doubted by the Confederates.

The steamer *Ella and Anna*, before mentioned, was captured by the U.S. Steamer *Niphon*. Before her surrender, the former attempted to run into the *Niphon*; but did not strike her exactly "midship," or she no doubt would have sunk her. Failing in this bold effort to thwart her pursuers, she surrendered to the *Niphon*; and while her officers, crew and passengers were assembling on deck, preparatory to leaving their vessel, the "acting Ensign of the *Niphon*"—a low bred creature—fired into the crowd, with a pistol, and wounded a seaman severely in the thigh.

Another seaman had been previously wounded in the shoulder by a fragment of a bomb shell thrown from the *Niphon*.[112] Both have been carried to the U.S. Hospital in Beaufort.[113]

Among the persons captured on the 10th. inst., on board the Steamer

---

111   The Confederate blockade-runner *Ella* left Bermuda at 9 a.m. on November 4, 1863, headed to Wilmington. On the evening of November 10, she was captured by the USS *Howquah* about thirteen miles north of Fort Fisher, outside Wilmington. *Official Records, Navy*, ser. 1, 9:297–298.

112   The commanding officer of the USS *Niphon* reported that the *Niphon* suffered three casualties from the ramming. The *Ella and Annie* suffered four casualties from shell or grapeshot fired by the *Niphon* to force her to surrender. There is no official reference to the events Rumley reports. *Official Records, Navy*, ser. 1, 9:291–292.

113   Captain Josiah Pender's Atlantic Hotel was seized and converted into Hammond General Hospital by Union authorities in April 1862. It served as a hospital until January 14, 1865. Powell, *Dictionary of North Carolina Biography*, 5:62–63; Doughton, *The Atlantic Hotel*, 5–53; entry dated January 14, 1865, Edmund Janes Cleveland Diary.

Ella and Anna, were two passengers—Mr. Gray of Georgia, and a lady who bears the name of Mrs. Anne Nichols. The lady has stated confidentially to a few citizens, that she is lately from Paris, and is bearer of dispatches from Vice-President Stephens, now in Paris, to the Confederate government.[114] Seeing she was about to be captured, she carefully destroyed the written dispatches, first tracing their substance in the book of memory, where the sharp eye of the Yankees cannot detect them. During the present war she has suffered imprisonment banishment and shipwreck, and now seems ready to face danger on flood or field in the cause of the south. She and Mr. Gray were ordered to New Bern on the 14th. inst.

November 17, 1863.

Loud peals of cannon at Fort Macon yesterday afternoon announced the arrival of Major General Benjamin F. Butler, U.S.A., who has been assigned to the command of the forces, and such territory as the United States government controls, in Virginia and North Carolina. He came by sea in the steamer *Spaulding.*

No man which this war has thrown upon the stage of action could be more unwelcome to these shores than this brute in human form. Yet, if he should visit the town, and it was announced here that he would, the people wanted to behold the murderer of Montport,[115] and the vile persecutor and defamer of the women of New Orleans. The troops stationed here were formed in line on the county wharf about sunset, and many of the male inhabitants of the town assembled near in expectation of his arrival, and they waited, till night drew her curtain over the scene,

---

114 This is a strange entry. Alexander Stephens (1812–1883), a former Whig congressman from Georgia, was vice-president of the Confederacy. However, contrary to what Rumley reports, Stephens never traveled to a foreign country during the Civil War. Schott, *Alexander H. Stephens of Georgia.* Neither Mr. Gray nor Anne Nichols is referred to in any of the official records of the capture of the *Ella and Annie.* I have been unable to identify them.

115 Rumley has misspelled the name of William Mumford. Union general Benjamin Butler had Mumford, a New Orleans gambler, executed for tearing down the U.S. flag that had been raised over the U.S. mint by Admiral David Farragut to signify the beginning of Union occupation of New Orleans in April 1862. Butler, *Autobiography and Personal Reminiscences,* 437–445.

and Butler did not come. This morning, we learn, he is on his way to New Bern. A citizen on the street, on hearing it announced, expressed the wish that the old villain may not stop this side of Hell.

November 20, 1863. [also listed as November 21, 1863 at end of paragraph]

Among the vessels in port is a pretty, trim looking barque of seven hundred, or eight hundred tons burthen, called the *Release.* This is the vessel which, with the steamer *Arctic,* was sent by the Hon. J.C. Dobbs,[116] Secretary of the U.S. Navy, in 1855, in search of Doctor Kane's "Arctic Expedition," who found the Doctor and his company at Lively in Greenland, and took them thence to New York.[117] The sight of this vessel revives many recollections of the thrilling narrative of the bold voyage who now sleep in death.

November 21, 1863. [also listed as November 24, 1863, at end of paragraph]

Deserters from the Confederate army have lately made their appearance quite frequently on our streets. Very few Carteret men are to be seen among them. They come here because they find a safe asylum in a place farther beyond the reach of Confederate power, than any other in the

---

116   James C. Dobbin (1814–1857), a North Carolina lawyer who had served as a U.S. representative from 1845 to 1847, was secretary of the navy from 1853 to 1857. Lanman, *Biographical Annals,* 142.

117   Dr. Elisha Kent Kane embarked on an expedition to the Arctic Circle on May 31, 1853. He was searching for a British expedition team that had gone missing. Kane's expedition became hopelessly trapped by the frozen waters, forcing his expedition to spend nearly two years in the Arctic regions. In May 1855, they abandoned their ship and carried their provisions in small boats over 300 miles of ice before reaching the open sea. They then sailed over 1,300 miles to Greenland. In 1855, the secretary of the navy, with congressional approval, outfitted the *Release* and the *Arctic* under a naval lieutenant to search for Kane. This search party found Kane and his crew in Greenland in September 1855. *New York Daily Times,* February 24, 1857.

state and where in case of the approach of a Confederate army, they can rush on board the Yankee vessels in the harbor and seek refuge at sea. They come in squads of four or five, and as soon as they set foot upon the place are besieged by Buffalo Recruiting officers (who are swarming over the county), and are wheedled, or frightened, into the Federal service. They are thus swelling the ranks of the pestilent army of "Buffalo Troops," the most deadly foes that any country ever reared on its own soil—serpents, whose venomous stings are aimed at the body that warmed them into life.

What revelations these traitors make to the military authorities here perhaps the world will never know. They tell no doubt of merchandise and letters carried from port into the Confederate lines, and who the carriers are. But fortunately, most of them are without intelligence enough to give much reliable military information. But we would not judge harshly of the motives of these poor stragglers. They are incapable of appreciating the momentous character of the struggle in which the south is now engaged, and the awful doom that awaits her if she succumbs to Federal power; or they would not desert her standard. They have served her faithfully through two years and a half of a frightful war. But they begin to doubt whether [the] goal she is striving for can ever be attained; and their spirits quail before the prospect of a long war with its privations and fierce diseases in camp, its perilous marches, and its more perilous fields of slaughter, while their hearts yearn for their families and friends who live within the Federal lines.

November 25, 1863.

In the pleasant little mansion lately occupied by Eli Smallwood Esq.,[118] on Front Street, is the office of the United States Provost Marshal of this place. Day after day, before the door of this office, between the hours of nine and two, can be seen a crowd of white men, and sometimes women,

---

118 Eli Smallwood (b. ca. 1783–1860) was a prosperous merchant from Craven County who owned property in Beaufort. He was buried in Cedar Grove cemetery in New Bern. Seventh Census, 1850: Craven County; Stapleford, *Cedar Grove Cemetery*, 56.

waiting admittance, to get passes or permits, or for the trial of some cause. An armed sentinel stands at the door and admits only one or two at a time. They are mostly people from the country, who have come to town to purchase necessary stores for their families. These they are allowed to procure only in very limited quantities, and before the necessary permit for this purpose is granted, the applicant is required to swear that the articles he or she desires to carry from the town are for the consumption of his or her own family. Sometimes negroes can be seen mingling in the crowd. They too are after passes or permits, or perhaps have come to bring suit against some white man or woman. All are upon a level there.

Verily the spectacle is a sad one; is a striking comment upon our political state; and makes the passerby feel like he was walking beneath the shadows of an Eastern despotism, where the light of liberty had gone out from.

December 1, 1863.

The Autumn of 1863 has passed away. Its many bright and genial days, its starry nights, and its agreeable temperature, marked it as the most beautiful and pleasant autumn ever witnessed by the present generation in this part of Carolina. A few days of cloudy weather, with moderate winds and rain, imparted to the season a pleasant variety, but no storms or wintry blasts—which generally intervene between the regular summer and the Indian summer—marred its delightful serenity. As its last hours were running out, the cold wind came, fresh from the frozen hills of the North, and with roaring, howling, freezing blasts, ushered in the first morning of winter.

A very noticeable feature of the new order of things established here are the negro schools which abolitionism reared up in the heart of the community. Two are now in full operation; one in the Baptist Church building, and the other in the African Church building; both taught by Yankee women.[119]

---

119 The two women referred to are Sarah D. Comings (b. ca. 1840) and Mary Brownson (b. ca. 1830). Both were from Vermont and worked for the American Missionary Association. American Missionary Association, *Eighteenth Annual Report of the American Missionary Association*, 26; *Freedman's Advocate* 1 (April 1864): 15; Seventh Census, 1850: Chittenden County, Vermont, and Essex County, Massachusetts. I thank Ronald E. Butchart for providing this information from his research.

There is nothing intrinsically wrong in teaching this benighted race—whether in freedom or slavery—to read and write, and the statutes of our state forbidding such instructions have been severely censured by enlightened men of the county. But, to have these institutions of Yankeedom forced upon us by a conquering enemy, in utter contempt of the laws of the state and the general southern sentiment on the subject, with other insults from the insolent foe, is exasperating beyond conception.

If the State of North Carolina had set their negroes free and established schools for their instruction, they would have looked upon the white population of the state as their benefactors, and the two races might have lived together on the same soil, with proper distinction, social and political lines between them, in some degree of harmony. But far different is the effect of the present scheme of emancipation and education upon the servile race. They know that the South is now struggling to perpetuate their bondage and their intellectual darkness. On the other hand they see that the Yankees are fighting for their freedom, and assure their determination to cut their bonds of servitude asunder even with the sharp edge of the sword! These fanatics tell them they design to elevate them, by giving them freedom and education, to a position of social and political equality with the whites, and dazzle their imaginations with pictures of a golden age now opening before them.

The effect of all this is to fill the minds of the negroes with mortal hatred of the whole white population of the state, as well as the whole south, and there can be no hope of harmony between them. Should the designs of northern fanaticism towards this race finally succeed in this war, what an awful future the white race will have before them! How dreadful their state, with this embittered foe turned loose in their midst! The liberty-loving inhabitants of Greece long ago realized the bitterness of subjugation. Our ancestors of England suffered the same in the olden time, when first the "Curfew tolled the knell of parting day,"[120] and there was

"Darkness in chieftain's hall!
Darkness in peasant's cot!
While Freedom, under that shadowy pall,
Sat mourning o'er her lot."[121]

---

120 Rumley is slightly misquoting the opening line of Thomas Gray's "Elegy (Written in a Country Courtyard)." The line actually reads, "The curfew tolls the knell of parting day." Stuart, *A Treasury of Poems*, 533.

121 Rumley is quoting a verse from the poem "The Curfew Song of England," by Felicia Hemans (1793–1835). Hemans, *Poetical Works*, 397.

And Poland and Hungary, in later days, have drunk the bitter cup. But neither of these nations had among them a black servile race, like the southern negro, to be let loose by their conquerors upon them, to laugh at their calamity and exult in their downfall. Happier was the fate of either of these nations than will be that of the white population of the seceded states, if they fall under the yoke of northern fanaticism. A night of darkness, worse than that of the middle ages, is gradually drawing its curtain around them. We, here, are already enveloped in its dismal folds. And the solemn tones of the church bells, as they announced the appointed hours for the opening of these negro schools, sound in our ears like the death knell of the social and political power of the white race of the south!

December 3, 1863.

Some sensation was excited in town today, by the arrival of Burton Stanton[122] of this county, as a prisoner of the Yankees. He is, no doubt, a Confederate soldier, though draped in citizen's clothes. In company with two other persons, he ventured too near the Federal lines on Newport, a day or two since, and encountered on the road Major Vernon[123] with a small party from the Federal camp. Shots were exchanged and Stanton killed the Major, and was afterwards captured. His two "brothers in arms" fled. The major, who is said to have been one of the best men in the Federal army, had the magnanimity in his dying moment to request that Stanton might be treated as a prisoner of war, and not harmed in his person, as he had only "done his duty as a soldier."

---

122 Burton H. Stanton (b. ca. 1834) was a farmer from Craven County. Stanton joined the Macon Mounted Guards, Company E, 41st North Carolina Regiment, on December 10, 1861. He attained the rank of corporal before he was captured in Carteret County in December 1863. Eighth Census, 1860: Craven County; Manarin and Jordan, *North Carolina Troops*, 2:219.
123 I have been unable to identify Major Vernon.

December 7, 1863.

The Northern papers come to us with shocking accounts of the defeat of the Confederate army at Chattanooga, late in November![124] We have some accounts also of the repulse of the Federal army in Virginia, but the light which beams from that quarter over the west. The news from the army of Bragg is bad enough, no doubt, in the Confederacy, where the sun is still shining but is depressing in the extreme to those friends of the south who are sojourning here in this dark "valley and shadow of death."[125]

This ends 1863.

---

124   After their defeat at Chickamauga, the Union Army of the Cumberland retreated to Chattanooga, where it was promptly besieged by Confederate general Braxton Bragg's army. Major General Ulysses S. Grant arrived in Chattanooga in October 1863, relieved Rosecrans of command, and reorganized the army. In November, he drove Bragg's army away from Chattanooga, culminating with a surprisingly successful assault up the imposing Missionary Ridge that overlooked the city on November 25, 1863. McPherson, *Battle Cry of Freedom*, 676–681.

125   This is a mild corruption of the fourth verse of the 23rd Psalm: "Yea, though I walk through the valley of the shadow of death, I will fear no evil."

1. James Rumley, whose portrait comes from a composite photograph of the 1875 Constitutional Convention. This is the only known photograph of the diarist who recorded his experiences during three years of Union military occupation. Photograph courtesy of North Carolina State Archives, PhC.31.

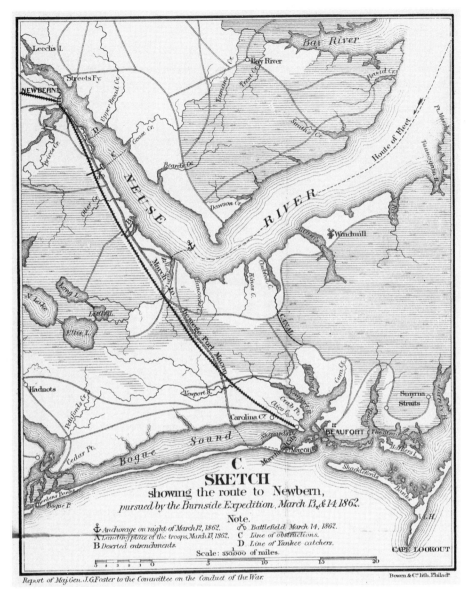

2. Map of General Burnside's expedition to capture New Bern and Beaufort. Prepared by General John G. Foster, who was commander of the Department of North Carolina from July 1862 until the fall of 1863. Source: William T. Sherman, George Henry Thomas, John Pope, John G. Foster, A. J. Pleasanton, Ethan Allen Hitchcock, Philip Henry Sheridan, James B. Ricketts, and Norman Wiard, *Supplemental Report of the Joint Committee on the Conduct of the War: Supplemental to Senate Report No. 142, 38th Congress, 2nd Session, vol. 2* (Washington, D.C., Government Printing Office, 1866).

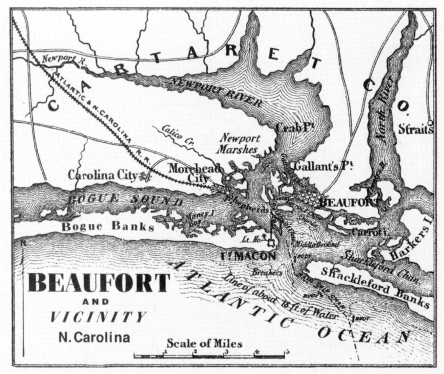

Map of Beaufort and surrounding area based on an inset from J. H. Colton's Topographical Map of North and South Carolina, A Large Portion of Georgia and Part of Adjoining States, published in New York in 1861.

3. Map of Beaufort and surrounding area based on an inset from J. H. Colton, *Topographical Map of North and South Carolina, A Large Portion of Georgia and Part of Adjoining States* (New York, 1861).

4. General Ambrose E. Burnside, who led the expedition that established Union control of New Bern and Beaufort in March 1862. Rumley complained that Burnside did not keep his promise to prevent runaway slaves from coming into Union lines. Burnside left the region in July 1862 to take command of a corps in the Army of the Potomac. Photograph courtesy of the North Carolina State Archives.

THE FLEET ASCENDING THE NEUSE RIVER.

5. Burnside's expeditionary force steaming up the Neuse River as it heads toward New Bern, March 1862. The force defeated a Confederate force and captured New Bern on March 14, 1862. Illustration from *Harper's Weekly*, April 5, 1862. Courtesy of the North Carolina Collection, University of North Carolina at Chapel Hill.

Bombardment of Fort Macon.

6. Union batteries bombarded Fort Macon for eleven hours on April 25, 1862. Rumley wrote, "The scene was one of painful interest to the inhabitants of Beaufort, many of whom had husbands, brothers or sons in the doomed fortification." Illustration from *Harper's Weekly*, May 17, 1862. Courtesy of the North Carolina Collection, University of North Carolina at Chapel Hill.

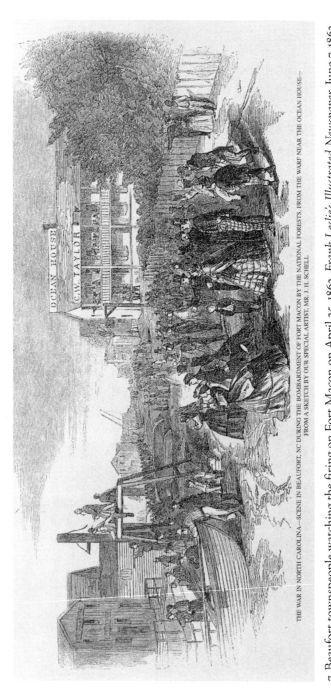

THE WAR IN NORTH CAROLINA.—SCENE IN BEAUFORT, NC DURING THE BOMBARDMENT OF FORT MACON BY THE NATIONAL FORESTS. FROM THE WARF NEAR THE OCEAN HOUSE—FROM A SKETCH BY OUR SPECIAL ARTIST, MR. J. H. SCHELL.

7. Beaufort townspeople watching the firing on Fort Macon on April 25, 1862. *Frank Leslie's Illustrated Newspaper,* June 7, 1862. Courtesy of the State Archives, Division of Archives and History, Raleigh, North Carolina.

THE WAR IN NORTH CAROLINA.—SURRENDER OF FORT MACON—INTERIOR—LOWERING THE REBEL FLAG, APRIL 28TH.—FROM A SKETCH BY OUR SPECIAL ARTIST, MR. J. H. SCHELL.—SEE PAGE 50.

8. The Fort Macon's garrison, which included two companies of Carteret soldiers, surrendered on April 26, 1862. The soldiers were paroled and allowed to return to their homes until formally exchanged in August 1862. Illustration from *Frank Leslie's Illustrated Newspaper*, May 17, 1862. Courtesy of the North Carolina Collection, University of North Carolina at Chapel Hill.

9. Craven County native Edward Stanly was appointed military governor of North Carolina by President Lincoln in April 1862. On June 7, 1862, Rumley claimed that Stanly "deeply laments the bad effects of the war on our slave population." Stanly felt it prudent not to enforce the fugitive slave law initially and ultimately resigned in protest of the Emancipation Proclamation. Courtesy of the North Carolina State Archives.

BEAUFORT, NORTH CAROLINA, FROM MOREHEAD CITY.—FROM A SKETCH BY OUR SPECIAL ARTIST, F. H. SCHELL.

10. An artist's rendering of Beaufort in the spring of 1864 as it appeared from the small village of Morehead City across the harbor. Illustration from *Frank Leslie's Illustrated Newspaper*, April 9, 1864. Courtesy of the North Carolina Collection, University of North Carolina at Chapel Hill.

11. This photograph of the Leecraft House at 307 Ann Street in Beaufort was taken in March 1862, soon after Union troops occupied the town. The house belonged to Captain Benjamin Leecraft, who had organized a company for Confederate service. Rumley lamented that the Union troops took control of the house and allowed the local black population to enter the house and take furniture and dresses of Leecraft's female family members. Courtesy of the North Carolina Collection, University of North Carolina at Chapel Hill.

THE EFFECTS OF THE PROCLAMATION—FREED NEGROES COMING INTO OUR LINES AT NEWBERN, NORTH CAROLINA.—[SEE PAGE 115.]

12. When Federal troops occupied New Bern and Beaufort, thousands of slaves escaped to find refuge within Union lines. Rumley complained in December 1862 that the town "is crowded with runaway negroes" who "have poured in upon us, until every available habitation has been filled with them." Illustration from *Harper's Weekly*, February 21, 1863. Courtesy of the North Carolina Collection, University of North Carolina at Chapel Hill.

THE CAMPAIGN IN NORTH CAROLINA—HEADQUARTERS OF VINCENT COLYER, SUPERINTENDENT OF THE POOR AT NEWBERNE—DISTRIBUTION OF CAPTURED REBEL SOLDIERS' CLOTHING TO THE CONTRABANDS.—From a Sketch by our Special Artist, J. H. Schell.—See Page 181.

13. The Federal government provided clothing and rations for thousands of escaped slaves in New Bern and Beaufort during the war. Many freedpeople worked as laborers for the Union forces or enlisted in the Union army. In this illustration, freedpeople are reporting to the Office of the Superintendent of the Poor in New Bern for rations or work orders. Illustration from *Frank Leslie's Illustrated Newspaper*, June 14, 1862. Courtesy of the North Carolina Collection, University of North Carolina at Chapel Hill.

14. Carteret resident Emeline Pigott regularly carried contraband mail and goods outside Federal lines to Confederate forces. On February 8, 1865, she was arrested and imprisoned while on one of these missions. Rumley documents the arrest of this "very respectable young lady." She was eventually released without a trial. Courtesy of Carteret County Historical Society, Morehead City, North Carolina.

1864

Beginning of 1864.

The swift but "noiseless foot of time"[1] treads the threshold of another year. The eventful year 1863 is now registered in the records of Eternity. It was ushered in, we well remember, under dark and gloomy auspices. It passed away as it entered veiled in the shadows of political night. It will form, with the year preceding it, a space in the annals of the past, clouded like a night of sorrows on a desert or an ocean, with no bright spots, no happy associations, on which memory hereafter will love to dwell. Its last hours were singularly marked by an angry commotion of the elements of nature. Heavy rain clouds over head, and all around the horizon, made the night intensely dark, while violent gusts of wind swept over the land, driving before them with terrible fury the thick falling rain. The thunder's startling—unusual at this season here—twice broke through the dark vault above us, with flashes of lurid lightning, and "passed away with a great noise."[2] The raging sea roared like a cataract, and the whole scene might well cause one to think of that terrible place which Dante saw,

"Where light was silent all; and bellowing there groaned

---

1 The actual line is: "Th' inaudible and noiseless foot of Time." *All's Well That Ends Well*, act 5, sc. 3, in Wright, *The Complete Works of William Shakespeare*, 893.

2 Rumley is quoting from 2 Peter 3:10: "But the day of the Lord will come as a thief in the night; in the which the heavens shall pass away with a great noise, and the elements shall melt with fervent heat, the earth also and the works that are therein shall be burned up."

A noise, as of a sea in tempest torn
By warring winds; stormy blasts of hell
With restless fury drove the spirits on."[3]
And so departed the old year.

The first day of the new year is a day of festival and rejoicing among the negroes. It is the first anniversary of the day on which Lincoln's imperial edict [set] them free. Beholding the crowd which assembled on Ann Street, under the flag of the United States, to celebrate the day, we could but wish that the statesmen of South Carolina who in December 1860 broke down the wall which separated us from northern abolitionism, could be here today and behold the fruits of their labors.[4]

Negro orators graced the occasion, depicting the horrors of slavery, and the blessings which their great and good President had conferred upon them. One of the orators, a northern mulatto[5] with some education, originally a runaway slave from North Carolina, sent here to recruit for the army, told his black hearers that their race would have not only their personal freedom, but political equality, and if this should be refused them at the ballot box they would have it at the cartridge box! That the war would emancipate the poor white men of the south, as well as the black; that McLellan[6] was a traitor, "and although he failed to take Richmond with 200,000 white soldiers, Butler would soon take it with twenty thousand negroes!"

---

3   This passage is from Canto V (of Hell) in Dante's *The Divine Comedy*. Eliot, *The Divine Comedy of Dante Alighieri*, 21.

4   Rumley is referring to South Carolina's secession from the Union on December 20, 1860.

5   Rumley is most likely referring to Abraham H. Galloway (1837–1870), a former slave who served as a spy and recruiting agent for the Union army and was an important African American leader in occupied eastern North Carolina during the war. After the war, Galloway served as New Hanover County's delegate to the state constitutional convention in 1868 and was twice elected state senator, in 1868 and 1870. Cecelski, *The Waterman's Song*, 179–189.

6   Major General George Brinton McClellan (1826–1885) was commander of the Army of the Potomac from August 1861 to November 1862. From June 26 to July 1, 1862, his army was driven away from Richmond, Virginia, by Robert E. Lee's Army of Northern Virginia, though McClellan outnumbered Lee's army by a considerable margin. Warner, *Generals in Blue*, 290–292.

January 1, 1864.

Butler seems determined to harass the people of the South wherever he goes. He is down upon us now with a frightful oath. The heartless devil does not intend any friend of the Southern Confederacy to rest easy under the shadow of his authority. Confessing his act, that the so-called oath of allegiance already forced down the unwilling throats of the people has proved ineffectual, he now requires all persons (except civil and military officers of the United States, and persons performing manual labor for their own support) to take and subscribe an oath, which for preservation as part of the history of our troubles is worth recording! "I do solemnly swear, in the presence of Almighty God that I will henceforth faithfully support and defend the Constitution of the United States and the union of the States thereunder, and that I will in like manner abide by and faithfully support all acts of Congress passed during the existing rebellion with reference to slaves so long and so far as not repealed, modified, or held void by Congress or by decision of the Supreme Court, and that I will in like manner abide by and faithfully support all proclamations of the President made during the existing rebellion having reference to slaves so long and so far as not modified or declared void by decision of the Supreme Court; so help me God."[7]

To the oath is attached a parole of honor as follows: "And we give our solemn parole of honor (to be enforced according to military law) that we will hold no correspondence with, or afford any aid or comfort to, the enemies or opposers of the United States, save as an act of humanity, to administer to the necessities of individuals who are in sickness or distress; and solemnly declare that this oath and parole are taken and given freely and willingly, without any mental reservation or evasion whatever, and with full intention to keep the same."

Even those persons who perform manual labor for their own support, who are excepted in the order of Butler, are not allowed passports to pass any of the picket lines, unless they take and subscribe to this oath and parole. The authors of this detestable oath deserve to be sent to Siberia

---

7   Though Rumley blames Butler for the oath, this is actually a modified oath of allegiance issued by President Lincoln in a proclamation on December 7, 1863. *Official Records, Army,* ser. 2, 6:680–681.

and linger during their remaining days under Russian despotism. The villainous and lying composition called an oath, will be mentally loathed and spurned by every decent white man in the south upon whom it is forced. None will regard it as obligatory.

"The pestilence that walketh in darkness"[8] is among us, in the form of small pox. Its ravages, so far, have been confined to the negroes; but the white population are filled with apprehension, and vaccination is the order of the day; very few negroes have died of small pox.

[January 24, 1864].

Last evening (being Saturday the 23rd. Jany) a Union meeting was held in the Court House. The writer of this note did not venture near enough to see or hear any of the proceedings, but is informed that the orators were Charles Henry Foster, Capt. Haley of Massachusetts,[9] and Lieut Eddin[10] of Wake County NC, all of whom belong to the 2nd. Regiment of N Carolina Volunteers, commonly called "Buffaloes." Their doctrines

---

8   Psalms 91:6.

9   There is no Captain Haley who served in either the 1st or the 2nd North Carolina Regiments (Union). Perhaps Rumley is referring to James M. Hervey (b.
ca. 1838), who served as captain of Company A, 1st North Carolina, until he
resigned on June 30, 1863. Hervey, who hailed from Worcester, Massachusetts,
enlisted in the 25th Massachusetts Regiment on September 12, 1861. He was
discharged on June 1, 1862, to accept a commission in the North Carolina Regiment. It is possible that Hervey remained in North Carolina after he resigned
from the army. James M. Hervey File, 1st North Carolina Infantry Regiment,
Compiled Military Service Records of Volunteer Union Soldiers Who Served
in Organizations from the State of North Carolina, Record Group 94.12.2;
Massachusetts Adjutant General's Office, *Massachusetts Soldiers, Sailors, and
Marines*, 3:7.

10   William Henry Eddins (b. ca. 1841), from Wake County, enlisted in the 2nd
North Carolina Infantry Regiment (Union) as a private on December 24,
1863, at Beaufort, North Carolina. He was promoted to sergeant and then
transferred to the 1st North Carolina Infantry Regiment (Union) on February
27, 1865. He was promoted to sergeant major, and there is no further record
of him. William Henry Eddins File, 2nd North Carolina Infantry Regiment,
Compiled Military Service Records of Volunteer Union Soldiers Who Served
in Organizations from the State of North Carolina, Record Group 94.12.2.

are radical and destructive. The presence of a negro (or rather a mulatto) on the bench with the speakers indicated what they were.

January 30, 1864.

During last week some Federal troops were landed at Morehead City, which caused some uneasiness among the friends of the south residing here. Extracts from Richmond papers, which appear in the Northern papers received today, show that the arrival of those troops was known at Wilmington and Richmond as early as could be desired.

February 1, 1864.

At 11 o'clock this morning, news reached this place from Morehead City that a telegraphic dispatch had just been received from New Bern, announcing the fact that the Confederates had appeared in force around that town; that an attack was hourly expected; and calling for all disposable armed force at this post. Later in the day intelligence came that some fighting had occurred ten or twelve miles above New Bern, and that some Yankees had been killed and five or six hundred had fallen into the hands of the Confederates, among whom was a company of "Buffaloes."[11] The pickets around Beaufort have been hurriedly called in, and the troops are rapidly getting off for New Bern. Great excitement among the troops, Yankee citizens and negroes.

February 2, 1864.

Dispatches from New Bern today state that the Confederates have appeared in force at several points in the vicinity of the town. On the south

---

11   On February 1, 1864, during the early stages of Major General George E. Pickett's unsuccessful attempt to take New Bern, Confederate troops crossed Batchelder's Creek, nine miles from New Bern, despite stiff Union opposition. The Confederate force captured most of Company F, 2nd North Carolina Infantry (Union) in the attack. *Official Records, Army*, ser. 1, 33:93, 95–96; Barrett, *The Civil War in North Carolina*, 202–207; Browning, "'Little-Souled Mercenaries?'" 337–363.

side they have captured and blown up a large Federal gunboat lying in the Trent,[12] and have opened fire upon Fort Totten.[13] It is also stated that the Federal pickets have been driven in from every point. The Confederate force is variously estimated at from 15,000 to 25,000, and said to be under Gen. Pickett.[14] A later report from Morehead City states that there has been fighting at Newport, and that the Federal barracks at that post has been captured. Heavy firing has been heard in that direction.

Later. Reliable news has reached us that the Block House of the Yankees, on Bogue sound, was attacked and captured by the Confederates today [after] severe fighting. It was garrisoned by troops from the 9th. Vermont.[15]

February 3, 1864.

Last night two Yankee cavalrymen who had retreated from Newport Barracks, taking the route across Clubfoot and Harlow's Creek canal, rode into Beaufort with the news that the Barracks surrendered to the Confederates late yesterday afternoon after some fighting, a part of the garrison escaping. This morning about 300 infantry from that garrison, who found their retreat towards Morehead City cut off and took the land

---

12   On February 2, 1864, as part of Pickett's drive on New Bern, Confederates under Commander John Taylor Wood seized and destroyed the USS *Underwriter* on the Neuse River, not the Trent River, as Rumley stated. *Civil War Naval Chronology*, 4:12–13.

13   Fort Totten was a star-shaped earthen redoubt on the western edge of New Bern, located between the Trent and Neuse rivers. The fort was erected by Union forces soon after the capture of New Bern. Pickett's troops made a demonstration but did not assault the fort. Barden, *Letters to the Home Circle*, 64–65; *Official Records, Army*, ser. 1, 33:54–55.

14   Confederate general George Edward Pickett (1825–1875), most famous for leading the failed charge on the third day of the Battle of Gettysburg, was commander of the Department of North Carolina in the winter and spring of 1864. He launched an unsuccessful attempt to recapture New Bern in February 1864. Heidler and Heidler, *Encyclopedia of the American Civil War*, 3:1518–1519.

15   Brigadier General James G. Martin's Confederate force drove the Union garrison from Newport Barracks on February 2, 1864. Many of the defenders were new recruits from the Ninth Vermont Infantry. *Official Records, Army*, ser. 1, 33:81–82, 84–86.

route to this place, arrived in town, many without knapsacks or guns, some without shoes, and some without hats. Supposing the Confederates intend to march upon Beaufort, the Yankee commandant here, Capt. Fuller,[16] who has been sent here with his company from Fort Macon, has erected barricades of sawed lumber and pine wood on Front and Market Streets and is planting cannon to defend the place. Some of the Yankee traders and terrified negroes are packing up their movables, intending to seek safety on board of vessels under the guns of Fort Macon. The Negro schools are suspended, and the teachers, male and female, are evidently preparing to slink off. It does the heart good to see these intruders upon our soil, and violators of our laws, quailing before the sound of Confederate cannon, and trembling at the approach of a power which they have long insulted and defied.

February 4, 1864.

A black cloud of smoke ascending from Newport indicates that the Confederates are still there, and are burning turpentine. A Yankee Lieutenant and five or six privates came in this morning, who fled from Newport on the evening of the 2nd., and traveled a long distance through the woods to evade the Confederates, who, they say, are scouting the country in that vicinity. There is now a decided panic in town among the Yankees, negroes and some citizens.

Afternoon. A steamer from New Bern, via Core Sound, brings intelligence that the Confederates, on the 3rd. inst., made two assaults on Fort Totten, and were repulsed with heavy loss![17] The Yankee garrison are recovering from their fright, sufficiently to perceive that the proper point for their defensive works is in the rear of the town, accordingly preparing to erect batteries there, and are pressing white citizens of the town into the work. Every one who can dodge them is doing so. The frightened Yankees seem to be very nearly bereft of their senses; and just at this time if twenty-five Confederate cavalry should suddenly appear on the back of the town, a general stampede of Yankees and negroes on the boats and

---

16 Captain Nehemiah Fuller of the 2nd Massachusetts Heavy Artillery had been placed in command of Beaufort by Colonel James Jourdan on February 1, 1864. *Official Records, Army,* ser. 1, 33:77, 485.

17 There were no such assaults upon Fort Totten.

flats at the wharves might be expected. A thick cloud of smoke is seen rising from the woods. Cry among the negroes is, "The rebels are coming." Some frightened creature from the country has come in and told the Commandant that the rebels are on the road marching for Beaufort! The Yankee cavalrymen are dashing up and down the road, and through the streets, as swift as if the devil himself was at their heels.

February 5, 1864.

Last night a Federal cavalryman rode through the streets about 10 o'clock, and ordered the citizens to extinguish their lights. Today the panic subsides. No news from New Bern.

February 6, 1864.

News received today is that the former report of the assaults upon Fort Totten were false. No such assaults were made. Report says the Confederates have retired from New Bern and Newport. All is quiet here.

February 7, 1864.

No additional news.

February 8, 1864.

It is rumored today that the Confederates are still hovering on the borders of Newport. A Federal force which lately went up from Morehead City, to reoccupy the Barracks there, quietly retreated on hearing that the Confederates were returning, but returned to their post as soon as they learned the report was false. Among these were seven or eight hundred troops who arrived in the *Spaulding* a few days ago, to reinforce the army at New Bern.

Twenty-four graves at the Block House on Bogue Sound, and seven at Newport, are the silent monuments of the strife at those places. The Block House and Barracks were destroyed.

February 9, 1864.

The story of the thirty-one graves is false. Nobody seems to know how many men were killed on either side. Some say not more than ten or twelve altogether. Perhaps we shall learn the truth after the war is over. These late movements of the Confederates have taught the Yankees a lesson. A single stroke by a small Confederate force swept away every vestige of their power between Morehead City and New Bern, and showed them by what a feeble tenure they hold their possessions in North Carolina. But the best of all is, they have waked up the negroes from their dreams of Yankee freedom, and security from danger, and inspired them with "fearful forebodings of the wrath to come."[18] When they saw the Yankee soldiers, who had boasted so much of their ability to protect them, fleeing, without guns, without knapsacks, and without hats and shoes, from a small force of the rebels they had taught these negroes to despise, the charm of Yankee invincibility was broken, and broken, we hope forever.

February 16, 1864.

The late operations of the Confederates against New Bern and Newport are drawing reinforcements from the North to the Federal army at Newport. Several steamers have, within a week past, landed troops at Morehead City. Today 1200 negro soldiers were landed there!

February 22, 1864.

Loud peals of cannon at Fort Macon, at an early hour this morning, reminded the inhabitants that this is the anniversary of the birthday of Washington. One would suppose the anti-slavery fanaticism pervading the ranks of the Federal army would hardly permit them to do such honor to the memory of a man who was a slaveholder. Twelve months ago the same day passed by without the slightest demonstration of respect for it

---

18   Rumley is making an allusion to a sermon preached by Rev. Andrew Fuller on the nature of those who disbelieve in God or defame the Bible. Fuller's sermon actually reads "the latter, either blinded by insensibility, or if awakened to reflection, in fearful forebodings of the wrath to come." Fuller, *The Works of Reverend Andrew Fuller*, 4:293.

by any of the military on the harbor. They have concluded that although the mortal remains of the patriot be within the bounds of rebeldom, and his memory is associated with the hated name of slavery, they cannot afford in the present crisis to lose the prestige of his great name, and they will do honor to themselves by honoring his memory.

The Yankees lately captured Capt. Spencer's company of guerrillas in Hyde County, and carried them to New Bern.[19] They arrived at Morehead City today (except a few who took the oath of allegiance at New Bern) and will be carried thence to Fortress Monroe. They are a youthful band, and have our wishes that they may be happy in their captivity, and may live to talk over their adventures to their grandchildren.

February 29, 1864.

Dispatches from New Bern last night indicate that the Yankees there are again in expectation of an attack. The frightened herd who have command here have gone a stride farther today with the citizens than any of our Yankee masters have gone before. They have summoned every man they could find who is so unfortunate as to be under forty-five years of age, and forced arms into their hands to kill their own brethren and friends with![20] This lawless and inhuman proceeding, violating the usages of all civilized warfare, has excited the deepest indignation in every southern breast. Among these citizens who have been armed are some who are traitors to the South, and traitors to humanity. But far the larger portion are heart and soul with the south, and cannot and will not be forced in

---

19   On February 16, 1864, a Union gunboat and a 30-man detachment of the 101st Pennsylvania Infantry Regiment under the command of Captain Robert W. McLaughlin of the 13th New York Heavy Artillery steamed up the Alligator River to Fairfield, in Hyde County, where a Confederate guerrilla organization under the command of Captain William H. Spencer was camped. In a heavy snowstorm, the Union force captured Spencer, his lieutenant, and twenty-six privates of the Confederate outfit. *Official Records, Army*, ser. 1, 33:154–155, 1053. Manarin and Jordan, *North Carolina Troops*, 15:408.

20   A letter by Beaufort treasury agent John Hedrick confirms that on March 1, 1864, "all able bodied citizens . . . were put under arms yesterday evening, for Provost duty." Browning and Smith, *Letters from a North Carolina Unionist*, 188.

any emergency to turn their arms against their own countrymen. Sooner than do it they will suffer to be shot, or will shoot the rascals who have armed them!

March 2, 1864.

Notice was issued today to all able-bodied negroes (colored men) to appear at the Provost Marshal office at 3 o'clock P.M. to be armed and drilled! In the meantime dispatches from New Bern announced that all was quiet there, so the Yankees recovered from their fright and did not arm or drill the negroes. The white citizens will be relieved from any further annoyance at present.

Of the Buffalo troops captured by the Confederates at Batchelor's Creek, above New Bern, nineteen who were recognized as deserters were hung on the 13th. and 16th. of February at Kinston.[21] The man who, of all men, is most to blame for the sad fate of these unfortunate men is Charles Henry Foster, who is now Colonel, or Lieut. Colonel, of the Regiment to which they belonged. He told them they could have no assurance of protection outside of the Federal army; that as enlisted soldiers the government was bound to protect them, but if they refused to enlist, they would probably be sent back to the Confederacy and turned over to the tender mercies of the rebels. He told them of the "old flag"; how it had protected them in former years, and how soon it would wave over a prostrate rebellion, and give ample protection to all who should gather under its folds. And the poor wretches were drawn into the snare. There are other deserters now in the Federal army whose eyes have been opened by the hanging at Kinston.

---

21   Twenty-two North Carolinians serving in Company F, 2nd North Carolina Infantry Regiment were tried and hanged for desertion by Confederates in Kinston. They had been captured in early February during Pickett's unsuccessful drive against New Bern. Some had belonged to regular Confederate army units, but the majority had been in home guard units. Compiled Military Service Records of Volunteer Union Soldiers Who Served in Organizations from the State of North Carolina, Record Group 94.12.2; Collins, "War Crimes or Justice?" 50–83.

March 25, 1864.

This is the second anniversary of the advent of the Federal army into Beaufort; and we enter today into the third year of the reign of "nigger-ism." The whole period has been a season of profound political and social darkness, a long dreary night of despotism, which is still without any sure token of coming day. Weary of hope deferred we often cry out "Watch-man, what of the night";[22] but no watchman can tell the hour of this worse than polar night! We think, however, we have passed "the zenith of its dark domain,"[23] and that ere long we shall see its "midnight blackness changing into gray."[24] The prospects in the south looks better. The late victory of the Confederates in Florida,[25] the failure of Sherman's land ex-pedition against Mobile,[26] and other reverses of the Federal army inspire new hopes of Southern independence.

---

22 "What of the Night?" is a hymn by John Bowring, 1825. See the entry for October 1862 in chapter 1 of this volume.

23 Rumley is slightly misquoting from Milton's *Paradise Lost*, bk. 1, lines 15–17: "The Day too short for my distress; and Night, / Even in the zenith of her dark domain, / Is sunshine to the colour of my fate." In Eliot, *The Complete Poems of John Milton*, 1.

24 Rumley is quoting from a poem by Charles Mackay entitled "Clear the Way!" "There's a midnight blackness changing into gray / Men of thought and men of action, / Clear the way!" In Bates, *The Cambridge Book of Poetry and Song*, 362.

25 Brigadier General Joseph Finegan's 5,000 Confederates defeated Brigadier General Truman Seymour's force of 5,500 Union soldiers near Olustee, Florida, on February 20, 1864. Heidler and Heider, *Encyclopedia of the American Civil War*, 3:1435–1437.

26 On February 3, 1864, Union General William T. Sherman departed Vicks-burg, Mississippi, with four divisions of infantry and a cavalry division. He let it be known that his target was Mobile, Alabama, in order to delude Confed-erate forces along his route. Instead, he marched on Meridian, Mississippi, capturing that town on February 14. After destroying many Confederate supplies and much of the Mobile and Ohio Railroad, Sherman returned to Vicksburg with his force. *Official Records, Army*, ser. 1, 34, pt. 2:266–267; Den-ney, *The Civil War Years*, 366–376.

March 27, 1864.

The Federal troops here have just returned from one of their plundering and disgraceful raids. They left here on the 23rd., inst., in a large steamer, and went by sea, with two flats in tow, to make a raid upon Swansboro; where they had been informed a vessel had gone in with supplies, as was supposed, for the Confederates. When they reached the inlet, the vessel was gone. They say but little about the trip; but it has leaked out that they were not permitted to land at Swansboro; the Confederates being too thick about there.

They burnt an old vessel, and then sneaked off. A portion of them took the route through Bogue Sound, in a flat, and stole over twenty negroes on their way which they brought to Beaufort.[27] The scoundrels appear to be chagrined by their failure, and look like a gang of baffled and disappointed thieves. Their black trophies will add to the nuisance with which the place is already cursed. If the abolition devils—men and women—who are here could be compelled to take these stolen negroes into their beds with them, we should heartily rejoice.

April 4, 1864.

Last night, about 11 o'clock, the assistant keepers of the Light House at Cape Look Out were suddenly surprised by the appearance of 15 or 20 armed Confederates, who promptly placed these assistants under guard, and took measures to blow up the Light House with powder.[28] The explosion however did not destroy the building; carried away about sixty feet

---

27 Colonel James Jourdan, with 200 men of the 158th New York Infantry, embarked on March 25, 1864, on a mission to Bogue Inlet to capture vessels engaged in illegal trade. Bad weather and enemy forces at Swansborough turned them away. They burned one schooner and captured twenty slaves. *Official Records, Army*, ser. 1, 33:257–258.

28 Saboteurs from the 67th North Carolina used a keg of powder to severely damage the Cape Lookout Lighthouse on April 3, 1864. *Official Records, Army*, ser. 1, 33:260–261; Clark, *Histories of the Several Regiments and Battalions*, 3:706.

of the lofty stairway; burst open the doors, shattered the windows and did other damage to the property. At 3 o'clock this morning the Confederates quietly departed, and embarked in the boat they came in, taking the direction of Core Sound. The released prisoners posted to Beaufort to report the strange affair. They report that the Confederates called themselves "Capt. Semmes,"[29] and stated they were about forty in number.

April 21, 1864.

The report is current here today, and is generally believed, that the Confederates (called by the Yankees, "rebels") have floated their Roanoke "ram" down the river to Plymouth, captured that place, and anchored the ram below the town.[30] The Yankees at New Bern are expecting a visit from the terrible beast, which they dread worse than an army of wild mountain bears. The women and children are pouring down from there in a stream. Many of the Yankee women are embarking for their Northern homes, never, we hope, to return to North Carolina. If the Yankees have lost Plymouth, they have lost it forever. Their power is waning in Carolina. May it soon be gone forever, "and like the baseless fabric of a vision, leave not a rack behind."[31] Could be a mistake.

---

29 Perhaps they named themselves after Raphael Semmes, a commander in the Confederate navy. Semmes was not involved in the attack. Heidler and Heidler, *Encyclopedia of the American Civil War*, 4:1730–1732.

30 The Confederate ironclad CSS *Albemarle* was constructed on the Roanoke River at Edwards Ferry, North Carolina, in 1863. On April 17, 1864, the *Albemarle* cast off from its moorings and joined General Robert F. Hoke's Confederate attack on the Union garrison under Brigadier General Henry C. Wessells at Plymouth, North Carolina. With the aid of the *Albemarle*, which drove away the Union naval forces helping protect the town, Hoke's army secured the surrender of Plymouth on April 20. Jordan and Thomas, "Massacre at Plymouth: April 20, 1864," 125; Heidler and Heidler, *Encyclopedia of the American Civil War*, 1:24–25, 3:1533–1534.

31 Rumley is condensing some lines from Shakespeare's *The Tempest*. The lines, uttered by Prospero, actually read "and, like the baseless fabric of this vision . . . leave not a rack behind." *The Tempest*, act 4, sc. 1, in Wright, *The Complete Works of William Shakespeare*, 1319.

April 22, 1864.

No further news from Plymouth today. We have just passed through one of the most inclement seasons ever known in this country, in the month of April. Although March was terribly severe, and everybody was look-ing for bright, warm days in April; yet until a day or two past, the latter month has more the rough aspect of winter, more suited to the polar regions than to Eastern Carolina. Heavy gales from every point of the compass have swept over the bleak and dreary coast; while over the earth has hung, from day to day, a dark drapery of wintry clouds, in whose cold and withering shade man and beast have shivered; the birds have failed to sing their wonted carols, and the anxious husbandman has refused to commit his grain to the cold wet bosom of the earth. But now the spring, with its bright sunshine and genial warmth, is upon us, all nature smiles at its approach; and we fancy we hear its voice of greeting, as uttered in the sweet song of Mrs. Hemans:

"I come, I come! Ye have called me long;
I come o'er the mountains with light and song,
Ye may trace my step o'er the wakening earth,
By the winds which tell of the violet's birth,
By the primrose stars in the shadowy grass,
By the green leaves opening as I pass." &c.[32]

April 23, 1864.

The Yankees have terrible accounts today from New Bern of the cap-ture of Plymouth, with the whole of Wessel's brigade of Yankees and a number of negroes and "Buffaloes," by the Confederates, who they say

---

32   This is a verse from Felicia Hemans's poem, "The Voice of Spring." Hemans, *Poetical Works*, 268–269.

indiscriminately slaughtered negroes and buffaloes![33] General Peck[34] announces in a General Order the fall of Plymouth and the capture of the entire garrison! The news falls heavy upon the Yankees and their sympathizers. It foreshadows their doom in North Carolina.

April 28, 1864.

At Washington, N. Carolina, the Yankees are hourly expecting the approach of the Confederates. They have permitted the "Buffalo" troops to fly from the coming storm. These wretched victims of Yankee lying and trickery, with their squalid and destitute women and children are flocking to Beaufort as their last place of refuge on the soil of their outraged and insulted state. They will now ask themselves and these Yankee authors of their ruin, where they are to fly when the approach of the Confederate arms shall warn them that there is no safety here for those who have taken up arms with negroes against their own country.

"Where for shelter shall the guilty fly,
When consternation turns the good man pale?"[35]

---

33   When General Robert F. Hoke's Confederate force of nearly 7,000 men captured Plymouth and the 2,800-man Union garrison under Brigadier General Henry Wessells, the Confederates purportedly executed an indeterminate number of African Americans and white North Carolinians serving in the Union Army. Recent historical investigation suggests that as many as fifty civilians and soldiers were massacred by Confederate forces. Jordan and Thomas, "Massacre at Plymouth," 125–197.

34   Major General John James Peck (1821–1878) was commander of the District of North Carolina, Department of Virginia and North Carolina. He was replaced by Major General Innis Palmer on April 28, 1864. Warner, *Generals in Blue*, 364–365; Sifakis, *Who Was Who in the Civil War*, 485, 495.

35   This is a verse from the Edward Young poem "Night the Ninth and Last: The Consolation." Young, *The Complaint*, 256.

April 29, 1864.

We have news today that Washington has been evacuated by the Federal troops.[36]

May 2, 1864.

The sad news comes today that Washington was fired by the Yankee troops or negroes, before its final evacuation, and that the larger portion of the buildings on Main Street was consumed by the fire. Two helpless women were burnt to death in their houses.

May 3, 1864.

A large bear suddenly appeared this morning on the north side of the town, and deliberately walked through the western part of it, towards Front Street. He did not seem inclined to follow the streets, and caring little for fences, he passed over several lots, when his march was successfully arrested on the lot occupied by Mr. Ensley west of Orange and north of Front Street. Here he was killed. A whole regiment of Confederates would not have created greater excitement than the bear caused for a few minutes. It turns out that the poor animal was a pet bear that had deserted from one of the Federal gunboats in the harbor and was only looking for better company.

May 5, 1864.

Cars arrived at Morehead City today. Telegraphic communication with New Bern has been cut off, and rumors have reached Morehead that a

---

36 After the fall of Plymouth, North Carolina, to Confederate forces on April 20, 1864, the Union garrison at Washington, North Carolina, abandoned the town as Confederate general Robert F. Hoke's forces approached. The garrison set fire to the town before fleeing, damaging many of the town's buildings. Heidler and Heidler, *Encyclopedia of the American Civil War*, 1:25.

Confederate force has occupied Croatoan station on the road and cut the wires.[37] Heavy cannonading has been heard in the direction of New Bern during the day.

May 6, 1864.

A steamer from New Bern brings news that the Confederates are in force on Neuse River, near Croatoan, and at other points near New Bern. An investment of the place is expected. Great excitement among the Yankees here. Citizens are called out, and arms forced into their hands.

May 7, 1864.

Various and conflicting rumors in reference to the Confederates are afloat today.

Afternoon. The report is that a heavy Confederate force is marching down upon Newport. The negroes are called out and armed!

At sunset, the news from Morehead City is that three Confederate deserters have come into the Yankee camp at Newport, who report that the whole Confederate force near New Bern has been suddenly called to Virginia![38] So ends this fight if the news be true, to the great relief and satisfaction of the Yankees and negroes, as well as another class; breasts have been disquieted, for the last few days, with the thoughts of the halter, or perpetual exile, but to the great disappointment of many others, who yearn for the approach of Confederate power, and like the mother

---

37   Croatoan Station was a railroad stop about ten miles southeast of New Bern and twenty miles northwest of Beaufort.

38   On May 2, 1864, General Hoke and his forces were ordered to Virginia to join Robert E. Lee's Army of Northern Virginia in preparation of its defense against the Union Army of the Potomac. Hoke's forces began withdrawing from New Bern on May 3, 1864. *Official Records, Army*, ser. 1, 36, pt. 2:941–943.

of Sisera look out at the window and cry through the lattice, "Why is his chariot so long in coming? Why tarry the wheels of his chariot?"[39]

May 23, 1864.

Since the news reached us about two weeks ago, that Grant's "Army of the Potomac" had moved towards Richmond[40] and that Butler's naval force had moved up James River,[41] no tongue can express the deep anxiety—the painful suspense, that has filled the breasts of Southern citizens in this town and county. First came the report that Petersburg was captured and the railroad torn up by Butler; but we knew enough of Yankee facility in lying to doubt it. Next came the "official dispatch" that Fort

---

39   Rumley is referring to a story from the biblical book of Judges. Sisera was the commander of the army of Jabin, a king of Canaan, who ruled over the Israelites. The Israelites, following Deborah's call, defeated Sisera's army in battle. He escaped, only to be killed by an ally's wife. The verse that Rumley quotes is from the Song of Deborah in the 5th chapter of Judges. The verse is from Judges 5:28.

40   Lieutenant General Ulysses S. Grant crossed the Rapidan River with the 118,000 men of the Union Army of the Potomac on May 4, 1864, in a campaign designed to attack General Robert E. Lee's 61,000-man Army of Northern Virginia. It led to the Battle of the Wilderness on May 5–6, 1864. McPherson, *Battle Cry of Freedom*, 718–725; Heidler and Heidler, *Encyclopedia of the American Civil War*, 4:2108–2113.

41   General Benjamin F. Butler sailed up the James River with a force of 30,000 Union soldiers on May 5, 1864. He disembarked his troops at City Point, where the James and Appomattox rivers merge, halfway between Richmond and Petersburg. Though his force greatly outnumbered the 5,000-man Confederate garrison defending Richmond, Butler inexplicably delayed his advance for over a week. By the time he moved on Richmond, Confederate reinforcements had arrived and managed to drive Butler back to the James River, where he went on the defensive, thereby posing no threat to Richmond. McPherson, *Battle Cry of Freedom*, 723–724; Denney, *The Civil War Years*, 400, 409.

Darling[42] had been stormed and taken by the valorous Butler, and Richmond surrounded, but knowing that the father of lies himself could not excel the Yankee officials in deluding the people with false dispatches, we doubted that also. Next came frightful accounts in the New York papers that Grant had "smashed up" Johnson's and Ewell's Divisions, captured 15,000 prisoners, with guns &c, and was rapidly driving Lee before him to Richmond; but knowing the [tendency] of these villainous papers in preventing and making the "worse appear the better side," we doubted these accounts also. They have all turned out to be false. And if the news received today can be credited, things are going well for the Confederates in Virginia. But the magnitude of the crisis and the vast armies and fleets of the beleaguering host appall us; and the thoughts of men are entirely turned from their ordinary channels, and directed with intense and all absorbing interest to the great conflict in Virginia.

May 28, 1864.

Five days more of anxiety and suspense have rolled by, and we are yet without any news from Virginia by which we can judge correctly how the tide of battle is running. Northern papers have been received today, and their contents are not favorable to the Confederate arms. But their well-established character for lying deprives them of all credit. The *New York News* and *Metropolitan Record* are exceptions to this class. Their tone is encouraging, and it is refreshing in this dark and perilous hour to read them.

A frightful mortality prevails among the unfortunate women and children who fled to this place on the evacuation of Washington. Every morning, for a fortnight past, from four to six corpses could be seen in the dead house at the U.S. Hospital (formerly the Pender Hotel),[43] where three of four hundred of these unhappy exiles have been crowded

---

42   Fort Darling was a Federal position near Drewry's Bluff on the James River south of Richmond, Virginia. On May 16, 1864, General P. G. T. Beauregard's 16,000-man Confederate force attacked and defeated General Benjamin Butler's 18,000-man Union army at this position. The Union forces suffered approximately 4,100 casualties while the Confederates suffered approximately 2,500. This battle ended Butler's attempt to capture Richmond. Long, *The Civil War Day by Day*, 503.

43   Hammond General Hospital.

together. Grave diggers and coffin makers are constantly at work. Measles and Pneumonia are the chief disease.

June 8, 1864.

More than a month has elapsed since the opening of the last campaign against Richmond, and yet we are without intelligence of any decisive results. Grant's "change of base" creates fresh solicitude.[44] We have good news, and we have had bad news. Hope, at times, rises high, but it resembles much the uncertain glory of an April day
"Which now shows all the beauty of the sun;
But by and by a cloud takes all away"[45]
Like fabled Tantalus in Hell,[46] we are tormented with disappointed hopes. We watch the progress of the struggle in Virginia with deep and fearful suspense, as we would watch the crisis of a fearful disease in some loved and valued friend whose death would involve our own ruin. The Northern papers bring us favorable news.

June 9, 1864.

A welcome little messenger in the shape of the *Raleigh Confederate*[47] of the 6th. of June, has found its way into our hands today. Nothing in the

---

44 Before beginning his Overland Campaign in the spring of 1864, Grant had the Aquia Creek Railroad built, connecting Aquia Creek, near the Potomac River, with Falmouth, Virginia, near Fredericksburg. Over this railroad his army would be supplied and wounded could be evacuated. When his army arrived outside of Richmond, Virginia, in early June 1864, the railroad was no longer necessary, as Grant could use the rivers that flowed through the peninsula to supply his army. Rumley's optimism undoubtedly stems from Grant's defeat at the Battle of Cold Harbor on June 3, 1864. *Official Records, Army*, ser. 3, 4:885.

45 *The Two Gentlemen of Verona*, act 1, sc. 3, in Wright, *The Complete Works of William Shakespeare*, 253.

46 For insulting the gods, Tantalus was set in a pool in Hades. When his thirst tormented him, he would stoop down but be unable to reach the retreating water. Whenever he reached for the luscious fruits hanging overhead, the wind would blow them out of his reach. Thus he was doomed to be forever thirsty and hungry, unable to satisfy either urge. Hamilton, *Mythology*, 237.

47 A weekly newspaper based in Raleigh, North Carolina.

form of a newspaper could have been more acceptable. It contains General Lee's official reports of the 4th., and other documents, which reveal the true state of affairs at Richmond, and present a most hopeful and glowing prospect of a final and complete sweep against the Yankee hordes who now menace the Confederate capital.[48]

June 21, 1864.

The northern papers come to us today filled with alarming accounts of the sudden crossing of James River by Grant, the marching of part of his forces upon Petersburg, the storming and capture of the place by Smith, and the tearing up of the Petersburg and Richmond Railroad by Butler.[49] The *New York Herald* declares unqualifiedly that Petersburg is in the possession of the Federal forces, and that the "end of the rebellion is near."

The *Times* is sanguine, and the *News*, the most reliable paper we receive from New York, says the report of the capture of Petersburg "is confirmed." We doubt.

---

48 General Lee's official report of June 3, 1864, documented the defeat of Grant's troops at Cold Harbor on that day. In a follow-up note on June 4, 1863, he wrote that the Confederate position was still unchanged. He did not refer to sweeping the enemy from Richmond, however. *Official Records, Army*, ser. 1, 36, pt. 3: 869, 874.

49 On June 12, 1864, General Grant began to march the Army of the Potomac across pontoon bridges over the James River. He intended to convince Lee that he was at Cold Harbor while initiating a surprise attack on the vital rail center at Petersburg, south of Richmond. General William F. Smith, commander of the Union XVIII Corps, was given orders to lead the attack. Smith delayed long enough to allow Confederates to organize a defense. In heavy fighting on June 16, 17, and 18, Confederates repulsed Smith's attacks on the city, and Lee, slow to react to Grant's movement, finally moved his army to defend the trenches around Petersburg. On June 22, a Confederate counterattack on the Federal left flank stopped their movement to cut the Weldon-Petersburg Railroad. The fighting had stabilized into a prolonged siege by the beginning of July. General Smith was relieved of command on July 19, 1864, for his failure to act promptly to take Petersburg. Denney, *The Civil War Years*, 422–431; Heidler and Heidler, *The Encyclopedia of the American Civil War*, 4:1820–1821.

June 22, 1864.

News comes to us by the underground communication today, direct from the Confederate lines, by which we learn that an attack was really made on the defense of Petersburg, on the 15th. inst., and the outer line of defensive works was carried by the enemy, but that the Confederate reinforcements arrived in time to check their further progress. Nothing about the tearing up of the railroad by Butler.

June 25, 1864.

The Yankees are returning from another plundering raid they have made upon the people of Lenoir, Jones, and Onslow counties.[50] A few days ago they gathered all their available force of infantry and artillery from this county and Craven, amounting, it was said, to two thousand or more. Most of them went off from New Bern by land, and we supposed their object was to destroy the "ram" near Kinston.[51] Some went by sea towards New River. The land force did not destroy the ram. At least we suppose they did not, as they say nothing about it. But being divided into different bands they mistook some of their own men for "rebs," shot at them, and killed a sergeant, and wounded several others. Their only trophies are stolen negroes, twenty of whom arrived here to-day. The naval part of the expedition captured a few poor fishermen somewhere near New River, and brought them to Fort Macon.

Since the foregoing was written, we learn that the land expedition

---

50   Rumley is conflating two nearly simultaneous raids. The first expedition was commanded by Colonel Peter J. Claussen of the 132nd New York and consisted of two infantry regiments and a detachment of artillery and cavalry, composing 832 men. They left New Bern and demonstrated in the direction of Kinston. The second expedition, led by Colonel James Jourdan and directed against the Wilmington and Weldon Railroad, took place June 20–25, 1864. Fifteen hundred men left Morehead City and reached Jacksonville before encountering a large Confederate force, which caused them to abort the mission. *Official Records, Army*, ser. 1, 40, pt. 1:814,816–819, pt. 2:420.

51   The CSS *Neuse* was an ironclad ram that the Confederacy built near Kinston, North Carolina. It was finished by the summer of 1864, but because of lack of ground support, it never attempted to attack New Bern. Bright, Rowland, and Bardon, *C.S.S. Neuse.*

brought into New Bern about 50 prisoners. It is whispered in secret circles that they came in minus 150 men, and brought in some of their men dead. But it is difficult to get the truth in such cases, until long after the events have ceased to be of interest.

Among the prisoners carried to New Bern is Colonel Faulk,[52] the Confederate Commandant at Kinston. He is said to be a fine looking, well dressed and dashing young officer, and attracts attention among the Yankees at New Bern.

The Dead before the war.

Although the events of this revolution are calculated to engross all the thoughts of men, we often pause, amid its frightful developments, and look back through the darkness of the present hour to the light of other days, while memory calls up the pale form of the dead—those who lived in our day but died before the war. The spirits of these departed patriots were often disquieted no doubt by apprehensions of an evil day ahead, for the signs in the political heavens constantly pointed to a national disruption; and they saw perhaps, dimly, the shadows of coming events. But they never contemplated the full measure of woe and misery that this barbarous war was to inflict upon the country or the blood and fire and desolation that now mark its track. The hour of that great darkness which was coming on their country, fell not upon them, and they were permitted—happily we think—to pass to their quiet resting places without beholding one of the darkest political nights that ever settled down upon any free people, and one of the bloodiest dreams ever enacted in the theatre of mankind. It is refreshing, in these gloomy hours, to visit their graves. In solemn silence there they slumber on, where the tramp of armies and the fierce hurricane of war, can never rouse them.

"The storm that wrecks the wintry sky
No more disturbs their deep repose,

---

52   Colonel George Nathaniel Folk (1831–1896) of the 65th North Carolina (6th North Carolina Cavalry), was captured around June 22, 1864, by a Union expeditionary force on a raid toward Kinston. Folk was held from June 22 to December 15, 1864, before being exchanged. Folk had been a lawyer and a state representative from Watauga County before the war. *Official Records, Army*, ser. 1, 40, pt. 1:814,816, pt. 2:420; Manarin and Jordan, *North Carolina Troops*, 2:457; Powell, *Dictionary of North Carolina Biography*, 2:215–216.

Then summer evenings latest sigh
That shuts the rose."[53]

July 4, 1864.

This day passed away quiet and gloomy. Nothing was done by the Yankees to honor the day. In Fort Macon there was some sort of celebration, but very little is known about it. The thoughts of the Yankees were too much occupied by affairs in Virginia for them to bestow much attention on the day.

We are informed that on the 30th. ulto, two soldiers belonging to the 3rd. New York Artillery went to the house of William T. Ward,[54] Esq., of Newport, and beat him on the head with a stick, inflicting ghastly wounds, until they supposed he was dead, when they rifled his pockets of seventy-five dollars in cash, and left him bloody and apparently dead on the floor. Some hours after their departure, Ward revived and succeeded in getting on his bed, where he was discovered by his friends covered with blood, with seven shocking wounds on the head. All of them were gashes, open to the skull. The ruffians who committed the deed have been identified, and arrested at Newport. When carried into the presence of Ward they were immediately recognized by him. His condition is thought to be critical. This is the first attempt at willful murder by Federal soldiers in this county.

July 7, 1864.

A change takes place to-day in the office of Provost Marshal of Beaufort. Capt. Bartlett[55] has been ordered to take command of the remains of his shattered regiment in Virginia—a Massachusetts Regiment, lately

---

53 Rumley is quoting a verse from an English hymn titled "The Grave." Thompson, *Songs in the Night*, 262.

54 Rumley is likely referring to William Ward (b. ca. 1824), a farmer from the Swift Creek region of Craven County. Eighth Census, 1860: Craven County.

55 Captain George W. Bartlett, Company K, 27th Massachusetts Infantry Regiment. Massachusetts Adjutant General's Office, *Massachusetts Soldiers, Sailors, and Marines*, 3:122.

commanded by Col. Lee,[56] who was in May last assigned to quarters in
Richmond. Col. Poor[57] of the 2nd N.C. Volunteers is appointed Provost
Marshal.

While the campaign at Richmond drags its slow length along, we are
startled by accounts of another invasion of Maryland by the Confederates, which has struck the whole north with a panic, and attracted all eyes
in the south.[58] Grant at Richmond and Sherman at Atlanta, are almost
forgotten, or at least cast in the shade, by this bold and unexpected movement into Maryland. That the Confederate authorities at Richmond, who
were supposed to be taxed to their utmost power of exertion to resist the
host who are trying to beleaguer their own capital, should be able to send
a formidable army to menace, and perhaps capture, the capital of their
enemy, seize the railroad, burn bridges, and do what they please generally
in Maryland, surpasses all Yankee conception of their power, and must
astonish the nations of Europe, who are watching, with deep interest, all
the incidents of this mighty contest. We shall wait for further news from
this new theatre of war with great anxiety.

---

56 Horace Clark Lee (1820–1884) was named colonel of the 27th Massachusetts
Regiment on September 20, 1861. He was captured at the Battle of Drewry's
Bluff, Virginia, on May 16, 1864. He was honorably mustered out of the ser-
vice on September 27, 1864. Denny, *Wearing the Blue*, 43; Heitman, *Historical
Register*, 624; Massachusetts Adjutant General's Office, *Massachusetts Soldiers,
Sailors, and Marines*, 3:122.

57 Lieutenant Colonel Walter S. Poor took command of the 2nd North Carolina
Regiment (Union) on March 30, 1864, soon after Charles Henry Foster was
mustered out of the regiment on March 25, 1864. Poor was placed in com-
mand of Beaufort on April 19, 1864. Walter S. Poor File, 2nd North Carolina
Infantry Regiment, Compiled Military Service Records of Volunteer Union
Soldiers Who Served in Organizations from the State of North Carolina,
Record Group 94.12.2.

58 General Jubal A. Early led a Confederate force of approximately 15,000 men
to the north side of the Potomac River on July 6, causing much consternation
and panic in Washington, D.C. After defeating a small Union force at the
Battle of Monocacy on July 9, Early's troops reached the Washington defenses
on July 11. Grant had detached the VI Corps from the Army of the Potomac
to meet this threat. Early's force, which was too weak to attack Washington,
retreated to the south side of the Potomac a few days later. McPherson, *Battle
Cry of Freedom*, 756–757.

Later. Late papers inform us that the Confederates have withdrawn from Maryland, with horses and cattle, and army stores, in abundance.

July 25, 1864.

Affairs at Richmond have ceased to excite great anxiety, and the eyes of the people are now turned to Atlanta. Every dispatch from that section places Sherman nearer to the city, until at last he has it within range of his guns. So say the Northern papers. Johnston[59] has met him and fought him repeatedly on his march, and no doubt destroyed a large portion of his army, but still, on he goes over piles of his dead, until he crosses the Chattahoochee,[60] and marches to the very suburbs of Atlanta, while Johnston falls back with the defenses of the city. This is indeed a dark cloud on the Southern horizon.

July 27, 1864.

Northern papers bring reports of the fall of Atlanta.[61] The news falls with a chilling and depressing effect upon every Southern heart.

July 28, 1864.

The papers today repeat the story of the fall of Atlanta, and its occupation by Sherman, after a bloody fight on the 22nd. But while the Yankees and traitors are shouting over the victory, a message from Raleigh, silent and unseen, comes through the underground route, announcing a terrible defeat of Sherman, somewhere near Atlanta; which must have occurred

---

59 Joseph E. Johnston (1807–1891) was appointed commander of the Confederate Army of Tennessee in December 1863. He opposed General William Sherman's army throughout north Georgia as Sherman moved toward Atlanta in the spring and summer of 1864. Johnston was relieved of command on July 17, 1864. He was replaced by General John Bell Hood. Heidler and Heidler, *Encyclopedia of the American Civil War*, 3:1083–1085.

60 The Chattahoochee is a river in north Georgia approximately twenty miles north of Atlanta. McPherson, *Battle Cry of Freedom*, 754.

61 The information was incorrect.

on the 22nd.[62] This is a bright streak of light over a cloudy sky. We are profoundly anxious for further news from that quarter.

August 1, 1864.

The tone of the northern papers is such as to leave no doubt of the defeat of Sherman by Hood on the 22nd., near Atlanta.

August 4, 1864.

Papers of the 30th. ulto. (Yankee) represent Sherman as gradually drawing his lines round Atlanta. Surely the Confederates will not suffer themselves or the place to be caught at last in the coil of the serpent.

August 8, 1864.

The *Raleigh Confederate* of the 3rd. inst. comes to us today, through some unknown channel.

It reports a brilliant success of the Confederates over Stoneman's Cavalry in Georgia about the 1st.[63] Sherman was still near Atlanta, shelling the place. Grant had mined and blown up a fort near Petersburg, killing about 100 Confederates. After the explosion he made a grand charge, took the position, but was soon repulsed with terrible slaughter. He

---

62   The information was incorrect. A Confederate force under General John Bell Hood had unsuccessfully attacked the Army of the Tennessee (Union), commanded by General James McPherson (under the overall command of William Sherman), on July 22, 1864. The Confederates suffered twice as many casualties as the Union army, though McPherson was killed in the battle. McPherson, *Battle Cry of Freedom*, 754.

63   On July 27, 1864, Major General George Stoneman set out from near Atlanta, Georgia, with nearly 2,000 Union cavalry troopers and two cannons on a raid to liberate Union prisoners of war held at Macon, Georgia, and Andersonville, Georgia. Arriving outside of Macon on July 30, Stoneman encountered many difficulties as he assaulted the town and called off the raid. He eventually ordered a retreat back toward Atlanta. On his retreat, he encountered fierce Confederate opposition. While some of his troops managed to escape, he and about 700 of his troops were forced to surrender to Confederate forces on July 31, 1864. Castel, *Decision in the West*, 436–442.

placed his negro troops in front. He lost altogether about 3500 men. The Confederate loss was about 800.[64]

August 9, 1864.

We have northern papers today. The *Herald* admits a great disaster to Grant. The *News* says he lost 9,000 men in the terrible fight which followed the blowing up of the fort, and wants his army withdrawn from Petersburg. He pronounces the campaign against Richmond a complete failure.

August 15, 1864.

Northern papers bring painful news of the entrance of a Federal fleet under Farragut into Mobile Bay, the surrender of Fort Gaines with 600 men, and the destruction of Fort Powell, and nearly the whole Confederate fleet in the bay.[65]

Affairs at Atlanta seem to be enveloped in a fog. No news from there and no news from Grant's army.

---

64 The Battle of the Crater took place near Petersburg, Virginia, on July 30, 1864. Soldiers of the 48th Pennsylvania Regiment, many of whom had been coal miners before the war, dug a 500-foot-long mine shaft under the Confederate position. A division of black troops had been designated to lead the charge, but lacking faith in the fighting abilities of black men and fearing the political backlash that would occur if the attack failed, General Grant ordered white troops to lead the assault. When the mine was detonated, a mismanaged attack followed that resulted in a Union defeat and nearly 4,000 Union casualties, while the Confederates suffered nearly 1,500 casualties. McPherson, *Battle Cry of Freedom*, 758–760; Heidler and Heidler, *Encyclopedia of the American Civil War*, 1:515–517.

65 Beginning on August 3, 1864, a combined Union force under the command of Admiral David G. Farragut began assaulting the forts that guarded the entrance to Mobile Bay, the Confederacy's last remaining Gulf Coast port. Farragut's seventeen-ship fleet destroyed the smaller Confederate fleet in the harbor and forced Confederates to abandon Fort Powell on August 6. On August 8, Confederate colonel Charles Anderson surrendered Fort Gaines to Farragut's forces. Heidler and Heidler, *Encyclopedia of the American Civil War*, 3:1342–1344.

An excellent order has lately been made by the Provost Marshal, Col. Poor, at this place, to the effect that no negroes should be permitted to occupy the houses or kitchens of white citizens, without the consent of the owners of the places. This will relieve some citizens of an intolerable annoyance.

Another good order has been made, requiring all negroes having fire arms and deadly weapons in their possession, to deliver them up to the Provost Marshal.

August 17, 1864.

Last night, when the negroes were holding one of their so-called religious meetings in the African Church, some marines from the navy, who don't like the negroes much, and wanted a little fun, raised the cry, near the church, that the rebels were coming. The cry was enough to break up the meeting. The negroes fled in every direction. "Old Bate" was offering up a prayer for the congregation, when the cry was heard. His faith in his maker instantly departed, and he trusted alone to [his] legs.

September 1, 1864.

The summer of 1864 has ended, and Grant has not yet taken Richmond. He dispatched to the Federal Secretary of War early in May last, after five days hard fighting, that he intended to "fight it out on this line if it takes all summer."[66] He soon abandoned that line, and has tried several others in vain. His last attempt was made on the line of the Petersburg and Weldon road. He started this two weeks ago, with 30,000 men, three or four miles south of Petersburg, and [is] still holding it. But a division

---

66   Rumley is quoting a line from a letter from General Grant to General Henry Halleck dated May 11, 1864. Portions of the letter were reprinted in many newspapers and the letter was well known by the end of the summer. *Official Records, Army*, ser. 1, 36, pt. 1:4.

of his forces got badly whipped at Reams station further south, on the 25th. ulto.[67]

Fort Morgan, at the entrance of Mobile Bay, has surrendered.[68] Clouds hover over Atlanta.

West of the Mississippi all looks well. The Yankees have entirely abandoned Texas. The Southern horizon generally looks bright. And so closes the summer of 1864.

September 5, 1864.

The negroes here are in great distress; an order has come from Butler that every able bodied male negro, without regular employment, shall be sent from this Military District to the army before Petersburg, immediately.[69] The poor wretches now see that the southerners were their best friends, and upon them they now call for help. Through the intercession of their former masters and others, many of them after being conscripted and imprisoned, are released, and saved from exile worse to them than death.

---

67 In his attempt to cut the Confederate supply lines to Petersburg, Virginia, General Grant had ordered General Winfield S. Hancock to take his II Corps to destroy several miles of the Weldon Railroad south of Petersburg. While destroying the track, Hancock's division was attacked by Confederate general A. P. Hill's corps. In the ensuing fight, the Union troops were forced to retreat after suffering over 2,700 casualties. Heidler and Heidler, *Encyclopedia of the American Civil War*, 4:1613–1614.

68 Fort Morgan was the easternmost fort guarding the entrance to Mobile Bay. After holding out for two weeks against constant Union bombardment by land and sea, it surrendered on August 23, 1864, granting the Union navy complete control of Mobile Bay. Heidler and Heidler, *Encyclopedia of the American Civil War*, 3:1342–1345.

69 On August 30, 1864, Major General Benjamin Butler issued an order that "all able-bodied colored men not now engaged in some regular permanent employment" would be given work as laborers at the rate of $16 per month. The order was posted in New Bern, and the workers were required to report to the provost marshal's office in New Bern. Few African Americans volunteered for this duty willingly; they were compelled to do so by Union officers in the region. *Official Records, Army*, ser. 1, 42, pt. 2:600, 653–654.

Never, in the days of negro traffic, was such a scene exhibited in Beaufort, as was witnessed yesterday (Sunday) at the jail, where these poor victims of abolitionism were imprisoned, preparatory to their transportation to Virginia.

September 12, 1864.

Atlanta has fallen.[70] It was evacuated on the 1st. inst., by the Confederates, and occupied by the Yankees.

September 26, 1864.

Several days ago news was telegraphed from New Bern to Morehead City that Mobile had been evacuated by the Confederates and occupied by the Yankees. The Yankees here firmly believed it, and of course predicted the speedy downfall of the "rebellion." Southern men doubted its correctness, and it now turns out to be false.

But sad reports come from the Shenandoah Valley in Virginia, to the effect that the forces there under Gen. Early met with a disastrous defeat from Sheridan's forces, on the 19th. inst.[71] One hundred guns were fired at Fort Macon today in honor of the victory.

October 1, 1864.

A dreadful pestilence is raging in New Bern. It is supposed to be yellow fever, and originated in the town. We learn with deep sorrow that James

---

70   The Confederate Army of Tennessee under General John Bell Hood evacuated Atlanta on September 1, 1864. On September 2, Sherman's army took control of Atlanta. McPherson, *Battle Cry of Freedom*, 774.

71   On September 19, 1864, Union general Philip Sheridan's 37,000-man army attacked Confederate general Jubal Early's 17,000 men at the Third Battle of Winchester, or Opequon. Sheridan suffered over 5,000 casualties and Early over 1,800, but Sheridan's superior force drove Early out of Winchester and south through the Shenandoah Valley. Gallagher, "Revisiting the 1862 and 1864 Valley Campaigns," 191; Heidler and Heidler, *Encyclopedia of the American Civil War*, 4:2132–2135.

W. Bryan, Esq. and his lady,[72] who lately arrived there from New York, have fallen victims to the disease.

October 3, 1864.

Capt. Lyons,[73] of the 2nd. Regiment of N.C. Troops, is now Provost Marshal at Beaufort, in place of Col. Poor, late Provost Marshal, who has been ordered to New Bern.

October 7, 1864.

The news that daily comes from New Bern is appalling. With steady strides the terrible pestilence walks in darkness, and destroys at noon day, in that scourged and unhappy town. Citizens, traders, officers and soldiers, all fall before the fell destroyer thick and fast as the leaves of autumn in the stormy blast. The names of James W. Bryan, Mrs. Bryan, John F. Jones,[74] Frederick J. Jones,[75] Oliver, and others well known here, are announced to us as among the fallen. Near a thousand persons have perished there, since the pestilence began.

---

72 Ann Mary Washington Bryan (1814–1864). Powell, *Dictionary of North Carolina Biography*, 1:255.

73 Charles A. Lyon (1838–1864) was captain of Company B, 1st North Carolina Infantry Regiment (Union). Lyon, a law student from Brookfield, Massachusetts, had enlisted in Company I, 24th Massachusetts Regiment, on September 6, 1861. He was discharged on June 1, 1862, to be commissioned in the 1st North Carolina. Lyon died of yellow fever at Beaufort on October 24, 1864. Charles A. Lyon File, 1st North Carolina Infantry Regiment, Compiled Military Service Records of Volunteer Union Soldiers Who Served in Organizations from the State of North Carolina, Record Group 94.12.2; Massachusetts Adjutant General's Office, *Massachusetts Soldiers, Sailors, and Marines*, 2:825.

74 John Frederick Jones (b. 1832) was a clerk in the Bank of New Bern. He was the son of Frederick J. Jones, the cashier of the bank. Eighth Census, 1860: Craven County.

75 Frederick J. Jones (b. ca. 1842) was the son of Frederick J. Jones, cashier of the Bank of New Bern. He was brother to John Frederick Jones. Eighth Census, 1860: Craven County.

At Beaufort, too, where the winds of autumn, fresh from the ocean, have heretofore been a sure guaranty of health, the angel of death has spread his wings on the breeze, and poisoned the breath of life.

"The blessed seals
"That close the pestilence are broke,
And groaning victims wail its stroke."[76]

One hundred and fifty persons, now lie stretched upon their beds in Beaufort, with a terrible fever. Whether it is yellow fever is a question yet to be settled. It is probably the same fever that prevails in New Bern. It has, here, some of the characteristics of yellow fever. Among them is the dark colored matter, which some of the sufferers eject profusely from the stomach, in cases which terminate fatally. But it is by no means certain that this is the black vomit of the horrible disease referred to. The fatal cases, up to the present hour, are not as numerous as we feared they would be. Among the deaths occurring here is that of Colonel Amory[77] of the U.S. Army, who commanded in the Beaufort District. He died this morning of the prevailing disease. His wife died a few days ago of the same disease. (Oct. 17th. 1864 Obituary—The death by yellow fever at Beaufort, N.C. of Colonel T.J.C. Amory 17th. Massa. Volunteers)[78]

October 16, 1864.

The pestilence still rages, and the arrows of death fly thick through the air. A number of estimable ladies have fallen. Among the men who have

---

76 Rumley is slightly misquoting a verse from Fitz-Greene Halleck's poem "Marco Bozzaris." The last line of the verse actually reads "And crowded cities wail its stroke." Bryant, *A Library of Poetry and Song*, 451.

77 Colonel Thomas J. C. Amory.

78 This parenthetical entry appears in the handwritten copy of Rumley's diary, though the obituary was published ten days after Rumley's entry for October 7.

died are John W. Morgan,[79] John P.C. Davis[80] and Henry C. Jones![81] Physicians have pronounced the disease to be yellow fever! The weather has long been dry and hot, and our town is crowded with refugees and negroes to its utmost capacity. Under the circumstances nothing but the sea air can save us from a dreadful scourge. The war news is bad, but men talk little of that now while death in a form more terrible than the battlefield is among them.

"And I looked, and behold a pale horse; and his name that sat on him was Death!"[82]

October 24, 1864.

Neither cool weather with frost, or medical skill and experience have yet materially checked the ravages of the fever. Deaths and new cases occur daily.

Capt. Lyons,[83] the Provost Marshal, died this forenoon. Josiah S. Pender[84] died at half past 6 o'clock P.M. Both died of the prevailing sickness.

October 27, 1864.

Ten or twelve new cases and some deaths have occurred since the 24th. Mr. Ballard, a citizen of Virginia, died at the U.S. Hospital, at 6 o'clock this morning.

---

79 John W. Morgan (b. ca. 1810) was a mechanic who lived at George W. Taylor's Ocean House Hotel in Beaufort. Eighth Census, 1860: Carteret County.

80 John Philpot Curtin Davis (1815–1864) was one of the wealthiest merchants in Beaufort and had served as town commissioner, county trustee, and member of the Board of Superintendents of Common Schools of Carteret County. *Cemetery Records of Carteret County*, 151; Eighth Census, 1860: Carteret County; *Beaufort Journal*, June 10, 1857; Minutes of the Carteret County Court of Pleas and Quarter Sessions, February 1861 and February 1862; North Carolina, 5:166, R. G. Dun & Co. Collection.

81 Henry C. Jones (b. ca. 1828) was a lawyer from New Bern. Eighth Census, 1860: Craven County.

82 Revelation 6:8.

83 Charles A. Lyon.

84 Josiah Solomon Pender. For biographical information, see note 12 in chapter 1 of this volume.

A dreadful feeling of insecurity pervades all classes, and men now realize the solemn thought of the poet, that
"The Spiders most attenuated thread
Is cord, is cable, to the slender tie
We hold on human life."[85]

November 4, 1864.

The pestilence has abated. Ten cases of the fever now exist, and those are not serious. Probably three hundred persons have been prostrated with the disease, but nearly nine-tenths of them are out of danger.

The disease, in some cases, assumed a most violent and fatal form. The sea air, and lateness of the season when it appeared, probably modified it essentially and saved Beaufort from the terrible ravages it made at New Bern. The following is the roll of death for the few weeks of the pestilence—soldiers not included.

The Roll of Deaths: John B. Guthrie,[86] William P. Marshall Jnr,[87] Bryan Longest,[88] John Cameron,[89] John W. Morgan, John P.C. Davis, Henry C. Jones, George W. Morse,[90] Robert Hancock,[91] Josiah S. Pender, [*blank*

---

85 Rumley is quoting a verse from Edward Young's poem "The Complaint: Night the First." Young, *The Complaint*, 17.

86 This is likely John B. Guthrie (b. ca. 1815), a merchant in Beaufort. He is listed as J. B. Guthery in the 1860 census and is identified as John B. Guthrie in the 1850 census. Seventh Census, 1850: Carteret County; Eighth Census, 1860: Carteret County.

87 William P. Marshall (b. ca. 1796) was a farmer living near Beaufort. Eighth Census, 1860: Carteret County.

88 This is likely B. H. Longest (b. ca. 1824), a master carpenter who lived in New Bern. Eighth Census, 1860: Craven County.

89 J. C. Cameron (b. ca. 1831) was a Beaufort mechanic who was originally from Massachusetts. Eighth Census, 1860: Carteret County.

90 G. W. Morse (b. ca. 1820) was a mechanic in Beaufort. Eighth Census, 1860: Carteret County.

91 Robert Hancock (b. ca. 1825) had enlisted in Stephen D. Pool's "Topsail Rifles," which became Company H of the 10th North Carolina. He was discharged for a disability on November 22, 1862. He was listed in the 1860 census as a farmer, but on his enlistment card he is identified as a tailor. Eighth Census, 1860: Carteret County; Manarin and Jordan, *North Carolina Troops*, 1:130.

space] Pearce, William Reed,[92] Samuel L. Howland,[93] David Morse, Jr,[94] Mr. Ballard of Virginia, Mr. Glen (transient), Mr. Phelps (transient), Mr. Conklin (clerk for Treasurer Agt),[95] Col. Amory, U.S.A. commanding the Post, and wife, Capt. Lyon (Provost Marshal), Col. Scameron U.S.A., Miss Mattie Morse,[96] Miss Annie Dill,[97] Mrs. Charity F. Ramsy,[98] Annie Potter,[99] Mrs. Abby Willis,[100] Miss Gibbs, Mrs. Sallie Ward, Mrs. Bettie

---

92 William H. Reed (b. ca. 1834) was a farmer from Craven County. Eighth Census, 1860: Craven County.

93 Samuel Howland (b. ca. 1820) was a fisherman from Smyrna, a community located northeast of Beaufort in Carteret County. Eighth Census, 1860: Carteret County.

94 David W. Morse, Jr. (b. ca. 1851), was the son of Beaufort mechanic David W. Morse. He died on October 16, 1864. Eighth Census, 1860: Carteret County; *Cemetery Records of Carteret County*, 168.

95 Mr. Conklin (first name unknown) was a clerk for Treasury Agent David Heaton (1823–1870). Browning and Smith, *Letters from a North Carolina Unionist*, 154, 229.

96 Martha Morse (b. ca. 1848) was the daughter of Beaufort mechanic David W. Morse. Her brother David, Jr., also died of the yellow fever epidemic. While another contemporary source mentions the death of "one of Dave Morse's daughters," no official record of the death has been located. Eighth Census, 1860: Carteret County; Browning and Smith, *Letters from a North Carolina Unionist*, 237.

97 Vienna [Vianna] Dill (b. 1848) was the daughter of Stephen L. Dill, a mariner from Beaufort, and his wife Elizabeth. She died on October 6, 1864. Eighth Census, 1860: Carteret County; *Cemetery Records of Carteret County*, 151.

98 Charity Jones Ramsey (b. 1811) was the wife of Isaac Ramsey, one of the wealthiest merchants in Beaufort. She died on October 9, 1864. Charity's daughter, Martha Washington Ramsey (1846–1864), had died of yellow fever on August 18, 1864. *Cemetery Records of Carteret County*, 161; Marriage Bond of Isaac Ramsey and Charity F. Jones, November 27, 1833, Carteret County; Eighth Census, 1860: Carteret County.

99 Ann Potter (b. ca. 1836) died on October 11, 1864. She was a schoolteacher in Beaufort and was the daughter of Beaufort postmaster W. J. Potter. Eighth Census, 1860: Carteret County; *Cemetery Records of Carteret County*, 161.

100 Abigail Hancock Willis (b. ca. 1808) was the wife of Beaufort mechanic Horatio Willis. She died on October 12, 1864. Eighth Census, 1860: Carteret County; *Cemetery Records of Carteret County*, 165; Marriage Bond of Horatio H. Willis and Abigail Hancock, November 29, 1832, Carteret County.

Lawinberg,[101] Ruth Hatchel[102] Mrs. Skarren, Mrs. Morse, Mrs. Nant, Miss Tuttle (Teacher),[103] Mrs. Johnson, wife of Lt. Johnson, U.S.A., Dr. Babbitt,[104] Mr. Page (superintendent of the negroes),[105] Mrs. Murphy, Mrs. Thoroughgood, Miss Nancy Thomas.[106]

November [n.d.], 1864.

Capt. A. Thompson[107] of the 9th. New Jersey Regiment, is Provost Marshal of Beaufort, in place of Capt. Lyons, deceased.

---

101   Elisabeth Lowenberg (b. ca. 1836) was the wife of Bendix Lowenberg, a Prussian-born merchant in Beaufort. *Eighth Census, 1860: Carteret County*; *Cemetery Records of Carteret County*, 158.

102   Ruth Hatchel (b. ca. 1858) was the daughter of Rebecca and W. Hatchell, a Beaufort mariner. *Eighth Census, 1860: Carteret County*.

103   Bliss Tuttle (b. ca. 1842) was a resident of New Haven, Connecticut, who was living in the home of her father, Miles Tuttle. Miss Tuttle joined one of the freedmen's relief organizations that came to Beaufort and New Bern to teach the freedmen. Benjamin, *The Great Epidemic in New Bern and Vicinity*, 36; *Eighth Census, 1860: New Haven County, Conn*.

104   Robert A. Babbitt (1841–1864) hailed from Vermont and enlisted in the 8th Connecticut Regiment in 1861. He was appointed surgeon at the Hammond General Hospital in Beaufort in 1862 and a year later became surgeon of the 1st North Carolina Regiment (Union). He died on October 17, 1864. Browning and Smith, *Letters from a North Carolina Unionist*, 50–51; Hewett, *The Roster of Union Soldiers, 1861–1865*, 11, part 2:533; Hemenway, *The Vermont Historical Gazetteer*, 2:1027.

105   Rumley is likely referring to Dr. Jesse Page. If so, Rumley incorrectly reported Dr. Page's death. Dr. Jesse William Page, a graduate of Bowdoin College, was an agent of the U.S. Sanitary Commission in New Bern. John A. Hedrick, U.S. treasury agent in Beaufort, confirms that Page suffered an attack of yellow fever but lived through it. Browning and Smith, *Letters from a North Carolina Unionist*, 242–247; Barden, *Letters to the Home Circle*, 105.

106   Nancy Thomas (b. 1799) lived with Beaufort lawyer C. R. Thomas and his family. She died on October 14, 1864. *Eighth Census, 1860: Carteret County*; *Cemetery Records of Carteret County*, 164.

107   Augustus Thompson was elected first lieutenant of Company F, 9th New Jersey Infantry Regiment on November 9, 1861. He was promoted to captain of the company on January 8, 1863. He was discharged from the army on February 9, 1865 (reason not given). Drake, *The History of the Ninth New Jersey Veteran Vols.*, 462.

November 13, 1864.

The pestilence has probably taken its final leave of Beaufort. The cold, hard winds, we hope, have swept it away. A daughter of Capt. Duncan (Ella)[108] died yesterday. But it is believed this case closes the list of victims of the most dreadful fever that raged in this place.[109] It has abated in New Bern.

November 28, 1864.

The shattered remnant of the 27th. Massachusetts Regiment of Infantry, lately from Virginia, has been sent to Beaufort for garrison duty.[110] The "buffaloes" are ordered to the west side of the harbor.

December 1, 1864.

Our town is crowded with refugees from various parts of the state—chiefly from the lower counties. Most of them are young men who have fled from the conscription. They scout the idea of Southern independence, speak very contemptuously of "Old Jeff" and the "rebel Confederacy," and seem to be Yankees in heart and soul. If they think they can abandon their country in this manner, in her hour of trial, and affiliate with her enemies, and not be remembered hereafter as deserters and traitors, we think they are mistaken. We pity their fate, if the day should come,

---

108 Ella Duncan (b. ca. 1851) was the daughter of Thomas Duncan Sr. (1806–1880), a wealthy Beaufort merchant. Eighth Census, 1860: Carteret County; North Carolina, 5:163, R. G. Dun & Co. Collection.

109 Ninety-one people, fifteen soldiers and seventy-six residents, died in Beaufort of yellow fever. Hand, "Epidemic of 1864," 4:296.

110 The 27th Massachusetts Regiment had seen much action in Virginia in May and June 1864 as part of General Benjamin Butler's ill-fated expedition against Petersburg by way of Bermuda Hundred, Virginia. The 27th suffered over 300 casualties (259 of them captured) at the Battle of Drewry's Bluff on May 16, 1864. It lost 104 more men at the Battle of Cold Harbor on June 2 and 3. By June 3, the regiment had suffered 488 casualties in less than a month. It suffered thirty-nine more casualties in attacks on the defenses of Petersburg on June 15 and 18. Massachusetts Adjutant General's Office, *Massachusetts Soldiers, Sailors, and Marines*, 3:120–121.

"That great avenging day
When Yankee power in the dust shall lay."[111]
When the south shall come forth victorious from this fiery contest and, though scorched and scathed it may be, with the smell of fire upon her garments, yet with the principle of life strong within her, will have the power and the will to punish her enemies and reward her friends.

December 20, 1864.

A Federal fleet which lately assembled in the harbor, sailed on the 18th., for parts unknown. Some of the vessels returned yesterday and today, with troops on board. And Satan has appeared also in the shape of Gen. Benj. F Butler, who is reported to be at Morehead City. This is his first appearance here in connection with this fleet. The signs are mysterious.

A vessel of considerable size (razed, to elude observation) containing over 200 tons of powder so placed and confined as to produce a terrific concussion when it explodes, was in the fleet, and has gone on its murderous errand. The Yankees have tried to keep the matter a profound secret. But the diabolical scheme has leaked out. The design is to run the vessel on the shore near Fort Fisher and then ignite the powder (by what means we do not know).[112] The contrivers expect by this concussion to kill the whole garrison, dislodge the guns of the fort, and cause the torpedoes in the river to explode. After all this they expect, of course, to land their men and take quiet possession of the fort.[113]

---

111 Rumley is paraphrasing a passage from Alexander Pope's translation of Homer's *Iliad*, bk. IV, line 196. The original passage reads: "That great avenging day / which Troy's proud glories in the dust shall lay." Pope, *The Iliad*, 1:140.

112 Fort Fisher is approximately 100 miles southwest of Beaufort.

113 In this attempt to take Fort Fisher, which was planned as a prelude to the capture of Wilmington, Major General Benjamin F. Butler commanded an army of about 6,500 men and Rear Admiral David D. Porter a fleet of fifty ships. Butler suggested beginning the attack by detonating a powder-filled ship near the fort. An unsuccessful attempt was carried out on the morning of December 24. Later in the morning, the navy bombarded the fort without inflicting serious damage. When Butler, whose army had landed north of the fort, discovered this fact and that a Confederate army was to his rear in Wilmington, he called for a retreat. The campaign was resumed in January 1865. Barrett, *The Civil War in North Carolina*, 262–271.

December 23, 1864.

Gen. Butler appeared in town today. His stay was short. He walked, with his officers, leisurely through the town, and back to the wharf where he had landed, and then departed for Morehead City, or his flagship in the harbor. His presence created no stir, nor even a ripple on the surface of the water.

December 24, 1864.

This morning, about a quarter past two o'clock, the inhabitants were roused from their slumbers by a sudden jar of their dwellings, like the shock of an earthquake, followed by a noise like the distant explosion of a bombshell. It was, beyond doubt, the explosion of the powder ship sent against Fort Fisher, that produced the jar and the noise.[114] Great anxiety is felt to hear from that quarter. The whole contrivance will no doubt turnout to be a Yankee humbug.

December 25, 1864.

By arrivals in port today, we learn that the powder ship was exploded somewhere near Fort Fisher yesterday morning, after 2 o'clock, but without any visible damage to the fort or garrison. A bombardment ensued, the result of which is not known. The fort is certainly not reduced. The incessant roar of artillery in that direction, which we can distinctly hear, although there is light breeze from the east, at the hour of 2 P.M., tells of a raging fight. The day is Christmas, as well as Sunday. Where the battle rages the festive song is the roar of cannon, and the feast, alas is probably a feast of blood.

December 26, 1864.

Not a word of intelligence comes from New Inlet today. No firing is heard in that direction. As we have a light west wind, and a vapory atmosphere,

---

114 At 1:40 a.m. on December 24, the *Louisiana*, which was packed with explosives, blew up close to the stronghold with little effect. Barrett, *The Civil War in North Carolina*, 262–271.

we should certainly hear the cannonading, if any were going on at Fort Fisher. What means the silence?

December 27, 1864.

The appearance of part of the Federal fleet in the offing, this morning, was the signal for various conjectures as to the result of the fight at Fort Fisher. But the truth soon became known, that the attack was signally defeated. The firing on Sunday is represented as awful. The fort was not damaged, but the fleet was badly peppered, and the loss of men on board was considerable. They are landing their dead and wounded at U.S. Hospital in town. What became of Butler's land forces we cannot learn. It is said that after landing and a fruitless attempt to march towards Fort Fisher, he reembarked and sailed for Fortress Monroe. Inexpressible relief and satisfaction are felt here by the friends of the South, at this signal triumph of the Confederacy.

December 29, 1864.

About twenty vessels, of heavy burthen, have made their appearance, and anchored outside the bar. They have not been seen here before; but they were part of the fleet which operated against Fort Fisher. Their draft of water is too great for this bar. The fleet, it is said, consisted of one hundred and fifty vessels.

December 31, 1864.

Since Sherman evacuated Atlanta and commenced his grand march through Georgia[115] which should be called a retreat, forced upon him by the operations of the Confederate Army, we have watched the campaign in the south and west with profound interest. While the rapid concentration of the Confederates in Georgia, and the hopeful tone of the proclamations and speeches there, inspired among us high hopes of

---

115   Major General William Sherman's Union army left Atlanta to begin the march to the sea on November 15, 1864. Long, *The Civil War Day by Day*, 597.

Sherman's overthrow, Hood's victorious march into Tennessee,[116] threw a radiance like the rainbow of promise over that clouded region. But alas, how fluctuating is the tide of victory in war. Hood has been defeated at Nashville,[117] and has retreated out of Tennessee, and Sherman has marched through Georgia destroying millions of dollars worth of property, and now reposes quietly in possession of Savannah![118]

---

116 Hoping to defeat Union forces in Tennessee and Kentucky and therefore force Sherman to abandon his march through Georgia or at least to himself link up with General Lee's army in Virginia, Hood marched his army of approximately 40,000 men into Tennessee. He was defeated in this endeavor. McPherson, *Battle Cry of Freedom*, 809–812.

117 Union forces under Major General George H. Thomas defeated General John Bell Hood's Army of Tennessee at the Battle of Nashville, December 15–16, 1864. Boatner, *The Civil War Dictionary*, 579–582.

118 After marching through Georgia, Sherman's army reached Savannah on December 10 and occupied the city on December 21. Long, *The Civil War Day by Day*, 608, 613.

1865

January 1, 1865.

The year 1864 has gone forever—but its painful memories will linger with us throughout this mortal life. It will be vividly remembered by the present generation in Beaufort and New Bern, and if history fails to record its events it will be heard of by many, for ages to come, through the dim light of tradition. Dark as was the political night that shrouded it, still darker shades descended upon it when the pestilence spread over us its raven wings and breathed upon us its poisonous breath. Thoughtful minds, who witnessed its scenes of woe, will long look back upon it with feelings of sorrow and pain; and though it has gone by forever, it will long cast its gloomy shadows over the sunny paths of life. And as those who lost their dearest friends during that mournful period now enter upon the scene of the New Year, and look back to those friends, who were with them this day one year ago, they may exclaim, in sorrow,
   "Alas, how changed!—We see nor hear
   All whom we saw in the vanished year:
   They are gone from amongst us in silence down:
   To thy voiceless realm, Oh! Death, are gone!"[1]

January 12, 1865.

The Federal fleet, which since the last attack on Fort Fisher has been lingering in and near this port, sailed, or rather steamed off today, and

---

1   I believe this is a piece of original verse by Rumley.

the general impression seems to be that it has gone to renew the attack on that stronghold at New Inlet. General Terry[2] commands the land forces.

January 15, 1865.

The fleet has certainly gone to New Inlet and renewed the bombardment of Fort Fisher. We learn by arrivals from sea that troops with artillery have been landed in force near Masonboro sound, and the sound of cannon in the direction of New Inlet plainly indicates that fighting is going on there today. The deep anxiety which is felt here by many to know the result no tongue can tell.

January 17, 1865.

Last night, a little after one o'clock, a noise was heard, and a frightful shaking of houses, similar to that experienced on the 24th. ulto., was felt throughout the town. A grand explosion occurred somewhere.[3] The thoughts of all were turned to Fort Fisher. Something awful may have occurred there.

12 O'clock M. By an arrival from New Inlet this morning, we get the painful news of the fall of Fort Fisher on the 15th. Several unsuccessful assaults were made upon it by marines and land troops. They finally succeeded in entering the fort, where a desperate fight ensued which lasted three hours.[4]

---

2   Brigadier General Alfred H. Terry (1827–1890) took part in Butler's failed attempt to take Wilmington in December 1864. In January, after Butler was relieved, Terry was given command of the same forces and captured Fort Fisher on January 15, 1865, closing the last port of the Confederacy. Warner, *Generals in Blue*, 497–498; *Official Records, Army*, ser. 1, 46, pt. 1:396–399.

3   In the early morning hours of January 17, Confederate forces blew up Fort Caswell on Oak Island, which guarded the southern approaches to the Cape Fear River. Fort Caswell was located approximately 120 miles southwest of Beaufort. *Official Records, Army*, ser. 1, 46, pt. 1:399–401.

4   Brigadier General Alfred H. Terry's Union army captured Fort Fisher on January 15, 1865. *Official Records, Army*, ser. 1, pt. 1:396–399.

Same day.—Went to New Bern in obedience to a summons to attend a trial in the Provost Judges Court. One who had before the war been a frequent visitor to that town cannot now walk through its streets, and miss the hundreds of familiar faces so lately seen there, without feelings of the deepest sadness. The houses are still there except such as have been destroyed by fire, and the stately elms, now leafless, are there; and the beautiful waters of the Neuse and Trent still flow there, and sparkle in the sunshine as bright as ever; but the citizens are gone, and with them has gone all the interest that attached to the place. Most of them left New Bern when Burnside captured the place. Of those who remained, the yellow fever last fall swept off the larger portion; and now, few remnants of the population of 1861 are to be seen there.

As we stood on Broad Street, and looked at the site of the Washington Hotel, now stripped of every vestige of its former habitation, and the place where the old market stood, and thought of the happy crowds of citizens who used to assemble at those places, and then turned to the site of the old Court House, and thought of the eloquent voices that were heard in the better days of the country, within those walls that have perished forever, it seemed like we were viewing a city of the dead. It was the hour of sunset. The sky was clear; the winds were hushed; and a solemn silence reigned over the scene, interrupted only by the footsteps of a few Yankee soldiers and negroes, and the mournful strains of martial music that now and then fell upon the ear, from a band of musicians not far off who were trying to enliven the dullness of the evening, but only increased the sadness of the moment.

"We felt like one who treads alone
Some banquet hall deserted,
Whose lights are fled, whose garlands dead,
And all but he departed."[5]

On the morning of the 19th., we left the place, with no desire to see it again until its wandering exiles shall be gathered home. Civil law has vanished from the place. Military despotism sits enthroned there, while negro fanaticism rules the hour, and a new race inhabit the dwellings and walk the streets of the Elm City. On arriving at Morehead City, the pain-

---

5   Thomas Moore, "Oft in the Stilly Night," in Ward, *The English Poets*, 4:322.

ful sight presented itself of forty or fifty wounded Confederate soldiers, taken prisoners at Fort Fisher and brought to the Hospital at that place. Many of them were badly wounded. They were poorly clad, were squalid in their appearance, and looked forlorn and wretched beyond description. Poor fellows; how the sight of them made the heart bleed. The Confederate prisoners who were not wounded have been carried to Fortress Monroe.

We learn that the terrible shock felt in Beaufort on the night of the 17th., or morning of the 18th., inst., was the concussion produced by the blowing up of Fort Caswell by the Confederates.

January 29, 1865.

Lieut. Gen. Ulysses S. Grant appeared in town today. He has touched at this port from sea on his way somewhere. He came over from Morehead City in a small boat with his staff. They walked quietly through the town and departed for Morehead. A scheme is no doubt on foot for the capture of Wilmington.[6]

February [n.d.], 1865.

Troops are arriving at Morehead City from the north and the general belief is that a march into the interior of our state from Morehead City or New Bern is designed. Preparations are being made to lay the track of a railroad as the army advances. A thousand workmen have arrived at Morehead City within a few days for the ostensible purpose of working on the road. Others are already at New Bern.

February 8, 1865.

A very respectable young lady was arrested today while on her way from town to her home in the country, on suspicion of being engaged in car-

---

6   Lieutenant General Ulysses S. Grant and Brigadier General I. N. Palmer met in Beaufort. Grant had come from City Point, Virginia, while Palmer had traveled by train from New Bern. *North Carolina Times* (New Bern), February 3, 1865; *Official Records, Army*, ser. 1, 46, pt. 2:267.

rying contraband goods and letters to the Confederates.[7] Some letters and sundry articles of merchandise were concealed on her person. She was searched by a committee of three negro women, and afterwards by three white Yankee women. The insolence of one of the negroes and one of the white women was quite as much as the proud spirit of the prisoner could brook.

February 13, 1865.

The lady has been sent to New Bern for trial.

Maj. Graves[8] of the 1st. N.C. Volunteers, has been for several weeks past, and now is, the Provost Marshal of this place.

February 28, 1865.

Up to the present writing nothing has been done with the case of the above mentioned lady. She is confined as a prisoner at New Bern, in a house on Pollock Street. Miss Emeline J. Pigott is the lady referred to.

Since the fall of Fort Fisher, the star of the Confederacy seems to be on the wane, and, as far as we can ascertain, a general despondency prevails in every state. Sherman continues his triumphal march over Con-

---

7   Emeline Jamison Pigott (1835–1919) was arrested on February 8, 1865, for carrying numerous contraband goods through the lines to Confederates. She was imprisoned briefly in New Bern before being released without a trial. "Sketch of Miss Emeline Pigott," in Levi Woodbury Pigott Collection; Calvin Jarrett, "The Spy Was a Lady," *Greensboro Daily News*, September 29, 1963; entries dated February 7 and 8, 1865, [Emeline Pigott] Diary, Benjamin Franklin Royal Papers; entries dated February 9, 10, and 17, Edmund Janes Cleveland Diary; *Old North State* (Beaufort, N.C.), February 11, 1865; *Cemetery Records of Carteret County*, 314.

8   Major Charles C. Graves, commander of the 1st North Carolina Regiment (Union), was taken prisoner in September 1864 when the mail boat he was on was captured. He was soon released and returned to his regiment in December 1864. *Official Records, Army*, ser. 1, 33:485, 1057; Charles C. Graves File, 1st North Carolina Infantry Regiment, Compiled Military Service Records of Volunteer Union Soldiers Who Served in Organizations from the State of North Carolina, Record Group 94.12.2.

federate territory, and Columbia, South Carolina, has fallen before him.[9] Wilmington and Charleston have been evacuated by the Confederates.[10] These events seem to indicate that the main pillars of the Confederacy are falling away. But they may have a very different significance to that great military mind that now controls the movements of the Confederate armies—General Robert E Lee.[11] We will not despair while such a man lives in hope.

March 1, 1865.

Transports are daily arriving at this port with troops, who are landed at Morehead City. Over twenty thousand, it is estimated, have arrived within a week. Many of them are from Sherman's army south. They are designed to march into the interior of this state. The contemplation of what may follow makes us shudder.

March 1, 1865.

The women of the town are in trouble. They are required to take the hated oath of allegiance to the government of the United States. From the youngest of the sex who have arrived at the age of discretion, to the oldest, whether decrepit from age, lame, halt or blind, no exception is made.[12] All who are able to travel from home are required to go in person

---

9   Units from Sherman's 60,000-man army entered Columbia, South Caro-
     lina, on February 17. By February 18, much of the city had been burned to
     the ground. Long, *The Civil War Day by Day*, 640; McPherson, *Battle Cry of
     Freedom*, 828–829.

10   Confederate troops evacuated Charleston, South Carolina, on February 18
     and Wilmington, North Carolina, on February 22. Long, *The Civil War Day
     by Day*, 640, 642; McPherson, *Battle Cry of Freedom*, 828–829.

11   Maj. Gen. Robert E. Lee was named general-in-chief of all Confederate forces
     on January 31, 1865. Denney, *The Civil War Years*, 524.

12   A Union soldier's diary confirms that after Emeline Pigott's arrest, Federal
     authorities required all women to take the oath of allegiance. Entry dated
     February 17, 1865, Edmund Janes Cleveland Diary.

to the Provost Marshal's office, through a motley, filthy, insolent crowd of negroes, Yankees and Buffaloes, to submit to the humiliation.

"What a fall is here, my countrymen!"

March 11, 1865.

Many thousand Federal troops marched from New Bern several days ago for Kinston. News comes to us that the place has fallen.

March 12, 1865.

The report of the fall of Kinston is contradicted. The Yankees were met by a large Confederate force this side of Kinston and were successfully resisted. Severe fighting occurred, but reports of the result are very conflicting.[13]

March 13, 1865.

Report says that great preparations are being made at New Bern for the Federal wounded soldiers, and the indications are that a good deal of fighting on that line is expected. Reinforcements for the army at New Bern are constantly arriving at this port, and are rapidly hurried to the front.

March 20, 1865.

Kinston has been evacuated by the Confederates, and occupied by the Federals. Probably some movement of Sherman, who, since he left Columbia, has been supposed to have designs upon North Carolina, has rendered the evacuation of Kinston necessary. The movement upon Kin-

---

13 On March 8–10, 1865, at the Battle of Wise's Forks, also known as the Battle of Kinston, Confederates under General Braxton Bragg slowed (but could not stop) the Union advance on Goldsboro. *Official Records, Army*, ser. 1, 47, pt.1:977–979, 1078–1079.

ston seems to us to be one of great importance. Perhaps the Confederates underestimate it. Sherman himself attaches much importance to it, we infer, from the fact that large reinforcements and supplies are sent here from the south to sustain it.

Our waters are covered with transports of every size, laden with men and supplies. Vessels laden with army stores, sent from the north to Port Royal,[14] after arriving at Port Royal, have been ordered with their cargo to this port.

March 21st., 1865.

Yesterday evening, a negro man was shot about a mile and a half from town, on the North River road, by some person unknown. The negro died. Nobody seems to care much about it. Before the war such an occurrence would have excited to a high degree the whole of this community.

March 25, 1865.

Federal forces from Kinston have occupied Goldsboro. News reaches us also that Sherman was at Fayetteville, on the 12th. inst. Prop after prop of the Confederacy falls before the Yankee host. We have rumors of a great fight between Sherman's forces and the Confederates somewhere between Goldsboro and Raleigh.[15] These rumors represent a three days' fight, commencing on Sunday the 19th. inst., in which the Confederates were victorious on the first day, but were totally discomfited on the third. We wait anxiously for more reliable intelligence.

---

14   Port Royal, South Carolina.

15   From March 19 to 21, 1865, at Bentonville, North Carolina, General Joseph E. Johnston's 20,000 Confederates battled the 30,000 Federals under General Oliver O. Howard that composed the right wing of Sherman's army. On March 21, Johnston's army retreated. Denney, *The Civil War Years*, 548–549.

March 28, 1865.

Papers inform us that a fight occurred on the 16th., at Averasboro, on the Cape Fear River, between Sherman's forces from Fayetteville bound to Raleigh, and the Confederates under Gen. Hardee,[16] in which the Yankees were checked with serious loss; and that another fight took place on the 19th. between Goldsboro and Raleigh between the Eastern Corps of Sherman's army, and the Confederates under Gen. Johnston[17] in which the Yanks were checked. The Yankees here say nothing about the matter.

March 30, 1865.

A sad looking consignment of more than two hundred negroes, mostly women and children, landed in town yesterday from a steamer in the harbor. They are from the South—probably from the rice fields of South Carolina and are some of Sherman's stolen trophies. Excepting perhaps the wretched victims of African slave trade, a more miserable looking, gaunt, ragged, black, smutty gang of negroes was never seen on God's fair earth. Some were already sinking under disease and tottered as they walked. Most of them were marched up to the Baptist Church, where four of them died last night. The grave will soon close over many more of them. Poor wretches! Their path to freedom will be strewn with their dead.

April 1, 1865.

The Yankee papers are in great glee over the disaster of the Confederates near Petersburg on the 25th. The Confederates took Fort Steadman, but

---

16 General William J. Hardee's small force of Confederates fought a delaying action against the left wing of Sherman's army under the command of General Henry Slocum at Averasboro, North Carolina. Slocum's troops drove the Confederates back on March 16, 1865. Denney, *The Civil War Years,* 547.

17 Battle of Bentonville, March 19–21, 1865.

afterwards lost it, with nearly 3000 men, chiefly prisoners.[18] So say the papers.

April 4, 1865.

Reports have reached here that a large United States steamer from Wilmington, bound North with 300 discharged soldiers and a large number of refugees on board, perished by fire off Hatteras a few evenings ago, and about 700 persons were lost.[19]

April 6, 1865.

Papers received today confirm the report of the disaster referred to. The name of the steamer was *Gen. Lyon*.[20] About 500 lives were lost.

April 6, 1865.

News came by the cars today of the fall of Richmond.[21] The papers give accounts of some fighting in that vicinity on the first and second inst., but leave the result in doubt. Dispatches later than the papers give the terrible

---

18   Robert E. Lee's Army of Northern Virginia launched an attack at Fort Stedman, a Union redoubt east of Petersburg, on March 25, 1865. Lee was trying to puncture Union lines to relieve the pressure on Petersburg by forcing General Ulysses S. Grant to retract his siege lines. The Confederates were initially successful before Union reinforcements drove them back, inflicting heavy losses on Lee's weakened army. Heidler and Heidler, eds., *Encyclopedia of the American Civil War*, 2:753.

19   The steamer *General Lyon* sailed from Wilmington, North Carolina, on March 29, 1865, with approximately 600 passengers, most of whom were discharged soldiers, paroled prisoners of war, and refugees. The steamer caught fire in the midst of a storm off Cape Hatteras on March 30, 1865, and burned to the waterline. Only thirty-four of the passengers and crew survived. *New York Times*, April 3 and 14, 1865; *Times* (London), April 27, 1865.

20   The steamer was named after General Nathaniel Lyon (1818–1861), who was killed at the Battle of Wilson's Creek, near Springfield, Missouri, on August 10, 1861. Warner, *Generals in Blue*, 286–287.

21   Richmond and Petersburg, Virginia, fell to Union forces on April 3. Long, *The Civil War Day by Day*, 665.

result. While we write, the bells of all the churches in town are ringing to tell the joy the Yankees feel over the news. Soldiers are running to and fro in wild delight.

April 9, 1865.

The news of the fall of Richmond has been confirmed. It was evacuated by the Confederates on the 2nd. inst., and was occupied by the Federals on the morning of the 3rd.

April 12, 1865.

News comes today of the surrender, by Gen. Lee, of the Army of Northern Virginia![22] This is too astounding to believe without confirmation. But one hundred guns were fired at Fort Macon on receipt of the news.

April 14, 1865.

The report, on the 12th., of the surrender of the army of Northern Virginia, is confirmed today. An illumination is ordered.

The friends of the Confederacy are pale with despair, and their countenance gives "signs of woe, that all is lost."[23]

The poor negroes lately brought here from the south are dying fast. They lie down on the bare ground and die, in the rear of the town, without any assistance from those of their own color or the devils who brought them here. A lady lately went out among them, and saw a woman lying on the sand, in the open air, dying, with sand on her face and in her mouth, dying. Oh, Philanthropy! "How many crimes are committed in thy name."[24]

---

22 Robert E. Lee surrendered the Army of Northern Virginia on April 9, 1865, at Appomattox Court House, Virginia. Long, *The Civil War Day by Day*, 670.

23 Milton, *Paradise Lost*, bk. 9, line 784, in Eliot, *The Complete Poems of John Milton*, 280.

24 This is a play on the purported last words of Madame Roland, wife of the duke of Orleans, before she was executed by guillotine on November 8, 1793, in France. Roland's words were, "O Liberty, how many crimes are committed in thy name!" Burke, *The Annual Register*, 281.

April 18, 1865.

Dispatches from Fortress Monroe to New Bern announce the sudden and violent death of Abraham Lincoln. He was shot in a Theatre on the evening of the 14th., inst. at Washington City. Seward and one of his sons were badly, perhaps mortally, wounded, at Seward's dwelling.[25] Seward was at his room where he had been confined some days by injuries received in his carriage while riding out. The numerous ships in the harbor have displayed their colors at half mast.

April 21, 1865.

The report of the death of Lincoln is confirmed. He was shot in the head by John Wilkes Booth,[26] at a Theatre, on the night of the 14th. and expired on the morning of the 15th. inst. The assassination was a horrible deed. But the poor murdered man has gone down to his grave with the blood of a million of his countrymen upon him, and followed no doubt by the secret curses of millions more. For a word of conciliation and friendship from him, four years ago, would have prevented the secession of the border states and might have saved the country without the shedding of one drop of blood. The people cannot forget his Emancipation Proclamation, calculated, and no doubt designed, to upheave and ruin the whole mass of Southern society, by insurrections with all their attendant horrors, nor can they forget that this grand, this unparalleled usurpation of power was followed by the arming of negroes of the south against their masters, an

---

25   President Lincoln and his wife attended Ford's Theater in Washington on April 14, where Lincoln was assassinated by John Wilkes Booth. On the same night, Secretary of State William H. Seward's son, Frederick, was gravely injured by Booth's fellow conspirator Lewis Powell (also known as Lewis Payne). Powell attacked Frederick in an unsuccessful attempt to assassinate Secretary Seward in Seward's home. Donald, *Lincoln*, 594, 597; Van Deusen, *William Henry Seward*, 413–415.

26   John Wilkes Booth (1838–1865) was a strongly pro-southern Virginia-born actor. After he assassinated Lincoln, Booth fled and was killed on April 26, 1865, when Union cavalry caught him in rural Maryland. Heidler and Heidler, eds., *Encyclopedia of the American Civil War*, 1:250–252.

outrage against humanity and civilized warfare, which will blacken the memory of the deceased President forever.

April 26, 1865.

Yesterday, a large meeting was held at the Front Street House to express the sense of the people in relation to the late assassination of the President of the United States. Mr. Rich,[27] Mr. Satterthwait,[28] Mr. Warren,[29] and Dr. Arendell[30] &c, were speakers. Their condemnation of the crime of assassination of the President was all right. But several speakers, and especially Mr. Satterthwait, took occasion to glorify, in strains of lofty grandiloquence, the "Old flag," which was displayed above their heads. Mr. S. seemed to have forgotten that those bright stars and stripes, since he saw them four years ago, had become the bloody ensign of a tribe of brutal fanatics and tyrants, and that the flag was now polluted by bands of armed negroes who had been taken from masters who had spent their lives in upholding and sustaining that Union it was intended to symbolize; that in this town it had been hoisted over negro recruiting offices, where runaway slaves were enlisted and armed against their masters, and in short, that it had been prostituted to the vilest purposes that ever dis-

27 Ulysses H. Ritch (1819–1866) was a Washington, North Carolina, shipbuilder and Unionist. After briefly serving as treasury agent in Washington in early 1864, he was appointed local special treasury agent for New Bern in May 1864. *North Carolina Times* (New Bern), May 18, 1864; David Heaton to Ulysses H. Ritch, 1864, Myers House Papers; Ulysses H. Ritch to Benjamin S. Hedrick, October 17, 1863, Benjamin Sherwood Hedrick Papers.

28 Fenner B. Satterthwaite was a delegate to the secession convention and the constitutional conventions of 1861–1862 and 1865–1866. He served as president of the Council of State from 1863 to 1864. Cheney, *North Carolina Government*, 179, 386, 825, 832.

29 Edward Jenner Warren (1824–1876) was a lawyer and old-line Whig. As a delegate to the secession convention, he supported North Carolina's withdrawal from the Union. He also represented Beaufort County in the state senate during the war. Powell, *Dictionary of North Carolina Biography*, 6:125–126.

30 Michael F. Arendell (1819–1894), a doctor and a member of a prominent Beaufort family, served as state senator from 1850 to 1854 and again from 1860 to 1865. *Cemetery Records of Carteret County*, 148; *Cyclopedia of Eminent and Representative Men*, 2:563–565.

graced a civilized nation. Oblivious memory. Half hour guns are fired at Fort Macon today in honor of the late President. This is the day, we understand, on which his body is interred at Springfield.[31]

April 27, 1865.

A dispatch has been received at Morehead City, we are told, announcing the surrender of Gen. Johnston, with all his forces, now stationed west of Raleigh in this state.[32] If this be true, the fate of the Confederacy is sealed. Its sun has set forever.

"And who would soar the solar height,
To set in such a starless night?"[33]

May 4, 1865.

The Hon. S.P. Chase,[34] the present Chief Justice of the United States, arrived in port today, in the U.S. Rev Cutter *Wagander*,[35] commanded by Captain Merriman.[36] A national salute was fired in his honor. Dr.

---

31 President Lincoln was buried at Oak Ridge Cemetery in Springfield, Illinois, on May 4, 1865, after a 1,700-mile trip by funeral train throughout the North. Heidler and Heidler, eds., *Encyclopedia of the American Civil War*, 3:1193.

32 General Joseph E. Johnston surrendered his Confederate army to General William T. Sherman on April 26, 1865, at the Bennett homestead near modern-day Durham, North Carolina. Denney, *The Civil War Years*, 563.

33 Rumley is slightly misquoting Lord Byron's poem "Ode to Napoleon Bonaparte." The actual verse reads: "But who would soar the solar height, to set in such a starless night." Bryant, *A Library of Poetry and Song*, 712.

34 Salmon P. Chase (1808–1873) was secretary of the treasury until he resigned the office in July 1864 in disagreement with Lincoln over how to administer Reconstruction. When Chief Justice Roger B. Taney died in October 1864, Lincoln appointed Chase to the position. Heidler and Heidler, eds., *Encyclopedia of the American Civil War*, 1:408–410.

35 The ship was actually named the *Wayanda*. *Official Records, Army*, ser. 1, 47, pt. 3:410–411.

36 James H. Merryman was captain of the *Wayanda*. In June 1863, he had participated in an attempt to recapture the revenue cutter *Caleb Cushing*, which had been captured by Confederates at Portland, Maine. Merryman and others captured the crew but only after the Confederates had scuttled the cutter. Niven, *Salmon P. Chase Papers*, 1:540n64; *Official Records, Navy*, ser. 1, 2:325–326.

Arendell and the writer of these notes, being invited on board, paid a visit to the distinguished gentleman.[37] He received us courteously and kindly, discoursed freely upon the present posture of affairs in North Carolina, and, for himself and the people of the North, expressed towards the people of this state the most friendly sentiments. While people of smaller minds are breathing out threatenings and slaughter against Jefferson Davis, it was gratifying to hear this man speak of the fallen chief in most respectful terms. He disclaimed any intention on the part of the government to deal harshly with the leaders of the late revolution. On the negro question, we were sorry to perceive, he gave indications of very radical views. He is evidently in favor of extending the right of suffrage to the race. We suggested to him that this question ought to be left to the Legislatures of the several states to settle for themselves after reconstruction. Rev. Dr. Fuller,[38] of Baltimore, and several other gentlemen,[39] accompany Mr. Chase. The latter goes to New Bern this after afternoon.

May 6, 1865.

Mr. Chase visited Beaufort today. He spent over an hour in the Court House, looking over old records and talking familiarly with several gentlemen present.[40] His exalted position prevents him from indulging in

---

37 Salmon P. Chase confirmed in his journals and in a letter to his daughter that Dr. Arendell and "Mr. Rumley Clerk of County Court" paid a visit to Chase aboard the *Wayanda*. Niven, *Salmon P. Chase Papers*, 1:538; 5:34–35.

38 Rev. Richard Fuller, D.D. (1804–1876) was a well-known Baptist minister of Seventh Baptist Church in Baltimore, Maryland. A native of Beaufort, South Carolina, Fuller had graduated from Harvard and worked as a lawyer in his hometown before becoming a minister and beginning his ministry in Baltimore in 1847. Fuller, who supported the Union, was well known for his discourses on the religious view of slavery. Howard, *The Monumental City*, 523–526.

39 One of the other gentlemen was Whitelaw Reid (1837–1912), a northern journalist and antislavery partisan who wrote a book about his tour of the South with Salmon P. Chase. He recorded his impressions of this encounter in his book *After the War*. Reid, *After the War*, 23–27.

40 Salmon P. Chase confirmed this engagement and Rumley's presence, saying "Went to Clerks office—Mr. Rumley Clk showed me old records 1724 and forward." Niven, *Salmon P. Chase Papers*, 1:540.

any harsh language towards the people of the south. He is all kindness. But we do not forget his antecedents.

May 20, 1865.

Nearly all the Confederate troops belonging to this county have returned to their homes. Refugees from Carteret and Craven, whom we have not seen for three years past, appear daily on our streets. Citizens and soldiers are passing up and down the country as they did in better days. The curtain which for three years past has hid the interior of our state from our view, is drawn up and we can now take an inside view. But we behold there nothing but the wreck and ruins of the late powerful Confederacy. Reports have reached us that Jefferson Davis, the late head of the Confederacy, has been captured in the southern part of Georgia while trying to reach the coast.[41] All the signs indicate that the Confederacy is lost, and that the war is over.

Therefore, "to thy tents O Israel,"[42] there to take counsel together.

The trans-Mississippi Army is the only Confederate force which has not surrendered.

Mr. Davis has been carried to Fortress Monroe and closely confined in one of the casemates of the Fort. Mr. Stevens, the late Vice President of the Confederate States has been arrested in Georgia and carried to Fort Warren.[43]

---

41   Confederate president Jefferson Davis and his family were captured by the 4th Michigan Cavalry Regiment near Irwinville, Georgia, early on the morning of May 10, 1865. Denney, *The Civil War Years*, 569.

42   1 Kings 12:16.

43   Confederate vice president Alexander Stephens was arrested at his home in Crawfordville, Georgia, on May 11, 1865, and was imprisoned in Fort Warren in Boston Harbor until his release in October 1865. Foote, *The Civil War*, 3:1012.

May 31, 1865.

News received today that that Trans-Mississippi Army under Gen. Kirby Smith has surrendered.[44] So ends the contest in the field. We must now look to the halls of legislation.

June 5, 1865.

The first time since the commencement of the late war, negro troops have been sent here to garrison the town.[45] The sight of them is most revolting to southerners. Their presence here is deeply humiliating to the citizens, who bear it however as best they can, hoping they will soon be relieved of the nuisance, and that this may be the last degree in degradation to which they may have to descend.

For three years past, we have dreaded, as one of the results of subjugation, that the north would insist on placing the negroes on an equality with the white man at the ballot box. That this was the design of the Lincoln Cabinet and Lincoln himself the late declarations of Mr. Chase and the present tone of the Black Republican Journals of the north clearly show. The dread of this revolting degradation has long darkened our hopes of the future. But when the hour had come for the scoundrels of the north to develop their infernal scheme, in the mysterious providence of God Lincoln was removed from the theatre of his power forever, and the executive power of the government passed into the hands of Andrew

---

44 General Edmund Kirby Smith surrendered his army in Galveston, Texas, based on terms drawn up in New Orleans on May 26, 1865. Denney, *The Civil War Years*, 575.

45 I have been unable to identify the specific unit to which Rumley is referring. The 14th Regiment, U.S. Colored Heavy Artillery, which numbered 1,085 men in May 1865, was stationed in Morehead City from November 1864 to August 1865, when they were removed to Fort Macon. It is possible that a company of this regiment was stationed in Beaufort briefly in June. Richard M. Reid, *Freedom for Themselves*, 256–260.

Johnson,[46] a Southern man by birth and education, who knows too much of mental incapacity of the negro, and too much of southern sentiments, even among Union men, to attempt to force the bitter cup of negro suffrage down the throats of his conquered and afflicted countrymen. His Proclamation of the 29th. of May, declaring William W. Holden[47] Provisional Governor of North Carolina, and directing preliminary measures [*for*] the reorganization of the state government, expressly recognizes the right of the state to control the whole question of suffrage! The proclamation disfranchises and proscribes a good many of our worthy citizens.[48] We wish this had not been the case. But the document removes the blackest cloud that hung over us. We therefore welcome it with inexpressible relief and satisfaction. It inspired new hopes within us and to our view cast a radiant light over the dark horizon of the future.

---

46   Andrew Johnson (1808–1875), a former senator and military governor of Tennessee, was elected as Lincoln's vice-president in the November 1864 presidential election and assumed the office of the presidency upon Lincoln's assassination. While Johnson wanted to reduce the political power of planters, he did not share the interest of Radical Republicans in guaranteeing civil rights for freed slaves in the South, which led to a contentious term during Reconstruction. Heidler and Heidler, eds. *Encyclopedia of the American Civil War*, 3:1071–1072.

47   William Woods Holden (1818–1892) was editor and publisher of the *North Carolina Standard* of Raleigh and leader of the state's wartime peace movements. He was later elected governor as a Republican in 1868 and was impeached and removed from office in 1871. Powell, *Dictionary of North Carolina Biography*, 3:169–170.

48   On May 29, 1865, Andrew Johnson issued two proclamations. The first granted amnesty and a pardon for all former Confederates who took an oath of loyalty to the United States, but it excluded fourteen classes of white southerners, including those who owned more than $20,000 worth of property before the war. The second proclamation appointed William Woods Holden as provisional governor of North Carolina and charged him with calling a convention to rewrite the state's prewar constitution. Eric Foner, *A Short History of Reconstruction*, 85.

June 11, 1865.

The presence of a negro garrison in Beaufort creates immense dissatisfaction among all classes of white citizens. Never during the darkest hours of the dark of the war have the whites realized such a sense of degradation as they now feel, and never have they felt so keenly the loss of liberty. These black imps of the demon of fanaticism, intoxicated with the idea of universal negro freedom, very naturally forget the limits of their military duties, and to show authority over the whites, go much farther, in many instances, in annoying citizens than Yankee soldiers have ever gone. Their "air," their "fantastic tricks," and their insolence of manner are bad enough to bear. But they go farther than these. A few nights ago, they interfered with a sailing party of white gentlemen and ladies as they were about leaving the wharf to take refreshing night air upon the water and broke up the party, although upon inquiry at the General's office, it seems the negroes had no authority to molest the company. But they were not punished. The negro sergeant went into a store where a white man, the proprietor, a transient resident, was talking rather boisterously to another, when the negro sergeant ordered the said proprietor to "stop it." The proprietor, not knowing how to act when accosted in such a manner by a negro, rebuked the rascal for his impertinence, upon which the negro seized him by the collar and calling his guard took the outraged man to the Provost's office. The man was discharged and the negro not even rebuked for the outrage as far as we knew. A negro who was not a soldier assaulted a white man in town, we are informed, and beat him severely. Several of these negro soldiers were present and encouraged the negro and deterred white citizens from interfering. They were heard to say they intended to let the white men know that they (the negro soldiers) would rule over them.

A retired Federal white soldier was assaulted on the road while going from town to his home in the country and severely beaten by two of the wretches for his well known hostility to them as soldiers. Some of their talk with each other, and with their sergeant, as to their behavior towards the whites in this place, has been overheard and is of such a character as to cause serious apprehension.

Steps will be taken to have them removed. Their presence has a bad effect upon the black population of the place, and if continued may produce serious consequences. Terrible is the darkness that is now upon us, and horrible when contrasted with the light of happier days, when we were under a white man's government, in the enjoyment of civil liberty and law. "Jerusalem remembered in the days of her affliction and of her miseries, all her pleasant things that she had in the days of old."[49]

June 15, 1865.

A meeting of the citizens was called at the Court House today to organize a police force for the Beaufort District. Capt. Butler[50] of the U.S. Army superintended the organization. Thirty-five citizens were enrolled and sworn in. Others will be enrolled in other parts of the county. When the company is armed, it is probable the negro garrison will be removed.

A full brigade of negroes is stationed on this harbor and is under the command of Gen. Bates.[51] Fort Macon, Beaufort, Morehead City, and points above, are garrisoned by these savage descendants of Ham.[52] A quartermaster at Morehead City shot one of them dead a few days ago for dis[orderly] and mutinous conduct.

June 24, 1865.

A large number of dischar[ged Confederate] prisoners have arrived at Morehead [City from] northern prisons, within a few da[ys' journey] to their homes. It is melancholy to [think how] many who were carried to those [ms. torn] will never return.

---

49   Lamentations 1:7.
50   I have been unable to locate this Captain Butler in any of the official sources.
51   There is no record of a General Bates in the Union army.
52   Slavery defenders justified slavery on the grounds that Africans were descended from Noah's son, Ham, whom Noah cursed for uncovering his father's nakedness. The belief is that Ham's sons settled Africa and were cursed to be the "servant of servants." Genesis 9:20–25.

"Far from their friends and from [*their native shore*]
Silent they sleep, and hear of [*wars no more*]."[53]

July 1, 1865.

Ten Justices of the [*Peace, appointed*] by the Provisional Governor, [*ms. torn*] today, and took the oa[*th*] [*ms. torn*] their qualification. [*The*] Commissioners appointed for the [*ms. torn*] met at the Court House and Orga[*nized*] [*ms. torn*] first steps taken in this place to [*ms. torn*] restoration of Civil Law. The [*ms. torn*]

July 4, 1865.

This ann[*iversary was celebrated*] by the negroes only. They got up [*ms. torn*] and marched up and down the [*ms. torn*] and then to the Oak grove east of [*ms. torn*] a most incendiary harangue was d[*elivered, we*] understand, by a mula[*tto named*] Galloway, heretofore mentioned ch[*ms. torn*] reference to negro suffrage,[54] a privilege [*ms. torn*] says the[*y*] must and shall have. The negroes [*ms. torn*] behaved well. The whites look sullen and sad. How can they be otherwise.

July 6, 1865.

The commissioners of the town having entered upon their duties, the Commanding General (Bates) has sent off the negro garrison, much to the relief and gratification of the whole white population.

---

53 Rumley is slightly altering a quotation from Alexander Pope's translation of Homer's *Iliad*, bk. III, lines 312–314. The verse actually reads: "Wrapt in the cold embraces of the tomb; Adorn'd with honours in their native shore, Silent they slept, and heard of wars no more." Pope, *The Iliad*, 1:118.

54 Rumley had previously discussed a speech Abraham Galloway (1837–1870) gave on black political rights in Beaufort in his first entry of 1864, titled "Beginning of 1864." For more biographical information on Galloway, see note 3 of chapter 3 in this volume.

August [n.d.], 1865.

All our exiles are now home. No military force is now stationed in our midst and our place begins to look natural. The dark night which settled upon us in March 1862 is passing away. And though the day upon which we are entering is not clear, and shadows rest upon the horizon, yet we hope, as the day advances, the clouds may roll away, and the skies may grow brighter than the early dawn assures, and over the day, we trust that no night of starless gloom like that we have passed through may ever come.

And here we close!

BIBLIOGRAPHY

Manuscript Collections

Alfred H. Martine Papers, 1862–1865. Southern Historical Collection, Wilson Library, University of North Carolina, Chapel Hill, North Carolina.

Alida F. Fales Papers. State Archives, Division of Archives and History, Raleigh, North Carolina.

Benjamin Franklin Royal Papers, 1713–1891. Southern Historical Collection, Wilson Library, University of North Carolina, Chapel Hill, North Carolina.

Benjamin Sherwood Hedrick Papers, 1848–1893. Rare Book, Manuscript, and Special Collections Library, Duke University, Durham, North Carolina.

Biographical Directory of the General Assembly Photo Collection. State Archives, Division of Archives and History, Raleigh, North Carolina.

Civil War Collection. American Antiquarian Society, Worcester, Massachusetts.

Daniel Read Larned Papers. Manuscript Division, Library of Congress, Washington, D.C.

David S. Reid Papers. State Archives, Division of Archives and History, Raleigh, North Carolina.

Edmund Janes Cleveland Diary, 1864–1865. Southern Historical Collection, Wilson Library, University of North Carolina, Chapel Hill, North Carolina.

F. C. Salisbury Collection. State Archives, Division of Archives and History, Raleigh, North Carolina.

George H. Johnston Papers, 1861–1871. Southern Historical Collection, Wilson Library, University of North Carolina, Chapel Hill, North Carolina.

Governor's Papers—John Willis Ellis. State Archives, Division of Archives and History, Raleigh, North Carolina.

Horace James Correspondence, 1852–1870. American Antiquarian Society, Worcester, Massachusetts.

James Manney Papers, 1847–1851. Southern Historical Collection, Wilson Library, University of North Carolina, Chapel Hill, North Carolina.

Levi Woodbury Pigott Collection. State Archives, Division of Archives and History, Raleigh, North Carolina.

Marriage Bonds. Carteret County, North Carolina. State Archives, Division of Archives and History, Raleigh, North Carolina.

Minutes of the Carteret County Court of Pleas and Quarters, 1858–1868. Volume 19. State Archives, Division of Archives and History, Raleigh, North Carolina.

Myers House Papers. George H. and Laura E. Brown Library, Washington, North Carolina.

Papers of James Chaplin Beecher. Schlesinger Library, Radcliffe Institute for Advanced Study, Harvard University, Cambridge, Massachusetts.

Papers of Joseph Barlow. United States Army Military History Institute, Carlisle, Pennsylvania.

R. G. Dun & Co. Collection. Baker Library, Harvard Business School, Harvard University, Cambridge, Massachusetts.

Records of Committees relating to Claims, 1794–1946, Southern Claims Commission, 1871–1880, Disallowed Claims, Record Group 233.8. National Archives and Records Administration, Washington, D.C.

Records of Named Departments. Department of North Carolina. Record Group 393.4. National Archives and Records Administration, Washington, D.C.

Records Relating to Volunteer Union Organizations. Record Group 94.2.4. National Archives and Records Administration, Washington, D.C.

Microfilmed Government Documents

Eighth Census of the United States, 1860. Multiple Counties. Population and Slave Schedules. National Archives, Washington, D.C. Microfilm available at University of Georgia Libraries, Athens, Georgia

Ninth Census of the United States, 1870. Carteret County, North Carolina. Population and Slave Schedules. National Archives, Washington, D.C. Microfilm, University of Georgia Libraries, Athens, Georgia

Seventh Census of the United States, 1850. Multiple Counties. Population and Slave Schedules. National Archives, Washington, D.C. Microfilm, University of Georgia Libraries, Athens, Georgia

Sixth Census of the United States, 1840. Carteret County, North Carolina. Population and Slave Schedules. National Archives, Washington, D.C. Microfilm, University of Georgia Libraries, Athens, Georgia

Newspapers and Periodicals

Beaufort News, 1923, 1929, 1937
Carteret County Telephone, 1881
Freedman's Advocate (New York), 1864
Greensboro Daily News, 1963
Halcyon and Beaufort Intelligencer, 1854
The Liberator (Boston), 1862
The Look Out (Beaufort, N.C.), 1910
New Bern Daily Progress, 1860–1863
New York Daily Times, 1857
New York Times, 1865
North Carolina Times (New Bern), 1865
Old North State (Beaufort, N.C.), 1865
Times (London), 1865

Primary Sources

Addison, Joseph. *Cato: A Tragedy.* Boston: Mean and Fleeming, 1767.

Allen, George. *Forty-Six Months with the Fourth R. I. Volunteers in the War of 1861 to 1865: Comprising a History of the Marches, Battles, and Camp Life, Compiled from Journals Kept While on Duty in the Field and Camp, by Corp. Geo. H. Allen, of Company B.* Providence: J. A. & R. A. Reid, Printers, 1887.

American Missionary Association. *Eighteenth Annual Report of the American Missionary Association.* New York: American Missionary Association, 1864.

Barden, John R., ed. *Letters to the Home Circle: The North Carolina Service of Pvt. Henry A. Clapp, Company F, Forty-fourth Massachusetts Volunteer Militia, 1862–1863.* Raleigh: Division of Archives and History, North Carolina Department of Cultural Resources, 1998.

Bates, Charlotte Fiske. *The Cambridge Book of Poetry and Song.* New York: Thomas Y. Crowell and Company, 1910.

Benjamin, W. S. *The Great Epidemic in New Berne and Vicinity: September and October 1864, by One Who Passed through It.* New Berne, N.C.: George Mills Joy, 1865.

Blackstone, William. *Abridgement of Blackstone's Commentaries.* Ed. William C. Sprague. 2nd ed. Detroit: Sprague Correspondence School of Law, 1893.

Boatner, Mark M., III. *The Civil War Dictionary.* Rev. ed. New York: Vintage, 1988.

Bouvier, John. *A Law Dictionary, Adapted to the Constitution and Laws of the United States of America, and of the Several States of the American Union: With Reference* to the Civil and Other Systems of Foreign Law. 14th ed. Philadelphia: J. B. Lippincott & Co., 1874.

Browning, Judkin, and Michael Thomas Smith, eds. Letters from a North Carolina Unionist: John A. Hedrick to Benjamin S. Hedrick, 1862–1865. Raleigh: Division of Archives and History, North Carolina Department of Cultural Resources, 2001.

Bryant, William Cullen, comp. A Library of Poetry and Song: Being Choice Selections from the Best Poets. New York: J. B. Ford and Company, 1872.

Burke, Edmund, ed. The Annual Register, or a View of History, Politics, and Literature for the Year 1793; a New Edition. London: Baldwin, Cradock, and Joy, 1821.

Butler, Benjamin F. Autobiography and Personal Reminiscences of Major-General Benjamin F. Butler: Butler's Book. Boston: A. M. Thayer, 1892.

Cemetery Records of Carteret County. Carteret Historical Research Association, n.d.

Chase, Salmon P. Advice after Appomattox: Letters to Andrew Johnson, 1865–1866. Ed. Brooks D. Simpson, Leroy P. Graf, and John Muldowny. Knoxville: University of Tennessee Press, 1987.

Cheney, John L., ed. North Carolina Government: 1585–1974, a Narrative and Statistical History. Raleigh: North Carolina Department of the Secretary of State, 1975.

Ciment, James, ed. Colonial America: An Encyclopedia of Social, Political, Cultural, and Economic History. 5 vols. Armonk, N.Y.: M. E. Sharpe, Inc., 2006.

Civil War Naval Chronology, 1861–1865. Washington, D.C.: Navy Department, 1961.

Clark, Walter, ed. Histories of the Several Regiments and Battalions from North Carolina in the Great War, 1861–' 65. Vol. 3. Goldsboro, [N.C.]: Nash Brothers, 1901.

Cyclopedia of Eminent and Representative Men of the Carolinas of the Nineteenth Century. Vol. 2. Madison, Wis.: Brant and Fuller, 1892.

Dana, Charles Anderson, comp. The Household Book of Poetry. 5th ed. New York: D. Appleton and Company, 1859.

De Forest, B. S. Random Sketches and Wandering Thoughts; or What I Saw in Camp, on the March, the Bivouac, the Battlefield and Hospital, while with the Army in Virginia, North and South Carolina, during the Late Rebellion. Albany, N.Y.: Avery Herrick, Publishers, 1866.

Denney, Robert E. The Civil War Years: A Day-by-Day Chronicle of the Life of a Nation. New York: Sterling Publishing, 1992.

Denny, J. Waldo. Wearing the Blue in the Twenty-Fifth Mass. Volunteer Infantry, with Burnside's Coast Division, 18th Army Corps, and Army of the James. Worcester, Mass.: Putnam & Davis, Publishers, 1879.

Drake, J. Madison. The History of the Ninth New Jersey Veteran Vols., A Record of Its

Service from Sept. 13th, 1861, to July 12th, 1865. Elizabeth, N.J.: Journal Printing House, 1889.

Dyer, Frederick H. *A Compendium of the War of the Rebellion.* 2 vols. Dayton, Ohio: Morningside Press, Broadfoot Publishing, 1994.

Eliot, Charles W., ed. *The Complete Poems of John Milton.* Vol. 4 of *The Harvard Classics.* New York: P. F. Collier & Son Corporation, 1937.

———. *The Divine Comedy of Dante Alighieri.* Trans. Henry F. Cary. Vol. 20 of *The Harvard Classics.* New York: P. F. Collier & Son Corporation, 1937.

Fuller, Andrew. *The Works of Reverend Andrew Fuller.* 8 vols. New Haven, Conn.: S. Converse, 1824.

Garraty, John A., and Mark C. Carnes, eds. *American National Biography.* 24 vols. New York: Oxford University Press, 1999.

Heidler, David S., and Jeanne T., eds. *Encyclopedia of the American Civil War: A Political, Social, and Military History.* 5 vols. Santa Barbara, Calif.: ABC-CLIO Press, 2000.

Heitman, Francis B. *Historical Register and Dictionary of the United States Army.* 2 vols. Washington, D.C.: Government Printing Office, 1903.

Hemans, Felicia Dorothea Browne. *The Poetical Works of Mrs. Felicia Hemans, Complete in One Volume.* Philadelphia: Grigg & Elliot, 1836.

Hemenway, Abby Maria, ed. *The Vermont Historical Gazetteer: A Magazine, Embracing a History of Each Town.* Burlington, Vt.: Miss A. M. Hemenway, 1871.

Hewett, Janet B., Noah Andre Trudeau, and Bryce A. Suderow, eds. *Supplement to the Official Records of the Union and Confederate Armies.* 100 vols. Wilmington, N.C.: Broadfoot Publishing Company, 1994–2001.

Hewett, Janet B., ed. *The Roster of Union Soldiers, 1861–1865.* Vol. 11, part 2, *P-Z. Kansas, Arkansas, Louisiana, North Carolina, Texas, Alabama, Florida, Georgia, Mississippi.* Wilmington, N.C.: Broadfoot Publishing, 1998.

Howard, George W. *The Monumental City, Its Past History and Present Resources.* Baltimore, Md.: J. D. Ehlers & Co., 1873.

James, Horace. *Annual Report of the Superintendent of Negro Affairs in North Carolina, 1864. With an Appendix Containing the History and Management of Freedmen in this Department up to June 1st, 1865.* Boston: W. F. Brown, 1865.

Lanman, Charles. *Biographical Annals of the Civil Government of the United States.* 2nd ed. Revised, enlarged, and completed by Joseph M. Morrison. New York: J. M. Morrison, 1887.

Lewis, Robert G., ed. *The Carteret County Cemetery Book.* Vol. 1. *Beaufort and East of Newport River.* Morehead City, N.C.: The Carteret County Historical Society, 2007.

Long, E. B. *The Civil War Day by Day: An Almanac, 1861–1865.* Garden City, N.Y.: Doubleday and Company, 1971.

Manarin, Louis H., and Weymouth T. Jordan, Jr., comps. *North Carolina Troops, 1861–1865: A Roster.* 15 vols. to date. Raleigh: Division of Archives and History, Department of Cultural Resources, 1966–.

Massachusetts Adjutant General's Office. *Massachusetts Soldiers, Sailors, and Marines in the Civil War.* 8 vols. Norwood, Mass.: Norwood Press, 1931–1935.

Matthew, H. C. G., and Brian Harrison, eds. *Oxford Dictionary of National Biography.* 60 vols. Oxford: Oxford University Press, 2004.

Niven, John, ed. *The Salmon P. Chase Papers.* 5 vols. Kent, Ohio: Kent State University Press, 1994.

Nye, Holden Ryan, and Gerherdus Landon Demarest. *Psalms and Hymns and Spiritual Songs: Compiled for the Use of Universalist Churches, Associations, and Social Meetings.* Cincinnati: Nye and Demarest, 1861.

Parker, Freddie L., ed. *Stealing a Little Freedom: Advertisements for Slave Runaways in North Carolina, 1791–1840.* New York: Garland Publishing, Inc., 1994.

Pope, Alexander. *An Essay on Man.* Ed. Maynard Mack. London: Methuen & Co. Ltd., 1950.

———, trans. *The Iliad of Homer.* Ed. Steven Shankman. New York: Penguin Books, 1996.

Powell, William S., ed. *Dictionary of North Carolina Biography.* 6 vols. Chapel Hill: University of North Carolina Press, 1979–1996.

———. *The North Carolina Gazetteer.* Chapel Hill: University of North Carolina Press, 1968.

Proceedings of the Annual Meeting of the Stockholders of the Atlantic and North Carolina Railroad. 49 vols. New Bern, N.C.: William J. Williams, printer, 1855–1904.

Raper, Horace W. and Thornton W. Mitchell, eds. *The Papers of William Woods Holden, 1841– 1868.* 2 vols. Raleigh: Division of Archives and History, North Carolina Department of Cultural Resources, 2001.

Reid, Whitelaw. *After the War: A Tour of the Southern States, 1865–1866.* Ed. and intro. by C. Vann Woodward. 1866; New York: Harper & Row, 1965.

Scott, Robert N., H. M. Lazelle, George B. Davis, Leslie J. Perry, Joseph W. Kirkley, Fred C. Ainsworth, John S. Moodey, and Calvin D. Cowles, eds. *The War of the Rebellion: A Compilation of the Official Records of the Union and Confederate Armies.* 128 vols. Washington, D.C.: Government Printing Office, 1880–1901.

Sifakis, Stewart. *Who Was Who in the Civil War.* New York: Facts on File Publications, 1988.

Spear, John M. "Army Life in the Twenty-Fourth Regiment, Massachusetts Volunteer Infantry, Dec. 1861 to Dec. 1864, 1892." Typescript. Massachusetts Historical Society, Boston, Mass.

Stanly, Edward A. *Military Governor among Abolitionists: A Letter from Edward Stanly to Charles Sumner.* New York: n.p., 1865.

Stapleford, Mary Louise, comp. *Cedar Grove Cemetery*. New Bern, N.C.: Historical Records Survey of North Carolina, 1939.

Stedman, Edmund Clarence, ed. *A Victorian Anthology, 1837–1895*. 1895; repr., New York: Greenwood Press, 1969.

Stuart, Sarah Anne, comp. *A Treasury of Poems: A Collection of the World's Most Famous and Familiar Verse*. New York: Galahad Books, 1996.

Thompson, Rev. A. C. *Songs in the Night: or Hymns for the Sick and Suffering*. Boston: J. E. Tilton and Company, 1863.

Thorpe, Thomas B. *The Hive of "the Beehunter": A Repository of Sketches, including Peculiar American Character, Scenery, and Rural Sports*. New York: D. Appleton & Company, 1854.

Tolbert, Noble J., ed. *Papers of John W. Ellis*. 2 vols. Raleigh, N.C.: State Department of Archives and History, 1964.

United States Naval War Records Office. *Official Records of the Union and Confederate Navies in the War of the Rebellion*. 30 vols. Washington, D.C.: Government Printing Office, 1894–1922.

Ward, Thomas Humphry. *The English Poets*. Vol. 4. *The Nineteenth Century: Wordsworth to Tennyson*. New York: McMillan and Co., 1894.

Who Was Who in America. Vol. 1. Chicago: A. N. Marquis, 1963.

Wright, William Aldis, ed., *The Complete Works of William Shakespeare*. Garden City, N.Y.: Garden City Books, 1936.

Young, Edward. *The Complaint, or Night Thoughts*. Hartford: S. Andrus and Son, 1851.

Secondary Sources

Bancroft, George. *History of the United States from the Discovery of the American Continent*. 8 vols. Boston: Little, Brown and Company, 1856.

Barrett, John G. *The Civil War in North Carolina*. Chapel Hill: University of North Carolina Press, 1963.

Battle, Kemp P. *History of the University of North Carolina*. Vol. 1. Raleigh, N.C.: Edwards and Broughton, 1907.

Blight, David W. *Race and Reunion: The Civil War in American Memory*. Cambridge, Mass.: Belknap Press, 2001.

Branch, Paul, Jr. *The Siege of Fort Macon*. Morehead City, [N.C.]: Herald Printing Company, 1982.

Bright, Leslie S., William H. Rowland, and James C. Bardon. *C.S.S. Neuse: A Question of Iron and Time*. Raleigh: North Carolina Office of Archives and History, 1981.

Brown, Cecil Kenneth. *A State Movement in Railroad Development: The Story of*

North Carolina's First Effort to Establish and East and West Trunk Line Railroad. Chapel Hill: University of North Carolina Press, 1928.

Brown, Norman D. "A Union Election in Civil War North Carolina." *North Carolina Historical Review* 43 (Autumn 1966): 381–400.

———. *Edward Stanly: Whiggery's Tarheel "Conqueror."* University: University of Alabama Press, 1974.

Browning, Judkin. "'Bringing Light to Our Land . . . When She Was Dark as Night': Northerners, Freedpeople, & Education during Military Occupation in North Carolina, 1862–1865." *American Nineteenth Century History* 9 (March 2008): 1–17.

———. "'Little-Souled Mercenaries?' The Buffaloes of Eastern North Carolina during the Civil War." *North Carolina Historical Review* 77 (July 2000): 337–340.

———. "Removing the Mask of Nationality: Unionism, Racism, and Federal Military Occupation in North Carolina, 1862–1865." *Journal of Southern History* 71 (August 2005): 589–620.

———. "'Visions of Freedom and Civilization Opening before Them': African Americans Search for Autonomy during Military Occupation." In *Struggles over Change: North Carolinians in the Era of the Civil War and Reconstruction,* ed. Paul D. Escott, 69–100. Chapel Hill: University of North Carolina Press, 2008.

Carter, Nathan Franklin. *The Native Ministry of New Hampshire.* Concord: Rumford Printing Company, 1906.

Castel, Albert. *Decision in the West: The Atlanta Campaign of 1864.* Lawrence: University Press of Kansas, 1992.

Cecelski, David S. *The Waterman's Song: Slavery and Freedom in Maritime North Carolina.* Chapel Hill: University of North Carolina Press, 2001.

Collins, Donald E. "War Crimes or Justice? General George Pickett and the Mass Execution of Deserters in Civil War Kinston, North Carolina." In *The Art of Command in the Civil War,* ed. Steven E. Woodworth, 50–83. Lincoln: University of Nebraska Press, 1998.

Crofts, Daniel. *Reluctant Confederates: Upper South Unionists in the Secession Crisis.* Chapel Hill: University of North Carolina Press, 1989.

Delaney, Norman C. "Charles Henry Foster and the Unionists of Eastern North Carolina." *North Carolina Historical Review* 37 (July 1960): 348–366.

Donald, David Herbert. *Lincoln.* New York: Simon and Schuster, 1995.

Doughton, Virginia Pou. *The Atlantic Hotel.* Raleigh, [N.C.]: Privately printed, 1991.

Elkins, Stanley, and Eric McKittrick. *The Age of Federalism: The Early American Republic, 1788–1800.* New York: Oxford University Press, 1993.

Farnham, Thomas J., and Francis P. King. "'The March of the Destroyer': The New

Bern Yellow Fever Epidemic of 1864." *North Carolina Historical Review* 73 (October 1996): 435–483.

Foner, Eric. *A Short History of Reconstruction.* New York: Harper & Row, Publishers, 1990.

Foote, Shelby. *The Civil War: A Narrative.* Vol. 2. *Fredericksburg to Meridian.* New York: Random House, 1963.

———. *The Civil War: A Narrative.* Vol. 3. *Red River to Appomattox.* New York: Random House, 1974.

Furguson, Ernest B. *Chancellorsville, 1863: The Souls of the Brave.* New York: Vintage Books, 1992.

Gallagher, Gary W. "Revisiting the 1862 and 1864 Valley Campaigns: Stonewall Jackson and Jubal Early in the Shenandoah." In *Lee and His Generals in War and Memory,* ed. Gary W. Gallagher, 182–198. Baton Rouge: Louisiana State University Press, 1998.

Gordon, Lesley J. "'In Time of War': Unionists Hanged in Kinston, North Carolina, February 1864." In *Guerrillas, Unionists, and Violence on the Confederate Home Front,* ed. Daniel E. Sutherland, 45–58. Fayetteville: University of Arkansas Press, 1999.

Grant, Daniel Lindsay, ed. *Alumni History of the University of North Carolina.* 2nd ed. Durham: Christian and King, 1924.

Hamilton, Edith. *Mythology: Timeless Tales of Gods and Heroes.* New York: New American Library, 1969.

Hand, D. W. "Epidemic of 1864." In American Public Health Association, *Public Health Papers and Reports: 1877–1878.* Vol. 4, 293–296. Boston: Houghton, Osgood and Company, 1880.

Harris, William C. *With Charity for All: Lincoln and the Restoration of the Union.* Lexington: University Press of Kentucky, 1997.

Johnson, Guion Griffis. *Ante-Bellum North Carolina: A Social History.* Chapel Hill: University of North Carolina Press, 1937.

Jones, Maxine D. "'A Glorious Work': The American Missionary Association and Black North Carolinians, 1863–1880." Ph.D. diss., Florida State University, 1982.

Jordan, Weymouth T., Jr., and Gerald W. Thomas. "Massacre at Plymouth: April 20, 1864." *North Carolina Historical Review* 72 (April 1995): 125–197.

Mallison, Fred. *The Civil War on the Outer Banks: A History of the Late Rebellion along the Coast of North Carolina from Carteret to Currituck.* Jefferson, N.C.: McFarland & Company, Inc., 1998.

McPherson, James M. *Battle Cry of Freedom: The Civil War Era.* New York: Oxford University Press, 1988.

Morris, Roy, Jr. *The Better Angel: Walt Whitman in the Civil War.* New York: Oxford University Press, 2000.

Muse, Amy. *Grandpa Was a Whaler: A Story of Carteret Chadwicks.* New Bern, [N.C.]: Owen G. Dunn Co., 1961.

Paul, Charles L. "Factors in the Economy of Colonial Beaufort." *North Carolina Historical Review* 44 (Spring 1967): 111–134.

Rable, George C. "'Missing in Action': Women of the Confederacy." In *Divided Houses: Gender and the Civil War,* ed. Catherine Clinton and Nina Silber, 134–146. New York: Oxford University Press, 1992.

Reid, Richard M. *Freedom for Themselves: North Carolina's Black Soldiers in the Civil War Era.* Chapel Hill: University of North Carolina Press, 2008.

Schott, Thomas E. *Alexander H. Stephens of Georgia: A Biography.* Baton Rouge: Louisiana State University Press, 1988.

Schweninger, Loren, and John Hope Franklin. *Runaway Slaves: Rebels on the Plantation.* New York: Oxford University Press, 1999.

Sharpe, Bill. "Completely Coastal Carteret." *The State* 21 (June 27, 1953): 3–5, 33–38.

Silber, Nina. *The Romance of Reunion: Northerners and the South, 1865–1900.* Chapel Hill: University of North Carolina Press, 1993.

Thierry, Augustin. *History of the Conquest of England by the Normans.* 2 vols. Trans. William Hazlitt. London: David Bogue, Fleet Street, 1847.

Van Deusen, Glyndon G. *William Henry Seward.* New York: Oxford University Press, 1967.

Ward, Adolphus William, George Walter Prothero, and Stanley Leathes, eds. *The Cambridge Modern History.* Volume 9. *Napoleon.* Cambridge: Cambridge University Press, 1907.

Warner, Ezra J. *Generals in Blue: Lives of the Union Commanders.* Baton Rouge: Louisiana State University Press, 1964.

Watson, Alan D. *A History of New Bern and Craven County.* New Bern: Tryon Palace Commission, 1987.

INDEX

African Americans: appropriating white property, 38; armed by Union army for emergency purposes, 127, 134; attitudes of JR toward, 7, 17, 18, 54, 60, 84, 85, 99, 179; celebrate Emancipation Proclamation, 50, 118; celebrate July 4th, 79; conflicting with white residents, 19, 179; as defendants, 61; discussions of suffrage for, 175, 178, 181; disliked by Union conscripts, 86; distressed over Union actions, 62, 147, 148; drafted as laborers by Union army, 147, 148; education in schools, 18, 22, 61, 98, 99; enlisted in Union army, 17, 18, 71, 73, 78, 84, 173; escaping slavery, 36, 37, 48, 86, 129; exulting in freedom, 55; garrison removed from Beaufort, 181; and good relationship with Yankees, 60; granted legal rights, 17; and housing, 61; as informants against whites, 37; murder of, 168; in naval service, 42; as plaintiffs in court cases, 47, 52, 53, 60, 61; population in Beaufort and New Bern, 16; as refugees in poor health, 169, 171; religious meetings, 146; removed from houses in Beaufort, 146; required to give up firearms, 146; smuggled on board ships by Union soldiers, 39, 40; as soldiers arriving at Morehead City, 125; as soldiers garrisoning Beaufort, 177, 179, 180; suspension of schools for, 123; violence against, by Union soldiers, 180; violence against whites, 179; work for Union army, 33

Albemarle, 130

Allen, John A., 31, 33, 36

American Missionary Association, 18, 61n23, 98n119

Amory, Thomas J.C., 82, 150, 153

Ann Street Methodist Church (Beaufort), 25

Arctic, 96

Arendell, Michael F., 3, 173, 175

Atlanta: battles of, 142–7; capture of, 148; Sherman's evacuation of, 158

Atlantic Hotel (Beaufort), 9; confiscated, 33; converted into hospital, 12, 94n113

Averasboro, battle of, 169

Babbitt, Robert, 154

Ballard, Mr., 151, 153

Bartlett, George W., 86, 91, 141

Bask, James, 91, 92

Bates, Gen., 180, 181

Beaufort, N.C.: African American schools in, 18; African Americans imprisoned in, 148; African American soldiers enlist in, 17, 18, 71, 73, 78, 84, 173; African American soldiers garrisoned in, 179, 180; antebellum economy in, 5–7; antebellum politics in, 8, 9; attack on, expected, 21, 121, 123, 124; capacity of harbor, 45, 46, 55; Confederate deserters in, 13, 96, 134, 155; ex-Confederates return to, 176; fire in, 90, 91; hospitals in, 94; map of, vicinity, 104; pictured, 111; police force organized for, 180; population of, 16; port of, 89; public subsistence stores in, 45; racial attitudes in, 8, 19, 20; residents of, compelled to take up arms, 21, 126; residents of, enlisting in Confederate army, 9, 10; residents of, enlisting in Union army, 13, 44, 45, 97; residents of, maintain loyalty to the state, 11, 65; resistance to Union occupation in, 20; runaway slaves flee to, 16, 36, 37, 48, 86, 129; slavery in, 7, 8; as staging area for Union expeditions, 21; Union

Judkin Browning is assistant professor of history at Appalachian State University in Boone, North Carolina, where he specializes in the Civil War and American Military History. He has published numerous articles in the *Journal of Southern History, Civil War History,* and *American Nineteenth Century History,* among others. He also co-edited *Letters from a North Carolina Unionist* (2001) with Michael Thomas Smith. Dr. Browning is currently finishing a manuscript on the effects of Union military occupation in eastern North Carolina during the Civil War.

New Perspectives on the History of the South
Edited by John David Smith, Charles H. Stone Distinguished Professor of American History
University of North Carolina at Charlotte

"In the Country of the Enemy": The Civil War Reports of a Massachusetts Corporal, edited by William C. Harris (1999)

The Wild East: A Biography of the Great Smoky Mountains, by Margaret L. Brown (2000; first paperback edition, 2001)

Crime, Sexual Violence, and Clemency: Florida's Pardon Board and Penal System in the Progressive Era, by Vivien M. L. Miller (2000)

The New South's New Frontier: A Social History of Economic Development in Southwestern North Carolina, by Stephen Wallace Taylor (2001)

Redefining the Color Line: Black Activism in Little Rock, Arkansas, 1940–1970, by John A. Kirk (2002)

The Southern Dream of a Caribbean Empire, 1854–1861, by Robert E. May (2002)

Forging a Common Bond: Labor and Environmental Activism during the BASF Lockout, by Timothy J. Minchin (2003)

Dixie's Daughters: The United Daughters of the Confederacy and the Preservation of Confederate Culture, by Karen L. Cox (2003)

The Other War of 1812: The Patriot War and the American Invasion of Spanish East Florida, by James G. Cusick (2003)

"Lives Full of Struggle and Triumph": Southern Women, Their Institutions, and Their Communities, edited by Bruce L. Clayton and John A. Salmond (2003)

German-Speaking Officers in the United States Colored Troops, 1863–1867, by Martin W. Öfele (2004)

Southern Struggles: The Southern Labor Movement and the Civil Rights Struggle, by John A. Salmond (2004)

Radio and the Struggle for Civil Rights in the South, by Brian Ward (2004, first paperback edition, 2006)

Luther P. Jackson and a Life for Civil Rights, by Michael Dennis (2004)

Southern Ladies, New Women: Race, Region, and Clubwomen in South Carolina, 1890–1930, by Joan Marie Johnson (2004)

Fighting Against the Odds: A History of Southern Labor Since World War II, by Timothy J. Minchin (2005; first paperback edition, 2006)

"Don't Sleep With Stevens!": The J. P. Stevens Campaign and the Struggle to Organize the South, 1963–1980, by Timothy J. Minchin (2005)

"The Ticket to Freedom:" The NAACP and the Struggle for Black Political Integration, by Manfred Berg (2005; first paperback edition, 2007)

"War Governor of the South": North Carolina's Zeb Vance in the Confederacy, by Joe A. Mobley (2005)

Planters' Progress: Modernizing Confederate Georgia, by Chad Morgan (2005)

The Officers of the CSS Shenandoah, by Angus Curry (2006)

The Rosenwald Schools of the American South, by Mary S. Hoffschwelle (2006)

Honor in Command: The Civil War Memoir of Lt. Freeman Sparks Bowley, 30th United States Colored Infantry, edited by Keith P. Wilson (2006)

A Black Congressman in the Age of Jim Crow: South Carolina's George Washington Murray, by John F. Marszalek (2006)

The Spirit and the Shotgun: Armed Resistance and the Struggle for Civil Rights, by Simon Wendt (2007)

Making a New South: Race, Leadership, and Community after the Civil War, edited by Paul A. Cimbala and Barton C. Shaw (2007)

From Rights to Economics: The Ongoing Struggle for Black Equality in the U.S. South, by Timothy J. Minchin (2008)

Slavery on Trial: Race, Class, and Criminal Justice in Antebellum Richmond, Virginia, by James M. Campbell (2008)

Welfare and Charity in the Antebellum South, by Timothy James Lockley (2008)

T. Thomas Fortune the Afro-American Agitator: A Collection of Writings, 1880–1928, by Shawn Leigh Alexander (2008)

Francis Butler Simkins: A Life, by James S. Humphreys (2008)

Black Manhood and Community Building in North Carolina, 1900–1930, by Angela Hornsby-Gutting (2009)

Counterfeit Gentlemen: Manhood and Humor in the Old South, by John Mayfield (2009)

The Southern Mind Under Union Rule: The Diary of James Rumley, Beaufort, North Carolina, 1862–1865, edited by Judkin Browning (2009)